THE EUROPEAN UNION SERIES

General Editors: Neill Nugent, William E. Paterson, Vincent Wright

The European Union series provides an authoritative library on the European Union, ranging from general introductory texts to definitive assessments of key institutions and actors, issues, policies and policy processes, and the role of member states.

Books in the series are written by leading scholars in their fields and reflect the most up-to-date research and debate. Particular attention is paid to accessibility and clear presentation for a wide audience of students, practitioners, and interested general readers.

The series editors are **Neill Nugent,** Professor of Politics and Jean Monnet Professor of European Integration, Manchester Metropolitan University, and **William E. Paterson,** Director of the Institute of German Studies, University of Birmingham.

Their co-editor until his death in July 1999, **Vincent Wright,** was a Fellow of Nuffield College, Oxford University. He played an immensely valuable role in the founding and development of The European Union Series and is greatly missed.

Feedback on the series and book proposals are always welcome and should be sent to Steven Kennedy, Palgrave Macmillan, Houndmills, Basingstoke, Hampshire RG21 6XS, UK, or by e-mail to s.kennedy@palgrave.com

General textbooks

Published

Desmond Dinan **Encyclopedia of the European Union** [Rights: Europe only]

Desmond Dinan **Europe Recast: A History of European Union** [Rights: Europe only]

Desmond Dinan **Ever Closer Union: An Introduction to European Integration** (2nd edn) [Rights: World excluding North and South America, Philippines and Japan]

Simon Hix **The Political System of the European Union** (2nd edn)

Paul Magnette **What is the European Union? Nature and Prospects**

John McCormick **Understanding the European Union: A Concise Introduction** (3rd edn)

Brent F. Nelsen and Alexander Stubb **The European Union: Readings on the Theory and Practice of European Integration** (3rd edn) [Rights: Europe only]

Neill Nugent (ed.) **European Union Enlargement**

Neill Nugent **The Government and Politics of the European Union** (5th edn) [Rights: World excluding USA and dependencies and Canada]

John Peterson and Elizabeth Bomberg **Decision-making in the European Union**

Ben Rosamond **Theories of European Integration**

Forthcoming

Laurie Buonanno and Neill Nugent **Policies and Policy Processes of the European Union**

Mette Eilstrup Sangiovanni (ed.) **Debates on European Integration: A Reader**

Philippa Sherrington **Understanding European Union Governance**

Also planned

The Political Economy of the European Union

Series Standing Order (outside North America only)
ISBN 0–333–71695–7 hardcover
ISBN 0–333–69352–3 paperback
Full details from www.palgrave.com

Visit Palgrave Macmillan's
EU Resource area at
http://www.palgrave.com/politics/eu/

The major institutions and actors

Published

Renaud Dehousse **The European Court of Justice**

Justin Greenwood **Interest Representation in the European Union**

Fiona Hayes-Renshaw and Helen Wallace **The Council of Ministers**

Simon Hix and Christopher Lord **Political Parties in the European Union**

David Judge and David Earnshaw **The European Parliament**

Neill Nugent **The European Commission**

Anne Stevens with Handley Stevens **Brussels Bureaucrats? The Administration of the European Union**

Forthcoming

Simon Bulmer and Wolfgang Wessels **The European Council**

The main areas of policy

Published

Michelle Cini and Lee McGowan **Competition Policy in the European Union**

Wyn Grant **The Common Agricultural Policy**

Martin Holland **The European Union and the Third World**

Brigid Laffan **The Finances of the European Union**

Malcolm Levitt and Christopher Lord **The Political Economy of Monetary Union**

Janne Haaland Matláry **Energy Policy in the European Union**

John McCormick **Environmental Policy in the European Union**

John Peterson and Margaret Sharp **Technology Policy in the European Union**

Handley Stevens **Transport Policy in the European Union**

Forthcoming

Laura Cram **Social Policy in the European Union**

Bart Kerremans, David Allen and Geoffrey Edwards **The External Economic Relations of the European Union**

Stephen Keukeleire and Jennifer MacNaughton **The Foreign Policy of the European Union**

James Mitchell and Paul McAleavey **Regionalism and Regional Policy in the European Union**

Jörg Monar **Justice and Home Affairs in the European Union**

John Vogler, Richard Whitman and Charlotte Bretherton **The External Policies of the European Union**

Also planned

Defence Policy in the European Union
Political Union

The member states and the Union

Published

Carlos Closa and Paul Heywood **Spain and the European Union**

Alain Guyomarch, Howard Machin and Ella Ritchie **France in the European Union**

Forthcoming

Simon Bulmer and William E. Paterson **Germany and the European Union**

Phil Daniels and Ella Ritchie **Britain and the European Union**

Brigid Laffan **The European Union and its Member States**

Luisa Perrotti **Italy and the European Union**

Baldur Thorhallson **Small States in the European Union**

Issues

Published

Derek Beach **The Dynamics of European Integration: why and when EU institutions matter**

Forthcoming

Thomas Christiansen and Christine Reh **Constitutionalizing the European Union**

Steven McGuire and Michael Smith **The USA and the European Union**

Also planned

Europeanization and National Politics

Understanding the European Union

A Concise Introduction

Third Edition

John McCormick

First edition 1999
Second edition 2002
Third edition 2005

Published by
PALGRAVE MACMILLAN
Houndmills, Basingstoke, Hampshire RG21 2XS and
175 Fifth Avenue, New York, N.Y. 10010
Companies and representatives throughout the world

PALGRAVE MACMILLAN is the global academic imprint of the Palgrave
Macmillan division of St. Martin's Press, LLC and of Palgrave Macmillan Ltd.
Macmillan is a registered trademark in the United States, United Kingdom
and other countries. Palgrave is a registered trademark in the European
Union and other countries.

ISBN-13: 978–1–4039–4450–4   hardback
ISBN-10: 1–4039–4450–4   hardback
ISBN-13: 978–1–4039–4451–1   paperback
ISBN-10: 1–4039–4451–2   paperback

This book is printed on paper suitable for recycling and made from
fully managed and sustained forest sources.

A catalogue record for this book is available
from the British Library.

A catalog record for this book is available from the
Library of Congress.

10   9   8   7   6   5   4   3   2
14 13 12 11 10 09 08 07 06

Printed and bound in China

Contents

List of Boxes, Tables, Figures and Maps   viii

List of Abbreviations   x

Introduction   xii

Acknowledgements   xix

1 **What is the European Union?**   1

   The international system   2
      Confederalism   6
      Federalism   9
   The logic of integration   12
      Functionalism   13
      Neofunctionalism   16
   Regional integration around the world   18
      The Americas   18
      Asia   21
      The Middle East   23
      Africa   24
   Conclusions   25

2 **The Idea of Europe**   27

   The changing identity of Europe   28
   Where is Europe?   36
   Europe today   39
      Political structures   39
      Administrative structures   45
      Economic structures   47
   Conclusions   50

3 **The Evolution of the EU**   52

   Domestic and international background   53
   First steps towards integration (1945–58)   58
   The European Economic Community (1958–86)   62
   Economic and social integration (1979–92)   67
   From Community to Union (1992–)   71
   Conclusions   77

v

4 The Institutions of the EU   79

    A constitution for Europe   80
    The European Commission   82
    The Council of Ministers   89
    The European Parliament   94
    The European Court of Justice   99
    The European Council   103
    Conclusions   106

5 The EU and the Member States   108

    The changing identities of the member states   109
    Understanding the policy process   115
    The politics of the budget   121
    The changing character of the EU   125
    Conclusions   129

6 The EU and its Citizens   131

    The democratic deficit   132
    The people's Europe   139
    Participation and representation   145
      European elections   146
      Referenda   148
      Interest groups   150
    Improving accountability   153
    Conclusions   155

7 Economic Policy   157

    The single market   158
      Physical barriers   159
      Fiscal barriers   162
      Technical barriers   163
    Effects of the single market   165
      Rights of residence   165
      Joint ventures and corporate mergers   165
      A European transport system   170
      Open skies over Europe   171
    Inside the euro zone   173
    Conclusions   179

8 **Improving the Quality of Life**   181

   Building an even playing field   182
   Agricultural policy   187
   Regional policy   194
   Social policy   197
   Environmental policy   201
   Conclusions   206

9 **The EU and the World**   208

   Building a European foreign policy   209
   Towards a European defence policy   214
   Europe as an economic power   220
   Relations with the United States   223
   Relations with eastern Europe   225
   Development cooperation   228
   Conclusions   231

Conclusions   233

Appendix: A Chronology of European Integration, 1944–2004   237

Sources of Further Information   240

Bibliography   243

Index   251

List of Boxes, Tables, Figures and Maps

Boxes

1.1 International organizations   4
1.2 Government or governance?   10
1.3 Regional integration: costs and benefits   15
2.1 Paneuropa   35
2.2 The standard of living   48
3.1 The Marshall Plan, 1948–51   57
3.2 The 1986 Single European Act   69
3.3 The 1992 Treaty on European Union   73
4.1 European Union law   83
4.2 Specialized EU institutions   95
4.3 Parties in the European Parliament   98
5.1 The division of policy authority   113
5.2 The rise of regional identity   115
5.3 Intergovernmental conferences   127
6.1 The knowledge deficit   136
6.2 Promoting European culture   142
7.1 Illegal immigration and terrorism   161
7.2 Europe and the aerospace industry   167
7.3 The European Central Bank   174
8.1 The Common Fisheries Policy   192
8.2 Principles of European environmental policy   203
9.1 The EU on the world stage   211
9.2 A European or an Atlantic defence?   215
9.3 The European superpower   226

Tables

0.1 The European Union: basic indicators   xiv
1.1 Regional integration associations   19
2.1 Political and administrative structures   40
4.1 The European Commissioners, January 2005   85
4.2 Presidents of the European Commission   86

4.3   Directorates-general and services of the European
      Commission   87
4.4   Votes in the Council of Ministers   93
4.5   Seats in the European Parliament, 2004–9   96
5.1   The European Union budget   122
9.1   The ACP states   229

Figures

1.1   Confederalism and federalism compared   7
4.1   The European policy process   91
6.1   Public opinion on EU membership   134
6.2   Turnout at European Parliament elections, 2004   147
8.1   Per capita GDP in the European Union   183
8.2   Unemployment in the European Union   184
8.3   Economic structure of EU member states   185
8.4   Population engaged in agriculture   193
9.1   The EU in the global economy   221

Maps

1.1   The European Union   xx
3.1   Growth of the EU, 1952–86   66
3.2   Growth of the EU, 1990–2004   75

List of Abbreviations

A-10	Accession-10, or the ten countries that joined the EU in 2004
ACP	African, Caribbean, Pacific
ALADI	Latin American Integration Association
APEC	Asia Pacific Economic Cooperation
ASEAN	Association of Southeast Asian Nations
CAP	Common Agricultural Policy
CFSP	Common Foreign and Security Policy
CoR	Committee of the Regions
COREPER	Committee of Permanent Representatives
DG	directorate-general
EADS	European Aeronautic Defence and Space company
EAGGF	European Agricultural Guidance and Guarantee Fund
EC	European Community
ECOWAS	Economic Community of West African States
ECSC	European Coal and Steel Community
ecu	European Currency Unit
EDC	European Defence Community
EEA	European Economic Area
EEC	European Economic Community
EFTA	European Free Trade Association
EMS	European Monetary System
EMU	economic and monetary union
EP	European Parliament
EPC	European Political Cooperation
ERDF	European Regional Development Fund
ERM	Exchange Rate Mechanism
ESDP	European Security and Defence Policy
ESF	European Social Fund
EU	European Union
EU-15	The 15 member states of the EU prior to the 2004 enlargement
FTAA	free trade area of the Americas
G8	Group of Eight industrialized countries
GAC	General Affairs Council
GATT	General Agreement on Tariffs and Trade
GDP	gross domestic product
GNP	gross national product
IGC	intergovernmental conference
IGO	intergovernmental organization
INGO	international non-governmental organization

IO	international organization
LAFTA	Latin American Free Trade Association
MEP	member of the European Parliament
NAFTA	North American Free Trade Agreement
NATO	North Atlantic Treaty Organization
OECD	Organization for Economic Cooperation and Development
OEEC	Organization for European Economic Cooperation
PR	proportional representation
SAARC	South Asian Association for Regional Cooperation
SAP	Social Action Programme
SEA	Single European Act
TEN	trans-European network
VAT	value-added tax
WEU	Western European Union

With the 2004 enlargement, a series of two-letter abbreviations were introduced (on the US model) for all the member states. They are as follows:

AT	Austria		IT	Italy
BE	Belgium		LT	Lithuania
CY	Cyprus		LU	Luxembourg
CZ	Czech Republic		LV	Latvia
DE	Germany		MT	Malta
DK	Denmark		NL	Netherlands
EE	Estonia		PL	Poland
EL	Greece		PT	Portugal
ES	Spain		SE	Sweden
FI	Finland		SI	Slovenia
FR	France		SK	Slovakia
HU	Hungary		UK	United Kingdom
IE	Ireland			

Introduction

The European Union has finally come into its own. After several decades of slow growth, peppered by controversy, doubts, achievements, failures, and disagreements, there is a new understanding of its global significance. History may show that the turning point was the March 2003 US-led invasion of Iraq. Until then, conventional wisdom held that the end of the cold war and the demise of the Soviet Union had left the United States as the world's only superpower, facing no significant political, economic, or military competition. But the controversy over the invasion suggested otherwise, because it showed that American global leadership was losing its lustre, and that Europeans – frequently submissive allies of the United States during the cold war – now had the stature to be heard on the biggest international issues.

While the governments of the member state were divided over how to respond to the invasion – Britain, Italy, Spain, and Poland took the side of the Americans, while France and Germany made clear their opposition – ordinary Europeans were not. Opinion polls across the EU found 70–90 per cent majorities opposed to the war, and rising support for an independent European foreign policy. Coincidentally, the controversy came just as the EU was completing two of the most significant projects in its history. First there was the adoption of the euro in early 2002, which provided the Europeans with a world-class currency that could compete directly with the US dollar in international financial markets. Then came the May 2004 enlargement of the EU to take in ten new mainly eastern European member states, extending the EU into the former Soviet Union, pushing its population to more than 450 million, and opening considerable new economic opportunity. These achievements had in turn built on another: the removal of the barriers to the movement of people, money, goods, and services that had made Europe the world's biggest capitalist marketplace.

This combination of events – economic integration at home, and disagreements abroad with US policy – has brought about a transformation in the global role of the European Union. Once a limited exercise in policy cooperation, the EU is now a global superpower, certainly in economic terms but increasingly also in political, diplomatic, and (potentially) military terms. Its member states are today approached by external actors less as individual countries and more as partners in a regional grouping that increasingly thinks and acts together.

At the core of this changing identity has been the EU's growing effectiveness as a trading bloc. Not only does it account for nearly one-third of world trade, but it has the biggest mergers and acquisitions market in the world (helping its corporations take on their American and Japanese competitors), and it negotiates as one in the meeting rooms of the World Trade Organization – witness the string of trade wars fought with the United States since the mid-1990s. Its member states do not yet always think together on foreign and security policy, but their record is improving, and the EU as a unit is having a growing impact on most of the major international problems of the day. Progress on military cooperation has been particularly problematic, but attempts to build a European military have accelerated in recent years, encouraged in part by disagreements with United States policy. And whatever European governments think, there is no denying how their citizens feel about Europe's place in the world: recent polls have found less than half in favour of a strong global US presence, more than half regarding the US as a major threat to world peace, and three-quarters favouring foreign policy independence for the European Union.

Of course not everyone agrees that European integration has been a good idea, nor is everyone ready to give it credit for bringing peace to the region, nor is everyone yet ready to acknowledge that the EU is a superpower. Europeans have mixed opinions about the wisdom of shifting powers from the member states to a new level of government, and opinion polls show that only half approve of the European Union, while the other half either disapproves or is not yet sure what to think. Critics point accusing fingers at 'interfering Eurocrats', and disapprove of the authority given to institutions that are portrayed (often correctly) as secretive, elitist, and unaccountable. They also question the extent to which integration can be credited with the economic growth and prosperity that has come to Europe since 1945, and worry about the loss of national sovereignty and identity.

But like it or not, the European Union is here to stay. Its member states have spun a web of links that would be difficult to unravel. Free trade and the free movement of people have dissolved the barriers that for so long reminded Europeans of their differences, and while national and regional identities are still alive and well, Europeans are no longer willing to fight each other to assert those identities. Fifteen years ago, the EU was only a marginal factor in the lives of most Europeans, but with the completion of the single market, policy cooperation on a wide range of issues, a supranational system of law to which they are all subject, the drafting of a European constitution, the adoption of the euro, eastern enlargement, moves towards a common foreign policy, and important global challenges that demand a response, it has become impossible to ignore.

This is an introductory book about the European Union, written for anyone who wants to understand how it works and what it means for the

Table 0.1   *The European Union: basic indicators (ranked by GDP)*

	Area (000 sq. km)	Population (million)	Gross domestic product (billion $)	Per capita gross national income ($)
European Union (25):				
Germany	357	82.5	2,400	25,250
UK	245	59.3	1,794	28,350
France	552	59.7	1,747	24,770
Italy	301	57.9	1,465	21,560
Spain	506	41.2	836	16,990
Netherlands	41	16.1	511	26,310
Belgium	33	10.3	302	25,820
Sweden	450	8.9	301	28,840
Austria	84	8.1	251	26,720
Denmark	43	5.4	212	33,750
Poland	323	38.2	209	5,270
Greece	132	10.6	173	13,720
Finland	338	5.2	161	27,020
Portugal	92	10.2	149	12,130
Ireland	70	3.9	148	26,960
Czech Republic	79	10.2	85	6,740
Hungary	93	10.2	83	6,330
Slovakia	49	5.4	32	4,920
Slovenia	20	2.0	26	11,830
Luxembourg	2	0.4	26	43,940
Lithuania	65	3.5	18	4,490
Cyprus	9	0.8	11	12,320
Latvia	65	2.3	10	4,070
Estonia	45	1.4	8	4,960
Malta	0.3	0.4	4	9,260
Sub-total	*3,994*	*454.1*	*10,962*	

Source: Population and economic figures from World Development Indicators database, World Bank website, http://www.worldbank.com. All figures are for 2003.

	Area (000 sq. km)	Population (million)	Gross domestic product (billion $)	Per capita gross national income ($)
Other Europe (13):				
Switzerland	41	7.3	309	39,880
Norway	324	4.5	221	43,350
Romania	238	22.2	60	2,310
Ukraine	604	48.4	50	970
Croatia	57	4.4	28	5,350
Bulgaria	111	7.9	20	2,130
Serbia/Montenegro	102	8.1	19	1,910
Belarus	208	9.9	17	1,590
Iceland	103	0.3	10	30,810
Bosnia/Herzegovina	51	4.1	7	1,540
Albania	29	3.2	6	1,740
Macedonia	26	2.0	5	1,980
Moldova	34	4.3	2	590
Sub-total	*1,928*	*126.3*		
Europe total	*5,922*	*580.4*		
Other (7):				
United States	9,364	291.0	10,881	37,610
Japan	378	127.1	4,326	34,510
China	9,598	1,288.0	1,409	1,100
Canada	9,971	31.6	834	23,930
Australia	7,741	19.9	518	21,650
Russia	17,075	143.4	433	2,610
Turkey	775	70.7	238	2,790
World	*133,567*	*6,271.7*	*36,356*	*5,500*

454 million people who live under its jurisdiction. Unfortunately confusion seems to be the order of the day – Europe has been busy integrating itself since the early 1950s, but three in four of its inhabitants confess to a poor understanding of the EU, its policies and its institutions, and about one in eight admit that they know nothing at all about how it works (see Box 6.1 on page 136).

This is a worrying state of affairs. As long as the confusion persists, Europeans will keep their distance from the EU, integration will continue to be driven by the elites who have made most of the major decisions since the outset, and the values and priorities of the European people may not be reflected in those decisions. A common criticism of the EU is that it is undemocratic, and that bureaucrats have too much power and too little accountability – but little will change unless Europeans learn how it works, and increase the pressure for accountability.

From my vantage point as a British citizen living in the United States, I have watched with interest as my fellow Europeans have strengthened their bonds. My annual trips back to Europe have allowed me to compare public and media responses to the EU on both sides of the Atlantic, and to gain the kind of perspective that distance often allows. At the same time my students at Indiana University have presented me with the challenge of convincing them why they should care about something that is happening several thousand kilometres away.

Part of that challenge involved finding a book that explained the EU clearly and approachably, but while publishing on the EU has been a major growth industry in recent years, there are remarkably few books that really introduce the EU, and even fewer that successfully convey the significance of the EU. Too many authors become bogged down in treaty articles and Eurojargon, and – the worst sin of all – they often make one of the most fascinating developments in European history sound dull and bureaucratic.

These problems prompted me to write *The European Union: Politics and Policies*, which was published in 1996 by Westview Press and aimed mainly at college and university classes on the EU in the United States and Canada. In 1997, Steven Kennedy at Palgrave asked me to write a shorter book that was more introductory and broad-ranging, and aimed at a wider readership. The first edition of *Understanding the European Union* was published in 1999, its main goal being to demystify the European Union, to help readers come to grips with this strange new economic and political entity, and to do all this as clearly and as concisely as possible.

Apparently it struck a note, a second edition was published in 2002, and this new edition follows in short order. Like its precursors, the third edition includes all the important details about how the EU works and what it does, and provides context by introducing, explaining, and assessing the history of the EU, the goals and motives behind European integration, the impact of integration on the member states, the changes the EU has made to the lives of Europeans, and the long-term implications of the European experiment. It also provides critical analysis of the EU, offering thoughts on where it has done well and not so well, and on where improvements need to be made. It is very much coloured by the important changes that have taken place in the EU in recent years, notably the adoption of the euro, the steps taken towards a constitution, the trans-atlantic rift over Iraq, and the 2004 eastern enlargement.

The third edition has been thoroughly revised and updated, and large parts of it have been fine-tuned in response to developments since the second edition. The chapters on policy have been reorganized, with a ninth chapter added to absorb the changes. Several new sections have been added, several boxes have been replaced, and the arguments and analysis have been developed. One thing that remains unchanged, however, is the personality of the book: *Understanding the European Union* remains an introduction. It does not set out to cover every aspect of European integration in depth, but instead takes the broad view, offering depth where necessary but ultimately providing a route map to the rapidly growing number of more specialist studies of the many different facets of the EU.

Chapter 1 looks at the nature of regional integration, exploring the motives behind international cooperation, showing how the EU is different from conventional international organizations, and placing it in context by briefly describing several other exercises in regional integration around the world.

Chapter 2 provides historical background by discussing the evolution of the idea of Europe, and showing how the terms 'Europe' and 'European' have changed and evolved. The chapter also includes a political, economic, and social survey of Europe today, which serves as a foundation for the discussions about integration in later chapters.

Chapter 3 offers a short history of European integration since 1945. It describes and explains the different steps in the process, from the creation of the European Coal and Steel Community, through the treaties of Rome, Maastricht, and Nice, to the completion of the single market, adoption of the euro, and the 2004 enlargement.

Chapter 4 looks at the five major European institutions – the Commission, the Council of Ministers, the European Parliament, the Court of Justice, and the European Council – and explains how they are structured, how they function, how they relate to one another and how they fit into the process of making European law and policy.

Chapter 5 assesses the relationship between the EU and its member states, and the changing character of the EU. It looks at the EU policy process broadly defined, focusing on the ways in which that process has changed the relationship among the member states, and between them and the EU institutions.

Chapter 6 does much the same for the relationship between the EU and its citizens. It looks at the problem of the democratic deficit, assesses public opinion about European integration, and examines the channels through which Europeans can influence the work of EU institutions, including elections, referenda, and the work of interest groups. It ends with a discussion of the need for democratic reform.

Chapter 7 focuses on the economic impact of European integration, with particular emphasis on the single market programme and its effects, and includes a discussion of the euro: where it came from, and its implications for European economic policy.

Chapter 8 looks at the various policy fields whose key motivation has been improving the quality of life for Europeans; these include agricultural policy, regional policy, social policy, and the environment. It describes the content of these different policy areas, and assesses their impact.

Chapter 9 puts the European Union in a global context. The chapter begins with a survey of the attempts that have been made to develop a European foreign and defence policy, then assesses the role of the EU as a global economic superpower and looks at the EU's relations with different parts of the world.

The book ends with a new set of conclusions, which attempt to place the European Union in its historical, political, and economic context, and to make some suggestions regarding the future based on past developments, notably those of the last few years.

Acknowledgements

I would like to thank my publisher Steven Kennedy for his usual excellent judgement and for his advice and prodding on this third edition. My thanks also to Neill Nugent and Willie Paterson for their work as series editors, to the three anonymous reviewers for their suggestions, and to all the production staff at Palgrave Macmillan. Finally my thanks and love to Leanne for her support, and for taking on more than her share of looking after our sons Ian and Stuart during the summer of 2004.

JOHN MCCORMICK

Map 1.1 *The European Union*

EU member states

Chapter 1

What is the European Union?

The international system
The logic of integration
Regional integration around the world
Conclusions

> *To understand Europe you have to be a genius or French.*
> Madeleine Albright, US Secretary of State, 1998

When we study world politics and economics, and try to understand our place in the global system, most of us think in terms of states, and of ourselves as citizens of one or other of those states. Maps of the world show continents and regions divided by state frontiers, demarcating areas that come under the administration of different governments and separate systems of law. When we travel from one state to another, we usually have to show passports or other documents, and are reminded that we are in transit until we return to the state to which we 'belong'.

We think in terms of states because they have been the primary actors in the global system for more than 200 years, and because the study of international relations has long meant the study of alliances, changing patterns of cooperation and conflict, and fluctuations in the balance of power between and among states. But the state is not the only kind of administrative unit, nor is it even necessarily the best. In fact there are many who argue that the state system is declining, its credibility undermined by its association in the first half of the twentieth century with the nationalist ideas that led to the outbreak of two world wars, and its inability since 1945 to deal with many of the demands of a modern global society.

Those who sought peace after the Second World War placed a new premium on cooperation instead of competition, but plans to build a new global order dominated by western Europe and North America were disrupted by the cold war. For critics of the state system, the cold war once again showed how states seemed unable to guarantee the safety of their citizens except through a balance of terror and violence with other states. The resulting tensions led to renewed support for the idea of peace through international cooperation, which led in turn to a dramatic growth in the number of international organizations after the Second World War, spearheaded by the United Nations and covering a wide field of different functions and policy areas.

The desire for peace also led to exercises in regional integration, the process by which countries remove the barriers to free trade and the free movement of people across national borders, integrate their markets, and build common sets of policies. The European Union is just one of those exercises, but the one that has evolved the furthest and brought the greatest changes for its citizens. Regional integration has also been attempted in North America, Latin America, the Caribbean, south and southeast Asia, and parts of Africa, but so far on a more modest scale. Some argue that the European Union could provide a model that might eventually lead to the breakdown of the state system, and to its replacement by a new community of bigger political and economic units and networks.

The European Union has become a major new actor on the world stage, has changed the lives of more than 450 million Europeans, and has changed the lives of everyone who trades with Europe. Yet it is still a puzzle and a mystery to most people, and we are still some way from agreeing just what it is. It is more than a typical international organization, because it has much greater powers over its members, but it is not yet a state or a superstate. So what is it? In an attempt to provide some answers, this chapter looks at the nature of international cooperation, and assesses competing ideas about how the EU has evolved, and what it has become. It also looks at other experiments in regional integration in order to place the EU in a broader perspective.

The international system

Look at a map of the world and you will find it divided into nearly 200 states. As a unit of administration, the state has dominated the way we think about political relations among humans for generations – some say since the Renaissance, some since the Peace of Westphalia which ended the Thirty Years War in 1648, and others since the beginning of the nineteenth century. A state is a legal and physical entity which has four key qualities:

- It operates within a fixed *territory* marked by borders, and controls the movement of people, money and goods across those borders.
- It has *sovereignty* over that territory and over the people and resources within its borders, and has the sole right to impose laws and taxes within its borders.
- It is legally and politically *independent*, and both creates and operates the system of government under which its residents live.
- It has *legitimacy*, meaning that it is normally recognized both by its people and by other states as having jurisdiction and authority within its territory.

None of these qualities is absolute, because there are practical limits to all four: there may be border disputes that interfere with the definition of a territory; there may be legal, economic or political difficulties that compromise the notion of sovereignty; no state is truly independent because they are all subject to some degree of economic or political pressure from outside; and levels of legitimacy vary according to the extent to which the citizens of a state (and the governments of other states) respect the powers and authority of that state.

Another complicating factor is that states may be divided within themselves into different nations. Where the state is a legal/political entity, a nation is a group of people tied together by history, language and culture. Occasionally, a nation will coincide with a state (for example, Japan is predominantly Japanese, Egypt is predominantly Arab, and so on), but most states are home to multiple different national groups. Thus Spain, for example, is a state, but its population is divided into multiple different nations, including Andalusians, Aragonese, Basques, Cantabrians, Castilians, Catalans, Galicians, Navarese, and Valencians. The result of this kind of multinationalism is that loyalty to the state is often divided, as are the identities of states.

The power of states has declined in recent years, for several reasons:

- The world has become more complex, with many interstate political and economic ties driven by the need to trade, build security alliances, and borrow money.
- People have become more mobile, with complex new patterns of emigration developing, and the rise of mass tourism that has broken down the psychological borders among states.
- The focus of people's allegiance has changed as national minorities within states have become more assertive and demanded greater self-determination, even independence in some cases (as with the Scots in Britain, the Kurds in Turkey/Iraq, and the Quebecois in Canada).
- States have been unable always to meet the demands of their residents for security, justice, prosperity, and human rights.
- The inability of states to provide all the needs of their consumers for goods and services has combined with the rise of multinational corporations in search of new markets and profits to change the nature of production, and to make state boundaries more porous.
- Revolutions in technology, science and communications – and the need to deal with shared problems such as terrorism, transboundary pollution, the management of illegal immigrants, and the spread of disease – have demanded new systems of regulation.

As the ability of states to respond to the needs of their residents has declined, so there has been growing international cooperation on matters of mutual interest. This cooperation has taken many forms, from the narrowly focused to the broadly idealistic, and has resulted in the development of many different methods and systems for promoting cooperation. The most common has been the creation of international organizations (IOs, see Box 1.1), within which different governments, interest groups, corporations, and other institutions cooperate. Such

---

Box 1.1 International organizations

Most definitions of an international organization (IO) describe a body that promotes voluntary cooperation and coordination between or among its members, but has neither autonomous powers nor the authority to impose its rulings on its members. The emergence of IOs has been a relatively recent phenomenon, underwritten by desires to encourage cooperation as a way of avoiding international conflict. In 1900 the world had just 220 IOs; by 1969 the number had grown to about 2,000, by 1981 it had reached 15,000 and it now stands at more than 50,000 (Union of International Associations home page, 2004).

There are different kinds of IO that have developed for different reasons and with different structures, methods and goals. Most fit broadly into two main categories:

- *Intergovernmental organizations* (IGOs) have national governments as members, and work to promote voluntary cooperation among those governments on matters of shared interest. IGOs have little or no autonomy in decision making, because their members make all the key decisions, and they usually have little or no ability to enforce those decisions. Examples include the United Nations, the Commonwealth, the World Trade Organization, the Organization for Economic Cooperation and Development (OECD), and the North Atlantic Treaty Organization (NATO).

- *International non-governmental organizations* (INGOs) are either bodies that work internationally outside government, or that consist of groups of national non-governmental organizations. They include multinational corporations such as Royal Dutch/Shell, Sony, or General Motors, but most are non-profit-making interest groups that cooperate in order to pursue the collective goals of their members, or to bring pressure on governments for changes in policy. Examples include the International Red Cross (relief activities), Amnesty International (human rights), and Friends of the Earth (environmental issues).

Much more rarely, there will be hybrid IOs that consist of a combination of government members and non-governmental organizations. One example is the Swiss-based World Conservation Union, which deals with issues relating to nature conservation and the protection of the environment.

cooperation usually involves the joining of equals, who each have the same voting power and meet to make decisions together.

Where governments participate in international cooperation, decision making is described as intergovernmental. The IOs are used as fora within which governments can meet, share views, negotiate, and work to reach agreements. Membership in the IOs is voluntary, and they lack the power to raise taxes, usually depending for revenue on contributions from their members. They do not have independent powers, their decisions being the result of the joint will of their members. They do not have the power to enforce their decisions, and normally cannot impose fines on recalcitrant members, or impose sanctions other than those agreed by the membership as a whole. In most cases, the only pressure IOs can impose on members is moral, or the threat of expulsion from the organization.

In some ways, the European Union looks much like a standard IO. It is a voluntary association of states in which many decisions are taken as a result of negotiations among the leaders of the states. Its taxing abilities are limited and its revenues small. It has few compelling powers of enforcement, and its institutions have little independence, their task being mainly to carry out the wishes of the member states. None of its senior officials are directly elected to their positions, most being either appointed or holding *ex officio* positions (for example, members of the Council of Ministers are such by virtue of being ministers in their home governments).

However, on closer examination, it is obvious that the EU is much more than a standard IO. Its institutions have the power to make laws and policies that are binding on the member states, and in policy areas where the member states have ceded authority to the EU, European law overrides national law. Its members are not equal, because many of its decisions are reached using a voting system that is weighted according to the population size of its member states. In some areas, such as trade, the EU has been given the authority to negotiate on behalf of the 25 member states, and other countries work with the EU institutions rather than with the governments of the member states. In several areas, such as agriculture, the environment, and competition, policies are driven more by decision making at the level of the EU than of the member states.

Where cooperation leads to the transfer of this kind of authority, we move away from intergovernmentalism and into the realms of supranationalism. This is a form of cooperation within which a new level of authority is created that is autonomous, above the state, and has powers of coercion that are independent of the state. Rather than being a meeting place for governments, and making decisions on the basis of the competing interests of those governments, a supranational organization rises above individual state interests, and makes decisions on the basis of the interests of the whole.

Debates have long raged about whether the EU is intergovernmental or supranational, or a combination of the two. Some of its institutions – notably the European Council and the Council of Ministers – are more clearly intergovernmental, because they are the meeting places for the representatives of the member states, and decisions are reached as a result of compromises involving different national positions. Some of the other institutions – notably the European Commission and the European Court of Justice – are more clearly supranational, because they avoid discussions of national interests, and focus instead on the general interests of the European Union. The interests of Europe, however, are ultimately defined by the cumulative national interests of the member states of the EU, making it difficult to conclude that the EU is either particularly inter-governmental or supranational in nature.

There is no question, however, that the EU institutions as a group constitute an additional level of authority in Europe, making decisions that impact both the governments and the residents of the member states. Thus it is critical that we understand the nature of the relationship among the EU institutions, the governments of the member states, and the residents of those states. The two concepts most commonly raised in the discussions about that relationship are confederalism and federalism.

Confederalism

A confederation is a loose system of administration in which two or more organizational units keep their separate identities but give specified powers to a central authority for reasons of convenience, mutual security, or efficiency. The members are sovereign and independent, and the central authority is relatively weak, existing at the discretion of the members, and doing only what they allow it to do. If states were to form a confederation, then the citizens of those states would continue to relate directly to their own governments, and only indirectly to the higher authority (Figure 1.1).

One example of confederalism in practice was the United States in 1781–88. Following the end of the war of independence, the original 13 states cooperated under a loose agreement known as the Articles of Confederation, or a 'league of friendship'. Central government could declare war, coin money, and conclude treaties, but could not levy taxes or regulate commerce, and founded its system of 'national' defence on a network of state militias. The Articles could not be amended without the approval of all 13 states, and treaties needed the consent of at least nine states. There was no national executive or judiciary, and the powers of the confederation lay in the hands of an elected Congress in which each state had one vote. Congress rarely met though, and had no permanent home, so its powers were exercised by committees with variable membership. The

Figure 1.1   *Confederalism and federalism compared*

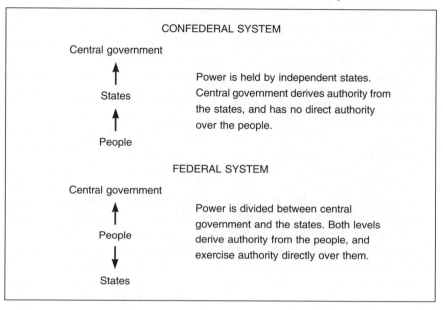

CONFEDERAL SYSTEM

Central government

↑

States

↑

People

Power is held by independent states. Central government derives authority from the states, and has no direct authority over the people.

FEDERAL SYSTEM

Central government

↑

People

↓

States

Power is divided between central government and the states. Both levels derive authority from the people, and exercise authority directly over them.

assumption was that the states might cooperate enough eventually to form a common system of government, but they did not. It was only in 1787 that work began on developing the federal system of government that we find in the United States today.

Confederalism was also used in Germany in 1815–71, when a 39-member confederation was created under the domination of Austria and Prussia following the Congress of Vienna in 1815. Based on the old Holy Roman Empire, it was more an empire than a new state. Few restrictions were placed on the powers of the member kingdoms, duchies, and cities, whose representatives met sporadically (just 16 times in the history of the confederation) in a diet in Frankfurt. Amendments to the constitution needed near-unanimity, and most other measures required a two-thirds majority. Regular business was conducted by an inner committee in which the 11 largest states had one vote each, and the smallest had six between them. There were no common trade or communications policies, and the development of a common army was frustrated by the refusal of smaller states to cooperate (Carr, 1987, pp. 4–5).

Switzerland, too, was confederal until 1798, and although it now calls itself a federation, it has given up fewer powers to the national government than has been the case with other federations, such as Germany, the United States, or Russia. Its 1874 constitution allocates specific powers to the federal government, the rest being reserved to the 20 cantons and six half-cantons. The Swiss encourage direct democracy by holding national referenda, have a Federal Assembly elected by proportional representation, and are governed by a seven-member Federal Council elected by the Assembly. More purely confederal systems in Europe today can be found in Bosnia and Herzegovina, and in Serbia and Montenegro.

The European Union has several of the features of a confederal system:

- The citizens of the member states do not relate directly to any of the EU institutions except Parliament (which they elect), instead relating to them mainly through their national governments. Despite their powers of making and implementing policy, the key institutions of the EU – the European Commission, the Council of Ministers, the European Council, and the European Court of Justice – derive their authority not from the citizens of the member states, but from the leaders and governments of the member states. They are run either directly by national government leaders (the Council of Ministers and the European Council), or are appointed by those leaders (the Commission and the Court of Justice).
- The member states still have their own separate identities, have their own systems of law, can sign bilateral treaties with other states, can act unilaterally in most areas of foreign policy, and can argue that the EU institutions exist at their discretion. There is no European government in the sense that the EU has obvious leaders – such as a president, a foreign minister, or a cabinet – with sole power to make policy for the EU member states. The most important elected political leaders in the EU are still the heads of government of the individual member states.
- There is no generalized European tax system. The EU raises funds in part through levies and customs duties, which are a form of tax, but the vast majority of taxes – income, corporate, property, sales, capital gains, and so on – are raised by national or local units of government, which also make tax policy.
- There is no European military or defence system. The armies, navies, and air forces of the member states still answer to the governments of the member states, although contingents have come together as the seeds of a European security force (see Chapter 9). In this sense they are the functional equivalent of the militias that existed in the American confederal system.
- The EU may have its own flag and anthem, but most of the citizens of the member states still have a much greater sense of allegiance to their own national flags, anthems, and other symbols, and there has been little progress towards building a sense of a European identity (see Chapter 6).

Interestingly, the concept of confederalism is rarely mentioned in conjunction with the EU. Most analyses of its character – and most political debates about its future – instead move directly to federalism, and revolve around the extent to which the EU is already federal in nature, or may become so. To a large extent this is due to the frequency with which Eurosceptics use anti-federalism as the core of their argument.

Federalism

A federal system is one in which at least two levels of government – national and local – coexist with separate or shared powers, each having independent functions, but neither having supreme authority over the other. Unlike a confederal system, where the higher authority does not exercise power directly over individuals, a federal government exercises power over both its constituent units and its citizens, and there is a direct relationship between citizens and each level of government.

A federal system usually consists of an elected national government with sole power over foreign and security policy, and separately elected local governments with powers over such issues as education and policing. There is a single national currency and a common defence force, a written constitution that spells out the relative powers of the different levels of government, a court that can arbitrate disputes between them, and at least two major sets of law, government, bureaucracy, and taxation. The cumulative interests of the local units tend to define the interests of the national government, which tends to deal with those matters better dealt with at the national rather than the local level.

There are several federations in the world, including Australia, Canada, Germany, India, Mexico, and Nigeria, but the best known and most thoroughly studied is the United States. It has been a federal republic since 1788, when nine of the original 13 states agreed to move from a confederal relationship to a federal union, voluntarily giving up power over such areas as common security, but retaining their own sets of laws and a large measure of control over local government. American states can raise their own taxes, and they have independent powers over such policy areas as education, land use, the police, and roads, but they are not allowed to make treaties with other states or foreign nations, or to have their own currencies, to levy taxes on imports and exports, or to maintain their own armies. Meanwhile, the federal government cannot unilaterally redraw the borders of a state, impose different levels of tax by state, give states different levels of representation in the US Senate (where each state has two representatives), or amend the US constitution without the support of two-thirds of the states. Meanwhile – an important point – the US constitution (in the Tenth Amendment) reserves to the states or the people all the powers not delegated to the national government by the constitution or prohibited by it to the states.

Box 1.2 Government or governance?

When we study politics, we inevitably look at government, or the institutions and officials (elected or appointed) that make up the formal governing structure of a state, and that have the power to make laws and set the formal political agenda. We examine how those institutions come to power, how they relate to one another, and how they relate to the people under their jurisdiction. But while the EU has a group of 'governing' institutions, there is no EU government as such. Instead, it is common to see the term 'governance' used in conjunction with the system of authority in the EU. This describes a system in which laws and policies are made and implemented without the existence of a formally acknowledged set of governing institutions, but instead as a result of interactions involving a complex variety of actors, including member state governments, EU institutions, interest groups, and other sources of influence.

At the heart of any discussion is the controversial question of sovereignty – what it is, who has it, and what impact integration has on the powers enjoyed by the member states. Sovereignty is usually defined as the right to hold and exercise authority. So a state is sovereign over its territory, for example, meaning it has the power to decide what happens within that territory, and to make laws that govern the lives of the people who live there. More specifically, sovereignty is usually said to lie in the hands of the person or institution that exercises control over the territory. In democratic systems, this usually means the national legislature. Theoretically, there are no legal constraints on a sovereign, only moral and practical ones – the sovereign is not answerable to any higher authority, but can only exert its powers to the extent that those under its authority will allow, and to the extent that it can practically implement its decisions.

In a democracy, the sovereign may not answer to any higher authority, but does answer to the people, because it is the will of the people that decides where sovereign power lies. So sovereignty lies with the people, even though sovereign power is usually exercised by the institution that the people elect to represent their interests. This means that the common complaint made by Eurosceptics that integration means a loss of sovereignty is not entirely accurate. Sovereignty has not been lost in the European Union, but rather has been redistributed. Where sovereign power was once monopolized by national governments in the member states, it is now shared by those governments and by the institutions of the European Union.

EU member states can still do almost everything that the states in the US model *cannot* do: they can make treaties, operate their own tax systems, maintain an independent military, and – with 13 of the 25 member states – use their own national currencies. The EU institutions, meanwhile, have few of the powers of the federal government in the US model: they cannot levy taxes, do not operate a common military, do not yet enjoy the undivided loyalty of most Europeans, and do not have sole power to negotiate all agreements on behalf of the member states with the rest of the world. The 'f-word' has proved a controversial element in several of the debates about how to change the structure and reach of the EU, and while the EU is far from being a full-blown federation, it does have some of the features of a federal system:

- It has a complex system of treaties and laws that are uniformly applicable throughout the European Union, to which all the member states and their citizens are subject, and that are interpreted and protected by the European Court of Justice.
- In those policy areas where the member states have agreed to surrender authority to the EU – including intra-European trade, the environment, agriculture, and social policy – EU law supersedes national law.
- It has a directly elected representative legislature in the form of the European Parliament, which has growing powers over the process by which European laws are made. As those powers grow, so the powers of national legislatures are declining.
- Although still small by comparison to most national budgets (just €100 billion, or $120 billion, in 2004), the EU budget gives the EU institutions an element of financial independence.
- The European Commission has the authority to oversee negotiations with third parties on behalf of all the member states, in those areas where it has been given authority by the member states.
- Twelve of the EU member states have their own currency, the euro. With its launch in 2002, they transferred monetary policy from their own national central banks to the European Central Bank in Frankfurt.

One way of looking at the practice of European federalism is to picture the EU as a network in which individual member states are increasingly defined not by themselves but in relation to their EU partners, and in which they prefer to interact with one another rather than third parties because those interactions create incentives for self-interested cooperation (Keohane and Hoffmann, 1991, pp. 13–14). It has been argued that the EU has become 'cooptive', meaning that its participants have more to gain by working within the system than by going it alone (Heisler and Kvavik, 1973). Once they are involved, governments of the member states must take some of the responsibility for actions taken by the EU as a whole, and find it increasingly difficult to blame the European institutions.

Federalism is not an absolute or a static concept, and it has taken on different forms in different situations and at different times according to the relative strength and nature of local political, economic, social, historical, and cultural pressures. For example, the US model of federalism was in place long before that country began its westward expansion, explicitly includes a system in which the powers of the major national government institutions are separated, checked, and balanced, and was adopted more to avoid the dangers of chaos and tyranny than to account for social divisions. Furthermore, it has changed over time as a result of an ongoing debate over the relative powers of national and local government. In India, by contrast, federalism was seen as a solution to the difficulty of governing a state that was already in place, and that had deep ethnic and cultural divisions; the national government has a fused executive and legislature on the British model, and while India is a federal republic like the United States, political reality has ensured that powers have often been much more centralized in the hands of the national government.

The most enthusiastic European integrationists would like to see a federal United States of Europe in which today's national governments would become local governments, with the same kinds of powers as the *Länder* governments have in Germany or state governments in the United States. Before this could happen, there would need to be – at the very least – a directly elected European government, a constitution, a common tax system, a single currency, and a common military, and EU institutions would have to be able to act on behalf of all the member states in foreign relations. But just how far the process of integration would have to go before there was a federal Europe is a debatable point. There is no reason why European federalism would have to look exactly like the US, Indian or even German models – it could be much looser.

The logic of integration

What are the motives behind regional integration, and how do they help explain the European Union? People or states usually cooperate or create alliances for one of four reasons:

- They may be brought together by force.
- They may come together out of the need for security in the face of a common external threat.
- They may share common values and goals, and reach agreement on how to govern themselves as a whole.
- They may decide that they can promote peace and improve their quality of life more quickly and effectively by working together rather than separately.

Interstate relations in Europe were long influenced and driven by the first two motives, but since 1945 there has been a shift to the third and the fourth. But just why and how the process of integration has evolved remains a matter of dispute, with competing theoretical explanations.

The study of international relations after the Second World War was dominated by realist theory, which argues that states are the most important actors on the world stage (because there is no higher power), and that states strive to protect their interests relative to each other. Realists talk about the importance of survival in a hostile global environment, and argue that states use both conflict and cooperation to ensure their security through a balance of power with other states. For them, the EU would be a gathering of sovereign states, which retain authority over their own affairs, give power to new cooperative bodies only when it suits them, and reserve the right to take back that power at any time. In short, realist theory argues that the EU exists only because the member states have decided that it is in their best interests. Realism is a pessimistic way of looking at the world, and was a response to the tensions that arose out of the nuclear age. It did not explain the rising tide of cooperation that followed the Second World War, and also left many unanswered questions about the motives behind international relations. Thus it began to fall out of fashion (although its principles have been revived by neoconservatives in the Bush administration in the United States), and most of the theoretical debates about European integration have since focused on two different sets of explanations: functionalism and neofunctionalism.

Functionalism

While realists talk about competition, conflict, and self-interest, functionalists focus more on cooperation. While realists talk about relations among governments, functionalists argue that the best people to build cooperation are technical experts, not government representatives. They talk of the internal dynamic of cooperation, arguing that if states work together in certain limited areas and create new bodies to oversee that cooperation, they will work together in other areas through an 'invisible hand' of integration. In short, functionalists argue that European integration has its own logic that the EU member states find hard to resist. Although membership involves contracts that could be broken, in reality they have an almost irresistible authority, and – in the case of the EU – integration has now become so much a part of the fabric of European society that if a state left the EU, the costs would outweigh the benefits.

Functionalism is based on the idea of incrementally bridging the gaps between states by building functionally specific organizations. So instead of trying to coordinate big issues such as economic or defence policy, for example, functionalists believed they could 'sneak up on peace' (Lindberg and Scheingold, 1971, p. 6) by promoting integration in relatively non-controversial areas such as the postal service, or a particular sector of industry, or by harmonizing technical issues such as weights and measures.

The thinker most often associated with these ideas was the Romanian-born British social scientist David Mitrany (1888–1975), who defined the functional approach as an attempt to link 'authority to a specific activity, to break away from the traditional link between authority and a definite territory' (Mitrany, 1966, p. 27). He argued that transnational bodies would not only be more efficient providers of welfare than national governments, but that they would help transfer popular loyalty away from the state, and so help reduce the chances of international conflict (Rosamond, 2000, p. 33). Ironically, Mitrany felt that peace could not be achieved by regional unification, because this would simply expand the problems of the state system, and replace interstate tensions with inter-regional tensions. Neither did he support the idea of world government, which he felt would threaten human freedom.

Writing in 1943, Mitrany argued for the creation of separate international bodies with authority over functionally specific fields, such as security, transport, and communication. They should be executive bodies with autonomous tasks and powers, he argued, and do some of the same jobs as national governments, only at a different level. This focus on particular functions would encourage international cooperation more quickly and effectively than grand gestures. The dimensions and structures of these international organizations would not have to be predetermined, but would instead be self-determined (Mitrany, 1966, pp. 27–31, 72).

Once these functional organizations were created, Mitrany argued, they would have to work with each other. For example, rail, road, and air agencies would need to collaborate on technical matters, such as the coordination of timetables, and agreement on how to deal with different volumes of passenger and freight traffic. As different groups of functional agencies worked together, there would be coordinated international planning. This would result not so much in the creation of a new system as in the rationalization of existing systems through a process of natural selection and evolution. States could join or leave, drop out of some functions and stay in others, or try their own political and social experiments. This could eventually lead to 'a rounded political system ... the functional arrangements might indeed be regarded as organic elements of federalism by instalments' (Mitrany, 1966, pp. 73–84).

Although it has been described as 'an approach rather than a tightly knit theory' (Taylor and Groom, 1975, p. 1), functionalism has dominated the theoretical debates since the 1950s about how the EU has evolved. The two men often described as the founders of the European Union, French businessman Jean Monnet and French foreign minister Robert Schuman, were functionalists in the sense that they opted for the integration of a specific area (the coal and steel industry) with the hope that this would encourage integration in other areas. As Schuman put it, 'Europe will not be made all at once or according to a single plan. It will be built through concrete achievements which first create a *de facto* solidarity' (Schuman Declaration, reproduced in Weigall and Stirk, 1992, pp. 58–9).

Box 1.3 Regional integration: costs and benefits

The opinions that Europeans have about regional integration are often based on a patchy grasp of how the EU has affected their lives, and are often coloured by the populist rhetoric of pro- and anti-European media, political parties, and political leaders. In the debate over the merits of integration, it has so far been easier to point accusing fingers at the costs than to outline the benefits. The costs most often quoted include the following:

1. Loss of sovereignty and national independence.
2. Loss of national identity as laws, regulations and standards are harmonized.
3. Reduced powers for national governments.
4. The creation of a new level of impersonal 'big government' in Brussels, leading to a new level of laws and regulations.
5. Increased competition and job losses brought by the removal of market protection.
6. Increased drug trafficking, crime and illegal immigration arising from the removal of border controls.
7. Problems related to controversial issues such as the Common Agricultural Policy.

For pro-Europeans, the benefits of integration include the following:

1. Cooperation makes war and conflict less likely.
2. The single market offers European businesses a larger pool of consumers.
3. Mergers and takeovers are creating world-leading European corporations, helping the EU better compete in the global marketplace.
4. There is greater freedom of cross-border movement within the EU.
5. It pools the economic and social resources of multiple member states.
6. Member states working together enjoy new global power and influence.
7. Poorer member states 'rise' to standards maintained by more progressive states.
8. Funds and investments create new opportunities in the poorer parts of the EU.
9. Democracy and capitalism are promoted in weaker member states.

As noted in Chapter 6, public opinion on integration has moved in cycles, with only about half of all Europeans supporting the idea, and a recent decline in the number of people who think that their country has benefited from membership. But – as also argued in Chapter 6 – very few Europeans know very much about the EU or about how it works.

Neofunctionalism

Studies of the early years of European integration led to the expansion of Mitrany's theories as neofunctionalism. This argues that preconditions are needed before integration can happen, including a switch in public attitudes away from nationalism and towards cooperation, a desire by elites to promote integration for pragmatic rather than altruistic reasons, and the delegation of real power to a new supranational authority (see Rosamond, 2000, Chapter 3). Once these changes take place there will be an expansion of integration caused by spillover: joint action in one area will create new needs, tensions and problems that will increase the pressure to take joint action in another. For example, the integration of agriculture will only really work if related sectors – say transport and agricultural support services – are integrated as well.

The forerunner of today's European Union was the European Coal and Steel Community (ECSC) (see Chapter 3). Founded in 1951, it was created partly for short-term goals such as the encouragement of Franco-German cooperation, but Monnet and Schuman also saw it as the first step in a process that would eventually lead to political integration (Urwin, 1995, pp. 44–6). Few people supported the ECSC idea at the start, but once it had been working for a few years, trade unions and political parties became more enthusiastic because they began to see its benefits, and pressure grew for integration in other sectors. Urwin notes that the ECSC approach was handicapped because it 'was still trying to integrate only one part of complex industrial economies, and could not possibly pursue its aims in isolation from other economic segments' (Urwin, 1995, p. 76). This was partly why – six years after the creation of the ECSC – agreement was reached among its members to achieve broader economic integration within the European Economic Community.

Neofunctionalist ideas dominated studies of European integration in the 1950s and 1960s, but briefly fell out of favour in the 1970s, in part because the process of integrating Europe seemed to have ground to a halt, and in part because the theory of spillover needed further elaboration. The most common criticism of neofunctionalism was that it was too linear, and needed to be expanded or modified to take account of different pressures for integration, such as changes in public and political attitudes, the impact of nationalism on integration, the influence of external events such as changes in economic and military threats from outside, and social and political changes taking place separately from the process of integration (Haas, 1968, pp. xiv–xv).

Joseph Nye (1971, pp. 208–14) gave neofunctionalism a boost when he wrote about taking it out of the European context and looking at non-Western experiences. He concluded that experiments in regional integration involve an integrative potential that depends on several different conditions:

- The economic equality or compatibility of the states involved. This was long the major concern behind allowing poorer eastern European and Mediterranean states to join the EU. At the same time, differences in the size or wealth of the member states may be less important than the presence of a driving force that helps bring them together, such as concerns about attempts by France and Germany to dominate the EU.
- The extent to which the elite groups that control economic policy in the member states think alike and hold the same values.
- The extent of interest group activity. Such groups play a key role in promoting integration if they see it as being in their interests.
- The capacity of the member states to adapt and respond to public demands, which in turn depends on the level of domestic stability and the capacity – or desire – of decision makers to respond.

On all these counts the EU has a relatively high integrative potential, in contrast to another key experiment in regional cooperation: the North American Free Trade Agreement (NAFTA) (see below). The United States may be a strong driving force, but it is much wealthier than Mexico, elite groups in Mexico are more in favour of state intervention in the marketplace than those in the United States and Canada, trade unions in the United States have been highly critical of NAFTA, and public opinion in Mexico is more tightly controlled and manipulated than in the United States and Canada. There is also widespread – but largely misinformed – criticism of NAFTA within the United States.

One of the responses to criticisms of neofunctionalism came in the form of intergovernmentalism, a theory which draws on realism and criticizes neofunctionalism for concentrating too much on the internal dynamics of integration without paying enough attention to the global context. Intergovernmentalism argues that while non-state actors play an important role in integration, the pace and nature of integration are ultimately determined by national governments pursuing national interests; they alone have legal sovereignty, and they alone have the political legitimacy that comes from being elected (Hoffman, 1964). A variation on this theme is liberal intergovernmentalism, a theory which emerged in the 1980s and 1990s, and combined the neofunctionalist view of the importance of domestic politics with the role of the governments of the EU member states in making major political choices. Proponents argue that European integration has moved forward as a result of a combination of factors such as the commercial interests of economic producers, and the relative bargaining power of important governments (for details, see Moravcsik, 1998).

Regional integration around the world

Whatever the pressures and motivations, Europeans since 1950 have built a complex web of economic, political, and social ties among themselves. Their successes and failures have drawn new attention to several other exercises in regional integration in other parts of the world. The motives have been similar or the same – peace through cooperation, security from neighbouring and distant enemies, the creation of greater economic opportunities, shared values, convenience, efficiency, and the self-interest of elites – but the levels of integration potential vary.

The Americas

The removal of barriers to trade has taken on a new significance for the United States, Canada, and Mexico, which are currently building a free trade area that – with a combined GNP of $11.8 trillion and a population of 420 million – is wealthier but smaller than the EU. It traces its roots to a bilateral free trade agreement born on 1 January 1989 between the United States and Canada, which became NAFTA when Mexico was admitted in 1992.

Compared to the EU, the goals of NAFTA were modest: to phase out tariffs on textiles, clothing, cars, trucks, vehicle parts, and telecommunications equipment over ten years; to phase out barriers to agricultural trade over 15 years; to allow banks, securities firms, and insurance companies access to all three markets; to open up the North American advertising market; to allow lorry drivers to cross borders freely; and to loosen rules on the movement of corporate executives and some professionals. National energy and transport industries are still heavily protected under NAFTA, there is nothing approaching the free movement of people, and all three member states can apply their own environmental regulations. No institutions have been created beyond two commissions to arbitrate disagreements over environmental standards and working conditions; special judges can also be empanelled to resolve disagreements on issues such as fishing rights and trade laws.

For some, NAFTA's real significance lay less in the content of the agreement than in the symbolism of its passage, representing (as it did at the time) a shift in US foreign policy and in the structure of a US economy gearing up for unparalleled competition from abroad. Certainly it is a much looser arrangement than the European Union, or even the European Economic Community in its early years. It is strictly intergovernmental, and although it has reduced trade restrictions, it has involved little surrender of authority or sovereignty.

Table 1.1 *Regional integration associations*

Europe	European Union (founded 1951, 25 members)
North America	North American Free Trade Agreement (1994, 3 members)
Latin America	Latin American Free Trade Association (1960–80, 7 members)
	Central American Common Market (1960, 5 members)
	Andean Group (1969, 5 members)
	Latin American Integration Association (1980, 11 members)
	Southern Cone Common Market (Mercosur) (1991, 4 members)
Caribbean	Caribbean Community and Common Market (1973, 14 members)
Pacific Rim	Asia Pacific Economic Cooperation (1989, 21 members)
Asia	Association of Southeast Asian Nations (1967, 10 members)
	South Asian Association for Regional Cooperation (1985, 7 members)
	Commonwealth of Independent States (1991, 12 members)
Middle East	Arab League (1945, 22 members)
	Council of Arab Economic Unity (1957, 13 members)
	Arab Cooperation Council (1989, 4 members)
	Arab Maghreb Union (1989, 5 members)
Africa	Central African Customs and Economic Union (1964, 6 members)
	East African Community (1967–78, revived 1999, 3 members)
	Economic Community of West African States (1975, 16 members)
	Economic Community of Central African States (1983, 10 members)
	Southern African Development Community (1992, 14 members)
	African Union (2001, 53 members)

Whether NAFTA will ever become anything like the EU remains to be seen. Neofunctional logic suggests it might, but many obstacles will need to be removed: Mexico's limited democracy and its centralist/corporatist ideas of government that run counter to traditions in the United States and Canada; large disparities in wealth, education, and per capita production;

concern among Canadians about the cultural dominance of the United States; significant gaps in mutual knowledge and understanding among the citizens of the three countries; and myths, misconceptions, and sheer ignorance about free trade.

While the United States and Canada are relative newcomers to the idea of regional integration, several much older exercises have been under way south of the Rio Grande since the 1960s, with mixed results. A combination of overly ambitious goals, persistent protectionism, authoritarian politics, and bad timing has undermined most of the agreements reached so far, forcing the participating states regularly to change their objectives and methods. The result has been a complex and constantly changing web of bilateral and multilateral free trade agreements.

The first step was taken with the signing in 1960 of the Treaty of Montevideo, creating the Latin American Free Trade Association (LAFTA). Seven countries – Argentina, Brazil, Chile, Mexico, Paraguay, Peru, and Uruguay – agreed to create a free trade zone by 1972, but the process was quickly derailed by the difficulties inherent in negotiating the abolition of trade barriers, the ambitious timetable, and the authoritarian nature of most of the governments involved. In 1969, Chile and Peru – frustrated by the lack of progress – joined Bolivia, Colombia, and Ecuador in the creation of the Andean Group, a more dynamic attempt at economic integration involving reduced taxes, a common external tariff, and investment in poorer industrializing areas.

Progress on LAFTA was undermined by domestic economic problems in most South American countries, so a new Treaty of Montevideo was signed in 1980, replacing LAFTA with the Latin American Integration Association (ALADI). With 11 members – the seven LAFTA members together with Bolivia, Colombia, Ecuador and Venezuela – ALADI emphasized the importance of regional preferences aimed at increasing exports, reducing imports and developing more favourable balances of trade as a prelude to regional integration. Although the replacement of authoritarian regimes by democratically elected governments augured well, the Latin American debt crisis of the 1980s discouraged those governments from opening up their markets.

The focus began to change in 1985–86 when Argentina and Brazil began to concentrate on the reduction of barriers to bilateral trade. Just as Franco-German cooperation provided the early engine for regional integration in Europe, the Argentina–Brazil nexus had a spillover economic effect on neighbouring states. In 1991 the effect expanded with the signing of the Treaty of Asunción between Argentina, Brazil, Paraguay, and Uruguay, creating the Southern Cone Common Market, or Mercosur. This has aimed at progressive tariff reduction, the adoption of sectoral agreements, a common external tariff, the agreement of free trade areas with neighbouring countries or subregional groups, and the ultimate creation of a common market. Bolivia and Chile are associate members.

A new dimension has been added to free trade in the Americas in recent years with US-led attempts to work towards a free trade zone covering the entire western hemisphere. The idea was raised in 1990 by President George H.W. Bush, who spoke of the possibility of a free trade area of the Americas (FTAA), stretching from Alaska to Cape Horn. It was taken up enthusiastically by President Bill Clinton, who played host to the leaders of 34 states at a 'summit of the Americas' in Miami in December 1994, the first meeting among leaders of American states for 27 years. They agreed a target date of 2005, with 'concrete progress' to have been made by 2000, and trade ministers have since held meetings to decide the agenda for negotiations. A second summit of the Americas was held in Santiago, Chile, in April 1998 formally to launch the negotiations. A third was held in Quebec City, Canada, in April 2001. However, while trade within regional subgroupings such as NAFTA, Mercosur, and the Central American Common Market has grown substantially in recent years, the FTAA has obstacles of a larger order to overcome.

Meanwhile, broader economic integration has been taking place around the Pacific Rim under the aegis of Asia Pacific Economic Cooperation (APEC). This is not so much an institution as a forum for the discussion of economic issues affecting 21 Asian, Pacific and American states, including Canada, China, Japan, Russia, and the United States. Although it has been promoted most actively since 1989 by the United States and Australia, China and Japan are now widely seen as the leading contenders for leadership of APEC. The medium-term goal is the creation of a free trade zone among these countries by 2020. Progress so far has been slow, and China appears to see Japan less as a partner than as a rival for leadership in the region. At the same time, the Japanese role is welcomed by many of its neighbours as offering a counterbalance to the economic weight of the United States.

Asia

The most important initiatives for Asian regional integration have come out of the Association of Southeast Asian Nations (ASEAN), established in August 1967 to replace an earlier organization founded in 1961. Headquartered in Jakarta, Indonesia, ASEAN has ten members: the founding states were Indonesia, Malaysia, the Philippines, Singapore, and Thailand, which were joined in 1984 by Brunei, in 1995 by Vietnam, and in 1997 by Burma, Cambodia, and Laos. From an initial interest in security issues (protecting the region from big-power rivalry and providing a forum for the resolution of intraregional problems), ASEAN has moved steadily towards economic cooperation and trade, its members agreeing in 1992 to create an ASEAN Free Trade Area by 2007.

ASEAN has a much looser institutional system than the EU. The major decision-making body is the Meeting of the ASEAN Heads of Government, or the ASEAN Summit (equivalent to the European Council). The first such summit took place in 1976, but no plans were made to meet regularly until the fourth summit in 1992, when it was decided that the heads of government would meet formally every three years and informally at least once in between. While summits lay down the general direction of ASEAN activities, foreign ministers meet annually (inviting along other ministers as and when necessary) to develop overall policies, and economics ministers meet annually to work on the development of free trade. In recent years, other ministers have also met more regularly to discuss energy, agriculture, tourism, and transport issues. When necessary, joint ministerial meetings take place to promote cross-sectoral coordination. A standing committee headed by a secretary-general takes care of business between ministerial meetings, providing a modest bureaucracy for ASEAN (ASEAN home page, 2004).

Further west, the most obvious candidate to head a regional economic grouping is India, with a population of just over one billion. India has been reluctant to become involved in regional economic arrangements, however, thanks mainly to strained relations with most of its neighbours, especially Pakistan, with which it has had three wars since 1947. India's giant presence has also caused an unequal distribution of power in south Asia, and successive Indian governments have preferred to deal bilaterally with other countries in the region. For their part, India's smaller neighbours fear that India would inevitably dominate a regional association, and use it to institutionalize its hegemony (Hardgrave and Kochanek, 2000, p. 431).

Despite these concerns, greater regional cooperation began slowly to emerge in the early 1980s, leading to the creation in 1985 of the South Asian Association for Regional Cooperation (SAARC) with seven members: Bangladesh, Bhutan, India, the Maldives, Nepal, Pakistan, and Sri Lanka. Together they are home to more than 1.4 billion people, or more than one-fifth of the world's population. Meeting in 1983, the foreign ministers of the seven countries agreed to promote 'collective self-reliance' in nine areas, including agriculture, transport, and telecommunications, and since 1985 the leaders have met at annual summits rotating among the different countries, with the host country assuming the chairmanship for that year.

The commerce ministers met for the first time in 1996, a move that was seen as recognition of the need to address what then Indian prime minister Narasimha Rao called 'neoprotectionism' among SAARC members, notably India and Pakistan. The seven countries had earlier agreed to set up a South Asian Preferential Trading Arrangement (SAPTA) with a view to encouraging the removal of tariff and non-tariff barriers and working towards the creation of a free trade area (SAFTA) by 2005. At the moment SAARC has no institutional arrangements, its goals are modest in comparison with those of the European Union, or even NAFTA, and the long-standing mutual distrust between India and Pakistan remains a considerable handicap.

The Middle East

The Middle East has had less success with experiments in regional integration than any other part of the world, which is ironic given the Islamic belief in a worldwide community of Muslims transcending race, language, and national identity. Greater cooperation among the states of the Middle East makes sense at many levels: several countries depend too much on a single commodity (oil); the profits of the oil producers could be used to invest in non-producers and help promote manufacturing in the region; cooperation would allow better control of the already considerable flow of workers to the oil-rich states, and intraregional trade could help the Middle Eastern states to reduce their dependence on oil exports to the West and to develop regional transportation networks. It might also underpin attempts to bring stability and democracy to one of the most volatile regions of the world.

There have been several attempts at regional cooperation. The first began in 1945 with the creation of the Arab League to promote political, economic, social, and military cooperation. The League is headquartered in Cairo, and currently has 22 members. A second step was taken in 1957 with the creation of the Council of Arab Economic Unity, whose goal is to promote economic integration. Headquartered in Amman, Jordan, it has 13 members. In 1965 the Arab Common Market was set up to promote economic cooperation and integration, but so far it has attracted only four members (Egypt, Iraq, Jordan, and Yemen). Finally, the Arab Monetary Fund was established in 1977 to promote economic and monetary integration. Headquartered in the United Arab Emirates, it has 19 members.

Why has the success of these organizations been so limited? Part of the problem stems from internal dissension, notably differences of opinion on how to deal with Israel: Egypt was expelled from the Arab League for ten years when it signed the 1979 peace treaty with Israel. Further divisions were caused by disagreement over how to respond to Iraq's invasion of Kuwait in 1990, and persist in the wake of the troubles following the 2003 US-led invasion of Iraq. Cooperation has been further undermined by differences among states over the interpretation of Islam, the fact that less than 10 per cent of trade in the Middle East and North Africa is intraregional, the dominance of oil in national economies, protectionist national economic policies, and severe cross-border restrictions on the movement of people. It will take a significant shift in attitudes and policies for the Middle East to create the right conditions for greater economic cooperation.

Africa

Africa to date has lacked high integrative potential, because of a combination of poverty, political instability, civil war, border disputes, and the often different political and economic agendas of African governments. This has not discouraged several groups of countries from building regional cooperative organizations. One early experiment was the East African Community, under which Kenya, Tanzania, and Uganda built elements of a single market and a customs union, operated a single currency, and developed a common transport system. The Community broke up in acrimony in 1977, in part because of the unbalanced benefits accruing to Kenya, but it was relaunched in 1999.

A more substantial experiment – but one that has its own problems – is the 16-member Economic Community of West African States (ECOWAS). Headquartered in Abuja, Nigeria, it was founded in 1975 and now has a total population of nearly 253 million people. ECOWAS set out to achieve first a customs union and then a full common market along the lines of the European Union. By harmonizing their policies on agriculture, industry, transport, and communications, and paving the way for the free movement of people and labour, its members felt they could change the balance of power between themselves and the richer Western countries. To promote cooperation, a development fund was created through which the wealthier ECOWAS members could channel investment funds to the poorer members.

Organizationally, ECOWAS revolves around meetings of the heads of government, which took place annually until 1997, when it was decided to hold them twice a year. A council of ministers, consisting of two representatives from each of the member states, meets twice a year to oversee the running of ECOWAS, which is left to a small secretariat and five commissions dealing with issues such as trade, customs, industry and transport. A tribunal meets to interpret provisions laid down in the founding treaty of ECOWAS and to settle disputes between member states.

ECOWAS faces many problems, including the persistent political instability of several of its members (notably Burkina Faso, Liberia, and Sierra Leone), the dominating presence of Nigeria (which accounts for about half of the population of ECOWAS and about half of its GDP), the unwillingness of smaller states to open their markets to Nigeria (suspecting the latter of working towards regional domination), and the often conflicting economic and trade policies of its members. It has nonetheless made progress in some areas, such as regional peacekeeping (including its contribution to monitoring a cease-fire in war-torn Liberia in 1990–93).

In July 2001, Africa launched the most ambitious attempt yet to build regional cooperation when the 37-year-old Organization of African Unity (OAU) was replaced by the African Union. Inspired by the European Union, the African Union is planning to set up an African central bank, a parliament, an executive commission, and a court. All 53 members of the OAU were potentially also members of the African Union, but since conflicts were under way in 21 of those countries, the integrative potential of the Union was questionable.

Conclusions

The European Union is the most highly evolved example of regional integration in the world, but – as this chapter reflects – it is far from being the only example. Clusters of states on every continent (or, at least, the elites of those states) have found that cooperation on a variety of issues is in their interests, so much so that several have decided to take that cooperation to another level. In other words, rather than simply working together on matters of mutual interest, they have transferred powers to decision-making systems that function above the level of the state. Some of these systems are informal, consisting of regular meetings among ministers or national leaders and agreement to reach decisions jointly rather than individually. Others are more formal and have moved beyond the intergovernmental level to involve the creation of supranational organizations and bodies of common law.

As a result, regional integration is a concept with which we are all becoming more familiar. This is especially true in Europe, because the laws and decisions that govern the lives of Europeans are being made less at the local or national level, and increasingly as a result of negotiations and compromises among the EU member states. Developments at the EU level are becoming as important for Europeans to understand as those in their national capitals. Not long ago an 'informed citizen' was someone who knew how their national system of government worked, how their national economy functioned and how their national society was structured. To be 'informed' now demands a broader horizon, and familiarity with a new set of institutions, processes, and political, economic, and social forces. It also demands an understanding of the character of the EU, and the extent to which it is a confederal or a federal association.

Yet Europeans are still some way from understanding how and why regional integration has happened, or even deciding whether or not it is a good idea. Europe has travelled a long road since 1945, and has survived political and economic crises to become an economic superpower that has enjoyed the longest period of general peace in its history. But to what extent can this be credited to the European Union? What would Europe look like today without the EU? Would it be richer or poorer, more or less peaceful? Is there anything that the rest of the world can learn from the European experience, and is there anything that Europeans can learn from the steps being taken towards regional integration in the Americas, Asia, or Africa?

Opinions on the value of regional integration – and its long-term prospects – will remain divided as long as they are confused and obscured by questions and doubts about the conditions that encourage integration, the logic of the steps taken towards integration, and the end product. Comparing the European case with other examples of regional integration around the world can give us more insight into its advantages and disadvantages, but we are still some way from agreement on what drives the process, and from understanding what we have created. Most confusingly, the goals of regional integration are only vaguely defined. How will Europe know when it has gone far enough? What exactly is the end goal? The next two chapters will attempt to answer these questions by looking at the evolution, structure, and effects of the European Union.

Chapter 2

The Idea of Europe

The changing identity of Europe
Where is Europe?
Europe today
Conclusions

Europe is a continent of energetic mongrels.
H. A. L. Fisher, British historian

We live in a European world. It is a multicultural world, to be sure, but most of it has been colonized at some point by one European power or another, and the majority of people live in societies that are either based on the European cultural tradition or influenced on a daily basis by the norms and values of that tradition. The 'world culture' described by the American political scientist Lucien Pye (1966) is ultimately European in origin, even if it is most actively promoted and exported by the United States (which is itself primarily a product of European culture).

It is all the more ironic, then, that the idea of Europe is so hard to pin down. We know where Europe sits on a map, but we have difficulty defining its physical and cultural boundaries and being sure about what makes it distinctive. Europeans have much that unites them, but much more that divides them. They have no common history, they speak many different languages, they have different social values, their views of their place in the world often differ, they have gone to war with each other with tragic frequency, they have often redefined their allegiance and their identity, and they have often redrawn their common frontiers in response to changes in political affiliations.

However, since 1945 the differences have slowly been replaced by common interests, goals and values, prompted in part by a redefinition of Europe's place in the world. Pressures to improve the way they managed their own affairs, to take on more responsibility for each other, and to deal with the uncertainties posed by changes in the Soviet Union and then in Russia initially made Europeans introverted (Wallace, 1992, p. 16). With the rise of the single market, the end of the cold war, and growing differences with the United States, however, Europeans have had to rethink their place in the world, and to accept the new responsibilities that come with renewed global power and influence. Outsiders have had to rethink their understanding of Europe, which is now less a collection of sovereign states and more a global superpower. North American and Japanese business and government leaders see the EU as a new source of competition for economic power and political influence, while most eastern Europeans and Russians see it as a new force for positive economic and political change.

Despite this redefinition of Europe, the idea of European unity that has taken root and expanded since 1945 is nothing new. In fact it is an old idea that has simply been revived and, more importantly, adopted voluntarily by a large number of Europeans for the first time. Monarchs, popes, generals, and dictators have dreamed about variations on the theme of unity since the Early Middle Ages, and intellectuals have written and spoken about unity as a means of defending Europe against itself and outsiders since at least the fourteenth century. The key difference between the times in which they wrote and the contemporary age is that there is now much wider political pressure and public support for the idea of integration.

This chapter will attempt to paint a portrait of Europe. It begins with a discussion of the meaning of the terms 'Europe' and 'European', providing a brief history both of the idea of Europe and of the arguments in favour of integration and unity, and setting the scene for developments after 1945 (covered in Chapter 3). The second half of the chapter is a political, economic and social profile of Europe at the beginning of the twenty-first century, which compares and contrasts the character of the member states of the EU and their neighbours.

The changing identity of Europe

Defining 'Europe' and 'European' has always been difficult, thanks to disagreements about the outer limits of the region and the inner character of its inhabitants. Today those inhabitants are experiencing political and economic change that is encouraging them to think of themselves less as Spaniards or Belgians or Poles and more as 'Europeans', but this is a trend that begs several questions. What is Europe, where does it begin and end, and what exactly does being a European mean? Is there a coherent and distinctive European identity and a set of core European values with which the inhabitants of the region can identify? When and how did the idea of European unity emerge, and how has it evolved?

Europe has never been united, and its history has been one of fragmentation, conflict, and changing political boundaries. Large parts of Europe have been brought together at various times for different reasons – beginning with the Romans and moving through the Franks to the

Habsburgs, Napoleon, and Hitler – but while many have dreamed of unification, it has only been since the Second World War that Europeans have finally begun to embrace the notion that nationalism might be put aside in the interests of regional cooperation. For the first time in its history, almost the entire region is engaged in a process of integration that is encouraging its inhabitants to think and behave as Europeans rather than as members of smaller cultural or national groups that just happen to inhabit the same land mass.

The word 'Europe' is thought to come from Greek mythology: Europa was a Phoenician princess who was seduced by Zeus disguised as a white bull, and was taken from her homeland in what is now Lebanon to Crete, where she later married the King of Crete. It is unclear when the term 'European' was first applied to a specific territory or its inhabitants, but it appears first to have taken on substance when Greeks began to settle on the Ionian Islands and came across the Persians. The expansion of the Persian Empire led to war in the fifth century BC, when Greek authors such as Aristotle began to make a distinction between the languages, customs and values of Greeks, the inhabitants of Asia (as represented by the Persians) and the 'barbarians' of Europe, an area vaguely defined as being to the north. Maps drawn up by classical scholars subsequently showed the world divided into Asia, Europe and Africa, with the boundary between Europe and Asia marked by the River Don and the Sea of Azov (Delanty, 1995, pp. 18–19; den Boer, 1995).

The Roman Empire – whose power was at its peak from approximately 200 BC to 400 AD – brought a substantial part of Europe under a common system of government for the first time. However, it was centred on the Mediterranean and took in North Africa and parts of the Middle East as well, and so was not exclusively European. Because the Romans were presiding over an empire, there was no prevailing sense that everyone living under Roman rule was part of a region with a common identity. Furthermore, the inhabitants of Europe were known as Franks or Romans by inhabitants of the Middle East and North Africa. The situation was further confused after the end of Roman hegemony in the last part of the fourth century AD, when Rome was invaded by the northern 'barbarians' and Europe broke up into feuding kingdoms. The invasions separated Europe culturally from its classical past, and the Dark Ages that followed witnessed substantial movements of people as different tribes – notably the Huns, the Vikings, and the Magyars – invaded other parts of Europe.

The birth of Europe is often dated to the Early Middle Ages (500–1050), with the emergence of a common civilization based on Christianity, with Rome as the spiritual capital and Latin as the language of education. The beginning of a sense of a European identity came with the development of a rift between the western and eastern branches of Christianity, the expansion of Frankish power from the area of what are now Belgium and the Netherlands, and the development of a stronger territorial identity in the face of external threats, notably from the Middle East. The retreat of Europeans in the face of Asian expansionism reached its peak in the seventh and eighth centuries with the advance of Arab forces across North Africa and into Spain and southern France. They were turned back only in 732 with their defeat by Charles Martel at Poitiers.

The term 'European' was used by contemporary chroniclers to describe the forces under the command of Martel (Hay, 1957, p. 25), but it did not become more widely used until the year 800, when Charlemagne was crowned Holy Roman Emperor by the Pope and was described in poems as the king and father of Europe. The Frankish Empire over which he presided covered most of what are now France, Switzerland, Austria, southern Germany and the Benelux countries. (As proponents of European unity in the 1950s liked to point out, this correlated closely with the territory of the six founding member states of the European Economic Community.) Although the Frankish Empire helped promote the spread of Christianity, it was quickly divided up among Charlemagne's sons after his death in 814, and while the Holy Roman Empire persisted until the middle of the fourteenth century, it was – as Voltaire later quipped – 'neither Holy, nor Roman, nor an Empire'.

Europe at the time was technologically backward in comparison with China, and was to remain peripheral to the development of civilization until well into the Middle Ages. Central authority declined and intra-European trade ended in the wake of further invasions from Scandinavia and central Europe, and feudalism became the norm as large landowners exercised growing authority over their subjects. By the beginning of the High Middle Ages in the mid-eleventh century, however, commerce had revived, agricultural production was growing, population was beginning to increase, towns were becoming centres of intellectual and commercial life, a new class of merchants was emerging, monarchs and the aristocracy were imposing greater control over their territories, and the threat of invasion from outside Europe had largely disappeared. In fact, through the crusades and the development of external trade, Europe – long the target of foreign invaders – now became the aggressor. As Christian armies came together from all over the region to take part in the crusades, Europe developed a tighter identity.

Safe from invasion, a European culture began to take root in the High Middle Ages, and by the fifteenth century it had become increasingly common for scholars to use the term 'Europe', which to outsiders became synonymous with 'Christendom'. Indeed the latter term was used more often than the former to describe the region. This was ironic given the turbulence that followed in the wake of famines, the Black Death and the

Hundred Years War (1337–1453), the emerging power of monarchs, and the challenges to the authority of the papacy that led to the Reformation and the growth of the modern state system. Europe became divided among a variety of Protestant churches and the Roman Catholic Church, and for much of the sixteenth and early seventeenth century was destabilized by religious warfare. Nonetheless Europeans began voyages of discovery to Africa, the Americas, and Asia, there was an expansion of education based on the classical works of Greek and Latin authors, and a scientific revolution was sparked by the findings of Copernicus, Sir Isaac Newton, and others. All these developments combined to give Europeans a new confidence and a new sense of their place in the world.

Delanty (1995, p. 42) argues that cultural diversity within Europe ensured that the idea of European unity was restricted to matters relating to foreign conquest. The earliest proponents of unity were motivated in part by their belief that a united Christian Europe was essential for the revival of the Holy Roman Empire and by concern about Europe's insecurity in the face of gains by the Turks in Asia Minor; most of the proposals for unity were based on the argument that the supremacy of the papacy should be revived (Heater, 1992, p. 6). A notable example was the suggestion made in 1306 by the French lawyer and diplomat Pierre Dubois (b. 1255). Noting that war was endemic in Europe despite the teachings of Christianity, Dubois suggested that the princes and cities of Europe should form a confederal 'Christian Republic', overseen by a permanent assembly of princes working to ensure peace through the application of Christian principles. In the event of a dispute, a panel of nine judges could be brought together to arbitrate, with the Pope acting as a final court of appeal (Heater, 1992, p. 10; Urwin, 1995, p. 2).

The Renaissance (roughly 1350–1550) saw the loyalty of individuals shifting from the Church to ideas based on individualism and republicanism, and the state system began to emerge, beginning in England and France. Under the circumstances, the idea of regional unity was far from the minds of all but a small minority of idealists. Among these were King George of Bohemia and his diplomatist Antoine Marini, who proposed a European confederation to respond to the threat posed by the Turks in the mid-fifteenth century. Their plan – which was remarkably similar to the structure eventually set up for the European Union – involved an assembly meeting regularly and moving its seat every five years, a college of permanent members using a system of majoritarian decision making, a council of kings and princes, and a court to adjudicate disputes (de Rougemont, 1966, p. 71).

The Church had become so divided by the end of the sixteenth century that the idea of a united Christian Europe was abandoned, and those who still championed the idea of European unity saw it as based less on a common religion than on addressing the religious causes of conflict and the growing threat of Habsburg power. These were the motives behind the Grand Design outlined by the Duc de Sully (1560–1641) in France in the early seventeenth century. He proposed a redrawing of administrative lines throughout Europe so as to achieve an equilibrium of power, and the creation of a European Senate with 66 members serving three-year terms (Heater, 1992, pp. 30–5).

One of those influenced by de Sully's ideas was William Penn (1644–1718), who in the middle of yet another war between England and France published *An Essay Towards the Present Peace of Europe* (1693), in which he proposed the creation of a European diet or parliament that could be used for dispute resolution. He suggested that quarrels might be settled by a three-quarters majority vote, something like the qualified majority voting system used today (see Chapter 4). This would be weighted according to the economic power of the various countries: Germany would have 12 votes, France ten, England six and so on (Heater, 1992, pp. 53–6; Salmon and Nicoll, 1997, pp. 3–6). In 1717 the Abbé de Saint-Pierre (1658–1743) published his three-volume *Project for Settling an Everlasting Peace in Europe,* in which he argued for free trade and a European Senate. (His ideas were later to inspire Friedrich von Schiller to write 'Ode to Joy' which – sung to Beethoven's Ninth Symphony – has become the European anthem (Heater, 1992, p. 85).)

Several prominent thinkers and philosophers subsequently explored the theme of peace through unity. For example Jean-Jacques Rousseau wrote in favour of a European federation; Jeremy Bentham, in *A Plan for an Universal and Perpetual Peace* (1789), wrote of his ideas for a European assembly and a common army; Immanual Kant's *Thoughts on Perpetual Peace* (1795) included suggestions for the achievement of world peace; and the Comte de Saint-Simon, in response to the Napoleonic Wars, published a pamphlet in 1814 titled *The Reorganization of the European Community,* in which he argued the need for a federal Europe with common institutions, but within which national independence would be maintained and respected.

For political figures, the desire to overcome Europe's political divisions usually led them to the narrow view that conquest was the best response, but found themselves foiled by the sheer size of the task and the resistance of key actors to changes in the balance of power. For example, the attempts by Charlemagne, Philip II of Spain and the Habsburgs to establish a European hegemony all failed, argues Urwin (1995, p. 2), because of the 'complex fragmented mosaic of the continent ... [and] the inadequate technical resources of the would-be conquerors to establish and maintain effective control by force over large areas of territory against the wishes of the local populations'.

The first attempt to achieve unity by force in modern times was made by Napoleon, who brought what are now France, Belgium, the Netherlands, Luxembourg, and parts of Germany and Italy under his direct rule. He saw himself as the 'intermediary' between the old order and the new, and hoped for a European association with a common body of law, a common court of appeal, a single currency, and a uniform system of weights and measures. In contrast to Napoleon's idealistic notion of unity, and despite rapid economic, social and technological change, nineteenth-century Europe was dominated by nationalism, which emerged during the French Revolution and led most notably to the unification of Italy in the 1860s and Germany in 1871. Nationalism led to rivalry among European states, both within Europe and further afield in the competition among those states for colonies.

The concept of a United States of Europe nonetheless continued to be promoted by nineteenth-century intellectuals such as Victor Hugo, who in 1848 declared that the nations of Europe, 'without losing [their] distinctive qualities or ... glorious individuality, will merge closely into a higher unity and will form the fraternity of Europe ... Two huge groups will be seen, the United States of America and the United States of Europe, holding out their hands to one another across the ocean'. However, political leaders did not embrace such idealistic notions, and a new wave of nationalism led instead to increased militarization and the outbreak in 1914 of the Great War, in which all the competing tensions within Europe finally boiled over. One of the results of the war was chaos in much of central Europe, but the peace arranged under the 1919 Treaty of Versailles avoided as many questions and problems as it addressed.

Before, during and after the war, philosophers and political leaders continued to put their minds to the question of how to encourage Europeans to rise above nationalism and consider themselves part of a broader culture, thereby helping them to address and remove the causes of conflict, and allowing Europe to defend itself against external threats. Dubois, Penn, Saint-Simon, and others had already explored such ideas, but they had all been writing in a vacuum of public interest. The horrors of the First World War now created an audience that was more receptive to the idea of European cooperation, and discussions involved not just intellectuals but political leaders as well. The most enthusiastic proponents tended to be smaller states that were tired of being caught up in big power rivalry, and several made practical moves towards economic cooperation. For example, Belgium and Luxembourg created a limited economic union in 1922, and in 1930 joined several Scandinavian states in an agreement to limit tariffs.

One of the best-known of the intellectual contributors to the debate about European unity was Count Richard Coudenhove-Kalergi, who proposed a Pan-European Union (Box 2.1). He failed to generate a mass following, but his ideas attracted the interest of a number of leading figures in the arts, such as Richard Strauss and Ortega y Gasset, and several current or future political leaders, including Georges Pompidou, Thomas Masaryk, Konrad Adenauer, Winston Churchill, and two French prime ministers, Edouard Herriot and Aristide Briand. Immediately after the war, the prevailing view in France was that European cooperation was an impossible dream, and that the best hope for peace lay in French strength and German weakness (Bugge, 1995, p. 102). Herriot was one of those who disagreed, and in 1924 he called for the creation of a 'United States of Europe', to grow out of the postwar cooperation promoted by the League of Nations.

For his part, Briand called for a European confederation working within the League of Nations, and in May 1930 distributed a memorandum to governments outlining his ideas (Salmon and Nicoll, 1997, pp. 9–14). In it he wrote of the need for 'a permanent regime of solidarity based on international agreements for the rational organization of Europe'. He used such terms as 'common market' and 'European Union', and even listed specific policy needs, such as the development of trans-European transport networks, and anticipated what would later become the regional and social policies of the EU. Although he is often described in France as one of the founding fathers of European integration, his memorandum was sidelined by the gathering tensions that led to the Second World War.

The rise of Nazism was focused on correcting the 'wrongs' of the Treaty of Versailles and creating a German 'living space'. Adolf Hitler spoke of a 'European house', but only in terms of the importance of German rule over the continent in the face of the perceived threat from communists and 'inferior elements' within and outside Europe. Many of the nationalist tensions that had built up in Europe during the nineteenth century – and had failed to be resolved by the Great War – now boiled over once again into conflict. Hitler was able to expand his Reich to include Austria, Bohemia, Alsace-Lorraine, and most of Poland, and to occupy much of the rest of continental Europe.

Following the end of the war in 1945, the ideological division of Europe added to its preexisting economic and social divisions, so that it became normal to think of the region as having multiple identities: the capitalist west, the socialist east, the industrial centre, the Mediterranean south, and the Nordic north. However, the end of the cold war in 1990–91 also brought an end to the ideological and social divisions that had been represented by the Berlin Wall and the Iron Curtain, and as the differences between east and west began to decline it became more normal to think of Europe as a whole.

Box 2.1 Paneuropa

The period of peace after the First World War saw the publication of a flood of books and articles exploring variations on the theme of European unity. The most influential of these were written by Count Richard Coudenhove-Kalergi (1894–1972), the son of an Austrian diplomat and his Japanese wife, and founder in 1922 of the Pan-European Union.

The problems facing Europe after the war convinced Coudenhove-Kalergi that the only workable guarantee of peace was political union, and he outlined his ideas in a book titled *Paneuropa,* published in 1923. He argued that while Europe's global supremacy was over, the internal decline of Europe could be avoided if its political system was modernized, with a new emphasis on large-scale cooperation. Changes in Europe could not happen in isolation from those in the rest of the world, however, and Coudenhove-Kalergi felt that the best hope for world peace lay in the creation of five 'global power fields':

- the Americas (excluding Canada)
- the USSR
- Eastern Asia (China and Japan)
- Paneuropa (including continental Europe's colonies in Africa and south-east Asia)
- Britain and its empire (including Canada, Australia, southern Africa, the Middle East and India)

He excluded the USSR from Europe because it was too diverse and did not have the democratic traditions necessary for the development of Paneuropa. He was uncomfortable about excluding Britain, but did so because he felt it was so powerful as to be a political continent in its own right. It could serve as a mediator with the United States, however, and could become part of Paneuropa if it lost its empire.

Coudenhove-Kalergi argued that an arms race among European states would be destructive and keep Europe in a permanent state of crisis. Instead, he proposed a four-stage process for the achievement of European union: a conference of representatives from the 26 European states, the agreement of treaties for the settlement of European disputes, the development of a customs union, and the drafting of a federal European constitution. He also suggested that English should become the common second language for Europe, since it was becoming the dominant global language.

Europeans still make many distinctions among themselves. Eastern Europe is still working to rid itself of the heritage of state socialism, and Germans still distinguish between those from the east and those from the west. Cultural and economic differences also continue to influence perceptions of Europe: the Mediterranean states to the south are distinctive from the maritime states to the west or the Scandinavian states to the north. However, compared with just a generation ago, the differences that separate Europeans have become less distinct and less obvious. Language differences still stand as a potent reminder of cultural divisions, but the increased mobility of Europeans, a communications revolution that has made Europe a smaller place, and the growth in trade that has put a greater variety of European products on the shelves of shops across the region have helped build a sense among Europeans that there is less to distinguish them from one another than they once thought.

Where is Europe?

Despite all the economic, social and political changes that have taken place in Europe since 1945, its identity remains ambiguous, for several reasons. First, few of the EU's member states are culturally homogeneous, and there is no such thing as a European race. The constant reordering of territorial lines over the centuries has created a situation in which every European state has national minorities, and several of those minorities – notably the Basques and the Irish – are divided by national frontiers. Many states have also seen large influxes of immigrants since the 1950s, including Algerians to France, Turks to Germany and Indians to Britain. Not only is there nothing like a dominant culture, but most Europeans rightly shudder at the thought of their separate identities being subordinated to some kind of homogenized Euroculture.

Second, residents of the EU speak more than forty languages, which are often vigorously defended as symbols of national identity and act as a constant reminder of the differences among Europeans; one of the factors that helped the development of the United States was the existence of a common language. Multilingualism in Europe also means that all official EU documents are translated into the 21 official languages of the member states, although the work of EU institutions is increasingly carried out in English and French. Supported by its rapid spread as the language of global commerce and diplomacy, the dominance of English grows, and it is slowly becoming the language of Europe. This worries the French in particular and other Europeans to some extent, but it is probably irresistible and will at least give Europeans a way of talking to each other, and perhaps help reduce the cultural differences that divide them.

Third, the histories of European states overlapped for centuries as they colonized, went to war, or formed alliances with each other. But those overlaps often emphasized their differences rather than giving them the sense of a shared past, and European integration grew in part out of the reactive idea of ending the conflicts that arose from those differences.

Historical divisions were further emphasized by the colonial interests of some European states, which encouraged them to develop competing sets of external priorities at the expense of cultivating closer ties with their neighbours. Even now, Britain, France, Spain, and Portugal have close ties with their former colonies, while Germany – for different reasons – has interests in eastern Europe.

Finally, and most fundamentally, the confusion over the definition of Europe arises out of uncertainty about its political and geographical boundaries. Every other continent is defined by its coastline, but while the western, northern, and southern boundaries of Europe are marked by the Atlantic, the Arctic, and the Mediterranean, respectively, it has no clear eastern boundary. Strictly speaking it is not even a continent (usually defined as a large, unbroken land mass), but is part of the Asian continent. However it has been seen as distinct from Asia for the last 2,000 years or more, even if no one can really agree on where Europe ends and Asia begins.

The eastern boundary of Europe is usually defined as running down the Ural Mountains, across the Caspian Sea, and along the Caucasus Mountains, but these are no more than geographical features that have been adopted despite political realities. The Urals, for example, were nominated as a boundary by an eighteenth-century Russian cartographer, Vasily Tatishchev, simply so that Russia could claim to be an Asian as well as a European power. If we continue to accept the Urals as a boundary, then six former Soviet republics – Belarus, Moldova, Ukraine, and the three Baltic states – are part of Europe. The three Baltic states (Estonia, Latvia, and Lithuania) have historically been bound to Europe, and are now members of the European Union, but questions remain about the orientation of Belarus, Moldova, and Ukraine.

The biggest problem with the Urals is that they do not mark the frontier between two states, but are deep in the heart of Russia. Russians have sometimes been defined – and have seen themselves – as European, and Russia west of the Urals was long known as Eurasia because of the distinctions imposed on the region by Europeans, but Russia today sees its political and economic interests as being significantly different from those of Europe. The most obvious problem with defining Russia as European is that three-quarters of its land area is east of the Urals, and more than forty ethnic minorities live in Russia, most of whom are unquestionably non-European.

In central Europe, changes in the balance of power long meant that the Poles, the Czechs, and the Slovaks were caught in the crossfire of great-power competition, which is why this region was known as the 'lands between'. The west looked on this area as a buffer zone against Russia, a perception that was helped by the failure of its people to form lasting states identified with dominant ethnic groups. During the cold war the distinctiveness of eastern Europe was emphasized by the ideological divisions between east and west, despite the historical ties that meant Poland was closer to western Europe than to Russia.

For their part, the Balkans occupy an ambiguous position between Europe and Asia, being a geographical part of the former but historically drawn towards the latter. They were long regarded as an extension of Asia Minor, and until relatively recently were still described by Europeans as the Near East (Hobsbawm, 1991, p. 17). The Balkans have long been regarded as a zone of transition between two 'civilizations', whether the term is applied to religions (the boundary between Islam, Catholicism, and Eastern Orthodoxy) or to political communities (the boundary between the eastern and western Roman empires, between the Habsburg and Ottoman empires, and more recently between Slavic-Russian, western, and eastern influences).

Historical maps of the region show how its affiliations have constantly changed: the Balkans have come under the Macedonians, the Romans, the eastern Roman empire, Slavic tribes, Christianity, the Kingdom of Hungary, the Venetians, and – from the sixteenth century until 1918 – the Ottoman Turks. Except during the Tito regime (1945–80), the region has never come close to being united, and the allegiance of its inhabitants has always been divided. These changes created what Delanty (1995, pp. 51–2) describes as 'frontier societies in the intermediary lands' between great powers. The Slavs in particular were divided between those who accepted Catholicism, Greek Orthodoxy, or Islam, which resulted in cultural heterogeneity in spite of the greater linguistic homogeneity among Slavs than among the peoples of western Europe (Delanty, 1995, p. 54). Slavs continue to have affiliations with Russia, which is part of the reason why NATO was wary about becoming too deeply involved in the conflicts in Bosnia and Kosovo in the 1990s.

Finally there is the question of Turkey, which most Europeans see as part of Asia Minor and part of the Islamic sphere of influence. However, we usually think of Europe and Asia as meeting at the Bosphorus, which means that about 4 per cent of Turkey lies in Europe. So is Turkey a European state? The EU agreed in December 2004 to open membership negotiations with Turkey, but Europeans have so far kept Turkey at a distance, expressing concern about its poverty, its large population and its mixed record on human rights. However, questions about the southeastern limits of Europe have not prevented the EU from giving membership to Cyprus, which is further from Brussels than most of Turkey.

The cold war has not been over for long, and most of us still find it difficult to ignore the political, economic and social distinctions that divided the countries on either side of the Iron Curtain; try as they might, most older Europeans still look on Hungary and Poland as being somehow different from Belgium and France. A further distinction has been added since the 1970s by the accelerating closeness among EU member states, which has divided Europe into countries that are members of the EU and those that are not. There is little question, however, that Europe is closer than it has ever been to being considered a region with common interests and a common identity.

Europe today

If its borders with Turkey and Russia are taken as its eastern limits, then Europe today consists of 38 countries: the 25 members of the EU, three other western European states (Iceland, Norway and Switzerland), and ten eastern European states. While there is a large measure of political, economic, and social cohesion in western Europe, which is expanding to eastern Europe, there are also significant differences, and these have had an impact on the process of integration. The leaders of the EU member states, for example, do not always meet as equals: their powers are based on often different political and administrative foundations, and they have different sets of economic and social priorities that sometimes oblige or encourage them to take conflicting positions at the negotiating table (see Chapter 5).

Political structures

Most European countries have political systems based on variations on the theme of parliamentary government (see Table 2.1). Its key features include direct elections to a representative parliament, the existence of multiple political parties, executive power vested in a prime minister who is the leader of the largest political party (or coalition) in parliament, a fusion of the executive and the legislature, and a monarch or figurehead president acting as head of state. Unlike the US system, where the roles of head of state and head of government are fused in the president, parliamentary systems have a symbolic head of state and a political head of government. Heads of state in Europe take several different forms:

- Eight countries – Belgium, Denmark, Luxembourg, the Netherlands, Norway, Spain, Sweden, and the UK – have monarchies. However, these are all constitutional monarchies, meaning that the monarchs have negligible political power and government is carried out in their name (they reign, but they do not rule). All are limited to ceremonial roles, and are given little opportunity to advise or influence the elected heads of government.

Table 2.1 *Political and administrative structures*

	Executive	Legislature	Government*	Administrative structure
Albania	President/PM	Unicameral	Majority	Unitary
Austria	President/Chancellor	Bicameral	Coalition	Federal
Belarus	Presidential	Bicameral	Non-partisan	Unitary
Belgium	Monarch/PM	Bicameral	Coalition	Federal
Bosnia and Herzegovina	Joint presidency	Bicameral**	Coalition	Confederal
Bulgaria	President/PM	Unicameral	Coalition	Unitary
Croatia	President/PM	Unicameral	Minority	Unitary
Cyprus	Presidential	Unicameral	Coalition	Divided
Czech Republic	President/PM	Bicameral	Coalition	Unitary
Denmark	Monarch/PM	Unicameral	Coalition	Unitary
Estonia	President/PM	Unicameral	Coalition	Unitary
Finland	President/PM	Unicameral	Coalition	Unitary
France	Dual executive	Bicameral	Coalition	Unitary
Germany	President/Chancellor	Bicameral	Coalition	Federal
Greece	President/PM	Unicameral	Majority	Unitary
Hungary	President/PM	Unicameral	Coalition	Unitary
Iceland	President/PM	Unicameral	Coalition	Unitary
Ireland	President/PM	Bicameral	Coalition	Unitary
Italy	President/PM	Bicameral	Coalition	Unitary
Latvia	President/PM	Unicameral	Coalition	Unitary
Lithuania	Dual executive	Unicameral	Coalition	Unitary

Country				
Luxembourg	Grand Duke/PM	Unicameral	Coalition	Unitary
Macedonia	President/PM	Unicameral	Coalition	Unitary
Malta	President/PM	Unicameral	Majority	Unitary
Moldova	Dual executive	Unicameral	Majority	Unitary
Netherlands	Monarch/PM	Bicameral	Coalition	Unitary
Norway	Monarch/PM	Unicameral	Coalition	Unitary
Poland	Dual executive	Bicameral	Coalition	Unitary
Portugal	Dual executive	Unicameral	Coalition	Unitary
Romania	President/PM	Bicameral	Majority	Unitary
Serbia and Montenegro	President/PM	Bicameral	Coalition	Confederal
Slovakia	President/PM	Unicameral	Coalition	Unitary
Slovenia	President/PM	Bicameral	Coalition	Unitary
Spain	Monarch/PM	Bicameral	Majority	Unitary
Sweden	Monarch/PM	Unicameral	Majority	Unitary
Switzerland	Presidential	Bicameral	Coalition	Federal
Ukraine	Dual executive	Unicameral	Coalition	Unitary
United Kingdom	Monarch/PM	Bicameral	Majority	Unitary

EU member states shown in **boldface**. PM = Prime Minister

* Situation as of December 2004

** Unicameral parliament in the Republic of Srpska

Notes: In Belarus and Cyprus, the president has the bulk of executive power. In Switzerland power is highly devolved. With dual executives, power is shared between a president and a prime minister. In all other systems, presidents and monarchs are largely figureheads.

Source: Based mainly on information in *Elections Around the World* at http://www.electionworld.org (2004).

- Most other European states have a figurehead president who has similar powers and a similar standing to that of a monarch, but instead of inheriting the job by an accident of birth, they are either appointed or elected to their position for a fixed term. In several countries – including Germany, Italy and Switzerland – the president is elected by the legislature; elsewhere he or she is elected directly by the people, but is not expected to be a political figure. The only slight exception is in Finland, where the president has a central role in foreign policy and can become involved in domestic policy if the situation allows.
- Several countries have a dual executive, or a mixed presidential/ parliamentary system of government: they include France, Moldova, Poland, Portugal, and Ukraine. Executive power is vested in the president, who is directly elected by the people, but legislative power is vested in the legislature, overseen by a prime minister and a council of ministers. If the president's party dominates the legislature, the president will have substantial powers over government – most notably, the president appoints the prime minister and the council of ministers, and also sets the political and legislative agenda. If the president's party is in a minority, however, the prime minister and council of ministers will come from a different party, base their power on their support in the legislature and will be much less obliged to the president.

Non-executive presidents and monarchs have the advantage of being able to act as symbols of national unity. They can provide stability and continuity, especially in the case of monarchs, who often outlast a succession of prime ministers – by 2004, for example, Britain's Queen Elizabeth had worked with ten prime ministers, and Sweden's King Carl Gustav with eight. In Italy various presidents have played a crucial role in helping deal with the disruptive effects of the frequent collapse of governments, and holders of that office have been known to become involved in public debates: President Cossiga, for example, came out in support of electoral reform in the wake of the financial scandals of the early 1990s and the subsequent collapse of the credibility of Italian political parties.

Presidents in countries with dual executives have a significantly different position within their domestic political structures, which gives them a different status at meetings with other European leaders. As noted above, when a president's party dominates the legislature, that president has considerable powers over the legislative programme and is in a strong position when it comes to negotiating international agreements. However, in the case of France, recent elections have resulted in presidents having to work with opposition party prime ministers. This was the case for President Chirac after the 1997 National Assembly elections: with the socialists winning the majority of votes, domestic affairs were taken over by prime minister Lionel Jospin, and Chirac could do little more than immerse himself in foreign affairs. Even there he found himself at a disadvantage in his discussions with other EU leaders because he could not rely on the backing of the National Assembly.

Executive power in most European states is vested in a head of government: the prime minister, or the chancellor in Germany and Austria. In contrast to the fixed term imposed on legislators in the United States, prime ministers and legislators in Europe are elected for a maximum term – usually four or five years (three years in Sweden) – and the leader has the power to call elections any time within that term. The main power of prime ministers lies in their virtual monopoly over appointments to senior government positions, and the fact that they can normally rely on parliamentary majorities that are strong enough to ensure the success of their legislative programmes. This is certainly true of prime ministers in states that regularly return majority governments, but less true of those with coalitions (where no one party has a majority, so two or more parties come together to form the government). While the former have substantial political powers, the latter (such as the leaders of Germany and Italy) must base their programmes on consensus and bipartisanship, and are limited by the need to achieve compromises that keep all the party groups within their coalition happy.

Almost all European legislatures are based on the parliamentary model, in which the government consists of a prime minister and cabinet that is answerable to – and usually part of – the elected legislative body. By definition, a legislature is where laws are introduced, discussed, amended if necessary, and either accepted or rejected. Most European parliaments have two chambers, a lower and more powerful chamber that is directly elected by the people, and an upper and usually less important chamber whose members may be elected directly or indirectly, or appointed. Austria, Germany, and the Netherlands have upper chambers whose members are elected or appointed by the state or local governments. Several smaller European states, including Cyprus, Estonia, Finland, Hungary, Latvia, Malta, Norway, Portugal, and Slovakia have only one chamber.

Europeans have a wide variety of political parties from which to choose at elections, with every part of the ideological spectrum represented. On the left, communists have seen their support declining significantly in recent years; in the west they receive far fewer votes than they did in the heyday of Eurocommunism in the 1970s, and in the east they have lost support since the end of the cold war (one exception being Poland where communists are still strong). The most enduring of the left-wing ideologies is social democracy, which now forms the foundation of political parties in almost every EU member state. A more conservative form of socialism, social democracy incorporates a belief in the welfare state and some degree of government ownership of services with a support for self-reliance and moderate positions on social issues.

The ideological right is dominated by Christian Democratic parties, which are active in most of the continental EU member states. More concerned than secular conservative parties about social issues, and more willing to support welfare as a means of avoiding social conflict, Christian Democratic parties have been particularly influential in Germany, France and Italy, where they have adopted more liberal positions than British and Irish conservatives. One of the effects of the European Parliamentary elections (see Chapters 4 and 6) has been to encourage social democrats and conservatives to form trans-European blocs, and while they do not as yet run on a European platform, these two blocs have consistently been the biggest in the European Parliament.

A recent phenomenon in national European politics has been the rise of political parties representing more focused sectors of society: these include greens, subnational and regionalist parties, and nationalist parties on the far right. Greens have done particularly well in Belgium, Germany, and some of the Scandinavian states, their views representing a backlash against unsustainable consumerism and economic development. Regional parties, while still small, have evolved in economically or culturally divided EU member states such as Belgium, Britain, and Italy. The far right, building on xenophobia and opposition to immigration, has had its biggest impact in Austria, Belgium, France, and Italy.

Electoral systems are far from standardized in Europe. Although most countries offer their voters proportional representation (PR), several different forms of PR are practised. The most common is the straight party list system, in which the country is divided into districts with multiple representatives, all parties field a list of candidates in each district, and the votes are shared out among the candidates according to the proportion of votes they receive. The most notable exception to the PR rule is Britain, which has a plurality or majority system (sometime known as first past the post), in which candidates from different parties compete against each other and the candidate who wins the most votes wins the seat, irrespective of whether or not they win a majority of votes. The Blair administration has introduced PR for European elections and elections to regional assemblies, and has debated the possibility of introducing PR for general elections.

The plurality system has two advantages: it usually results in one party winning a clear majority (and so contributes to governmental stability), and it assigns a single member of the legislature to each electoral district, allowing constituents to develop political and psychological links with one representative. However, the system tends to be unfair in that the proportion of seats won by competing parties is often different from the proportion of votes cast: parties that have solid blocs of support around a country turn those into legislative seats, while parties whose support is strong but more thinly spread often come second, and win fewer seats. This was particularly obvious in the 2001 British elections, when the governing Labour party won 41 per cent of the votes, but nearly 63 per cent of the seats in the House of Commons, while the opposition Conservatives won 32 per cent of the votes, but only 25 per cent of the seats.

PR is more representative of voter preferences, but voters are represented by a group of legislators rather than just one. More problematically, the system also results in more parties winning seats in the legislature, making it less likely that any one party will win a majority. The result is usually a coalition government, whose member parties have to compromise their policy goals in order to maintain the coalition, and may only have a small majority. The majority of European states are governed by coalitions, which generally function well. But they can also create instability, the most extreme case of which is found in Italy, which has had nearly sixty governments since 1945, some of which have lasted only a matter of weeks before collapsing. In order to promote stability, Italy changed its electoral system in 1993 from one based exclusively on PR to one using a combination of PR and winner take all.

The result of this variety of political structures is that the power of the individual leaders of the member states is often based on different foundations, which may affect their ability to negotiate with their counterparts. For example, British, Greek, or Spanish prime ministers who head a strong majority in their respective legislatures are able to adopt a relatively uncompromising position in intra-EU negotiations, while French presidents without a legislative majority, or Dutch or Danish prime ministers who lead a finely balanced coalition government, may be in a weak negotiating position and more inclined to follow than to lead.

Administrative structures

Government in European states tends to be highly centralized. All but five are unitary systems, meaning that all significant power is focused at the national level. Unitary administration means that a state has two or even three levels of government, with the national government being responsible for foreign and defence policy, managing the national economy, welfare policy, transport, environmental management, industrial development policy, and other matters that are considered as best dealt with from a national perspective. Meanwhile a network of local units of government –

which come under labels as varied as municipality, commune, county, parish, district, borough, province, department, or region – are usually responsible for overseeing public services such as land use planning, policing, local transport, schooling, public housing, refuse collection, road maintenance, and social services. However, they lack independent powers, and answer ultimately to national government for their authority.

The exceptions are Austria, Belgium, Germany, and Switzerland, which are federations in which national government coexists with local units of government with their own independent powers and responsibilities, and powers are more decentralized. (Bosnia is a confederation between Bosnia and Herzegovina, and the Republic of Sprksa.) Federalism usually works best in large countries where strong local government makes sense simply for reasons of convenience, or in countries that have significant social divisions and where decentralization gives different groups more power over their own affairs. The United States is often taken as the model of federalism, an arrangement that was used as a means of bringing the original 13 colonies together under a joint system of government.

Federalism in Switzerland is rooted in differences in language and religion, so that the populations of individual cantons speak French, German, or Italian, and are either mostly Protestant or mostly Catholic (Gallagher *et al.*, 1992, p. 137). In contrast, federalism in Germany was encouraged by the occupying powers after the Second World War as a means of decentralizing the German state, and several of the *Länder* created under the new system had no historical traditions. Federalism is sometimes proposed as a possible answer for the problems of culturally or historically divided societies such as Britain, which is already experiencing federalizing tendencies as Scotland, Wales, and Northern Ireland become used to their new regional assemblies.

As noted in Chapter 1, federalism at the European level has become controversial in recent years, being regularly used by Eurosceptics as a red flag with which to warn against the loss of powers by EU member states. They often talk of the possibility of a federal European government, associating the term with such notions as 'big government' and 'loss of sovereignty'. The Thatcher and Major governments in Britain were particularly leery of the idea, federalism becoming a critical issue for the latter during the debate over the Maastricht treaty. The draft included the objective of achieving a federal Europe, but British opposition led to the removal of all references to the idea, and the wording of the treaty was eventually changed to read 'an ever closer union among the peoples of Europe'.

However, it is questionable whether most Europeans really understand how federalism works, since so few of them have experienced it first-hand. It is also questionable whether a federal Europe – should it ever be created

– would have the same characteristics as a federal Austria or Germany. There is no one fixed definition of federalism; in some cases (such as India and Russia) national government is relatively strong, in others (such as Switzerland) it is relatively weak, and in almost all cases the balance of power between national and local government changes according to economic and political realities. This has certainly been the case in the United States, where there has long been a debate about which level has the advantage in that balance. The seeds of a federal European government have been planted, but whether they will eventually flower, or whether the confederal arrangement that exists at the moment will be retained, remains to be seen.

Economic structures

All European states are predominantly free-market capitalist systems, meaning that most economic activity is driven – and prices set – by supply and demand, and governments limit their intervention in the marketplace. This has been particularly true in the west since the 1980s, when the Thatcher government privatized many state-owned industries and services, and several continental European states followed suit. It has also been true in the east since the collapse of the Soviet Union brought an end to state socialism in former Soviet client states. The size of the public sector in most countries has declined markedly since the early 1990s, and free-market enterprise and competition have grown. (Of course, there is no such thing in practice as a purely capitalist system – governments always intervene in some way in the market, for example through regulation, price controls, or rules on competition.)

European states are also predominantly post-industrial, meaning that their economies have gone through a transition from agriculture to industry to a heavy reliance on services. The latter are economic activities that do not produce tangible commodities, for example the retail sector, food services, banking, insurance, and other financial activities. Services in most European states account for about 64–73 per cent of gross domestic product (GDP), industry for about 25–32 per cent, and agriculture for 1–3 per cent. In eastern Europe agriculture still plays a bigger role, accounting for 3–7 per cent of economic output (see Chapter 8 for more details). The poorer European states tend to have the largest agricultural sectors: while only 2–4 per cent of Britons, Danes, Germans, and Swedes work in agriculture, 12–15 per cent of Greeks and Portuguese are so employed, 18–20 per cent of Latvians, Lithuanians, and Poles, 40 per cent of Romanians, and 52 per cent of Moldovans (World Bank, 2004).

Western Europe has experienced substantial economic growth since 1945, and prosperity has spread to eastern Europe in recent years, but the levels of growth and prosperity have always differed from one region to another (see Box 2.2). Broadly speaking there is an economic heartland in the centre of Europe, running from northern Italy across Switzerland to the Benelux countries and neighbouring parts of France and Germany, and

---

Box 2.2 The standard of living

Assessed by almost any objective measure of the quality of life, western Europeans are among the most privileged people in the world. They have access to an advanced system of education and health care, an extensive and generous welfare system, a vibrant consumer society, and a sophisticated transport and communications system. An African infant is 21 times more likely to die at birth than a European infant, and the average European can expect to live 24 years longer than the average African and 18 years longer than the average Indian. Europeans enjoy almost universal literacy, employed Europeans enjoy more paid holiday leave and leisure time than almost anyone else, and the provision of shelter and nutrition is more than adequate. One author even argues that the quality of life of Europeans is eclipsing that of Americans, long thought of as living in the world's most socially privileged country (Rifkin, 2004).

Much can be attributed to the philosophy adopted by most western European governments after the Second World War that the state should provide a wide range of basic social services, creating a safety net through which even the poorest and the most underprivileged would not be allowed to slip. Hence every EU-15 member state has some form of state education and national health care, and the provision of care for children and the aged has increased as the number of lone-parent families and retirees has grown. Most European states even do well in comparison with the United States, which has the most technologically advanced health care in the world but lacks a national health service, and is one of the richest economies in the world yet still has 15 per cent of its people living in poverty.

Not all of Europe's welfare policies have succeeded, and it is one of the great ironies of life in modern industrialized democracies that considerable want continues to exist in the midst of plenty. Poverty has not gone away and in several places has worsened, creating considerable differences across Europe. For example, while the number of children living in poverty stands at 4–10 per cent in Germany, the Netherlands, and Sweden, it is as high as 16–18 per cent in Britain and Italy. However this is still much better than in the United States, where the figure is nearly 30 per cent (statistics quoted in Bradford, 1998, p. 265). On all these indicators, the A-10 countries (the ten countries that joined the EU in 2004) still lag behind, but the benefits of EU membership will likely help them in much the same way as it has helped Greece, Ireland, Portugal, and Spain, improving economies of scale so that the biggest European corporations are now able to compete more effectively with those from the United States and Japan.

continuing across the Channel from London to the English Midlands. This is the area where most industry and energy production is focused, with the greatest concentration of population, the highest levels of GDP, and the fewest people working in agriculture.

More generally, Europe has pockets of economic dynamism and under-development. The highest levels of activity are found in the economic heartland, particularly in the Rhineland, around northern Italian cities, and in and around Paris, Rotterdam, and London. These have neighbour-ing zones of balanced economic development, with a combination of prosperous agriculture, moderate urban growth, light industry, and ser-vices. Balanced against these areas are the depressed industrial regions of Europe, such as the Ruhr, the English Midlands, and south Wales. Finally, the periphery of Europe tends to be the most underdeveloped, either because it has lacked adequate investment, because it is remote and sparsely populated or – in the case of most of eastern Europe – because it is less industrialized and still suffering the effects of Soviet-style central planning.

The single market programme has exacerbated the differences by promoting cross-frontier competition, allowing industry and business to move to the areas of maximum efficiency and greatest profits, and promoting the movement of workers. At the same time, though, EU regional policies have helped provide more investment for poorer regions, and social policies have helped place workers on a more equal footing (see Chapter 8). The single market has also helped promote trans-European corporate mergers and joint ventures.

Economic differences are reflected in population numbers. Europe is one of the most densely populated regions of the world: overall population density is about 115 people per square kilometre compared with 30/sq. km in the United States, and 9/sq. km in Russia. Within the EU, population density varies from nearly 470/sq. km in the Netherlands to about 110–130/sq. km in the Czech Republic, Denmark, France, Hungary, Poland, and Slovakia, to a low of 20/sq. km in Finland and Sweden; the spread reflects environmental factors and different levels of industrializa-tion. The most densely populated parts of Europe are also among the wealthiest: northern Italy, western Germany, the Benelux countries, and southeastern England. The most sparsely populated include the poorest or the coldest: much of eastern Europe, central Spain, northwest Scotland, Iceland, and Scandinavia.

Not surprisingly, the greatest population growth is taking place in and around the major centres of industry and services, and new residential and leisure areas. Capital cities have seen growth since the mid-nineteenth century, their attraction lying in their role as administrative, cultural, service, and prestige centres, their central position in national transport networks, their large marketplaces, and their need for pools of skilled labour (Minshull and Dawson, 1996, p. 209). Regions of postwar industrial redevelopment, such as the Rhine valley in Germany and the West Midlands in Britain, have also seen sustained population growth. Meanwhile rural and peripheral regions and declining industrial areas have undergone steady depopulation. These trends have made Europe one of the most urbanized parts of the world. While only 78 per cent of Americans live in towns or cities, the figure for Belgium is 97 per cent, and for Denmark, Germany, the Netherlands, Sweden, and Britain is in the range of 83–90 per cent. For more sparsely populated or agricultural western European states such as Austria, Finland, Greece, and Ireland – and for A-10 countries – the figures are in the 60–70 per cent range.

The European Union has become the world's biggest trading power, and its exports and imports have grown rapidly since 1945, thanks in large part to the growth of intra-European trade. Worldwide exports from the EU consist mainly of manufactured goods, machinery, machine tools, motor vehicles, electronics, telecommunications equipment, aerospace products, chemicals, clothing, consumer durables, and agricultural products, while major imports include oil, agricultural products, and raw materials. The EU member states still actively protect their sovereignty in many different areas, but when it comes to economic issues it has become more realistic to think of them collectively – the completion of the single market, the substantial easing of the movement of people and capital, the power of the European Commission to negotiate on behalf of the EU as a whole on trade issues, and the conversion in 12 member states to a single currency have all taken Europe to the brink of full economic union (see Chapter 7).

Conclusions

The idea of European unity is nothing new. The conflicts that brought instability, death, and changes to the balance of power in Europe over the centuries prompted many to propose unification – or at least the development of a common system of government – as a means to the achievement of peace. The rise of the state system undermined these proposals, but interstate conflict ultimately reached a level at which it became clear that only cooperation could offer a path to peace. The two world wars of the twentieth century – which in many ways began as European civil wars – emphatically underlined the dangers of nationalism and of the continued promotion of state interests at the expense of regional interests.

The new thinking has dramatically altered the idea of Europe over the past two generations. The eastern and southeastern borders of Europe may have maintained their historical tradition of change, but in the post-industrial and democratic west, the nature of the internal relationship among the states that make up Europe has changed out of all recognition. For the first time, the concept of European unity has found a widespread audience. The audience may not always have been enthusiastic, but there has been a generational shift since 1945 as those who witnessed the horrors of the Second World War are superseded by those who have known nothing but a general peace in the region. Where intellectuals and philosophers once argued in isolation that the surest path to peace in Europe was cooperation, or even integration, the costs of nationalism are now more broadly appreciated, ensuring a wider and deeper consideration of the idea of regional unity.

Europeans still have much that divides them, and those differences are obvious to anyone who travels across the region. There are different languages, cultural traditions, legal, education and health care systems, social priorities, cuisines, modes of entertainment, patterns of etiquette, styles of dress, ways of planning and building cities, ways of spending leisure time, attitudes towards the countryside, and even sides of the road on which to drive (the British, Irish, Cypriots, and Maltese drive on the left, everyone else on the right). Europeans also have differences in the way they govern themselves, and in what they have been able to achieve with their economies and social welfare systems.

Increasingly, however, Europeans have more in common. The economic and social integration that has taken place under the auspices of the European Union and its precursors since the early 1950s has brought the needs and priorities of Europeans closer into alignment. It has also encouraged the rest of the world to see Europeans less as citizens of separate states and more as citizens of the same economic bloc, if not yet the same political bloc. Not only has there been integration from the Mediterranean to the Arctic Circle, but the 'lands between' – which spent the cold war as part of the Soviet bloc and part of the buffer created by the Soviet Union to protect its western frontier – are now becoming part of greater Europe for the first time in their history. The result has been a fundamental redefinition of the idea of Europe. In the next chapter we will look at the steps taken by European governments to build the European Union, the underlying motives of integration, and the debates involved in the process.

Chapter 3

The Evolution of the EU

Domestic and international background
First steps towards integration (1945–58)
The European Economic Community (1958–86)
Economic and social integration (1979–92)
From Community to Union (1992–)
Conclusions

> *We must build a kind of United States of Europe.*
> Winston Churchill, former British prime minister, 1946

The idea of 'Europe' has been with us for centuries, but significant efforts to promote voluntary European unity date back less than sixty years. It was only after the Second World War that all the theories about the possible benefits of European integration were finally tested in practice. There were several false starts, but the most critical first step was taken on 9 May 1950, at a press conference held at the French Foreign Ministry in Paris. To the attendant journalists, French foreign minister Robert Schuman announced a plan he had discussed with the French businessman and bureaucrat Jean Monnet and West German chancellor Konrad Adenauer under which the coal and steel industries of France and Germany would be brought together under the administration of a single joint authority.

Other countries were invited to take part, but only Italy and the three Benelux countries expressed interest. Nevertheless, this modest experiment involving six western European states was the first step that would lead to the European Union as we know it today. The original priorities were threefold: postwar economic construction, the desire to prevent European nationalism leading once again to conflict, and the need for security in the face of the threats posed by the cold war. At the core of this thinking was concern about the traditional hostility between France and Germany, and the argument that if these two could cooperate they might provide the foundation for broader European integration.

The six members of the European Coal and Steel Community, founded in 1952, went on to create the European Economic Community in 1958, with a more ambitious set of goals. These included the development of a common agricultural policy, agreement on a common external tariff for all goods coming into the Community, and the development of a single market, within which there would be free movement of people, goods, money, and services. Membership of the EEC expanded in 1973 with the accession of Britain, Denmark, and Ireland, followed in the 1980s by Greece, Portugal, and Spain.

Plans for the single market were threatened by economic problems and disagreements about what needed to be done to remove the internal barriers to trade, but the problems were addressed in 1986 with agreement of the Single European Act, which set a five-year deadline for completion of the remaining tasks. The single market is now in place, 12 of the member states have adopted a common currency, ten new mainly eastern European countries joined the EU in 2004, membership of the EU now stands at 25 countries with more than 450 million people, a controversial draft of a new European constitution has been agreed, and progress has been made on developing common policies in a wide range of issues. The achievements have been remarkable, but many Europeans are still ambivalent about the European Union, and question the wisdom of integration. And while membership has grown, doubts remain about the many items of unfinished business on the European agenda.

This chapter provides a brief history of European integration since the Second World War, describing the key steps that have been taken during the evolution of the EU, and their underlying motives. It moves from the Treaty of Paris to the Treaties of Rome, on to the construction of the single market and early attempts to bring about economic union and common social and foreign policies, and ends with the treaties of Maastricht, Amsterdam, and Nice, the adoption of the euro, and the debate over enlargement and the constitution. The European Union is a work in progress, however, so there are many changes yet to come.

Domestic and international background

The European Union was born out of the ruins of the Second World War. Before the war, Europe had dominated global trade, banking and finance, its empires had stretched across the world and its military superiority had been unquestioned. But Europeans had often gone to war with each other, and their conflicts undermined the prosperity that cooperation might have brought. Pacifists hoped that the Great War of 1914–18 might prove to Europeans the futility and brutality of armed conflict, but it was to take yet another conflagration finally to convince them that they needed to fundamentally rethink how they related to each other if a lasting peace was to be achieved.

The Second World War resulted in the death of more than 40 million people and caused widespread devastation. Cities lay in ruins, agricultural production was halved, food was rationed and communications were disrupted by the destruction of bridges, railways and harbours. While the physical damage caused by the First World War had been relatively restricted, every country involved in this latest conflict sustained heavy casualties and physical damage. The war also dealt a severe blow to European power and influence, clearing the way for the emergence of the United States and the Soviet Union as superpowers, and creating a nervous new balance in the distribution of political influence in the world.

Against this troubled background a number of European leaders revived the argument that European states should set aside their differences and build bridges of cooperation aimed at removing the causes of war, and perhaps even promoting European economic and political union. The argument had a new significance given the scale of the postwar reconstruction effort, but Europeans had different opinions about its merits:

- France had been destabilized by the trauma of wartime collaboration, and was to suffer further blows to its national pride with the defeat of French forces in Indochina in 1954 and the Suez crisis in 1956. Three times in less than a century it had gone to war with Germany, and three times had suffered substantial losses; it was time now to take the steps needed to remove the threat posed by Germany, once and for all.
- Germany was shamed, introverted, and occupied by four allied powers, who had divided the country into a socialist eastern sector and three capitalist western sectors. The Christian Democratic government of Konrad Adenauer (1949–63) set about aligning West Germany with the western alliance and rebuilding West German respectability, goals which fitted well with the idea of regional economic integration.
- Austria too was divided into separate zones of occupation, but had been relatively undamaged by the war and was able to return to its constitution of 1920, and quickly to hold democratic elections. It declared itself neutral in 1955, but was pulled increasingly towards economic integration with its western neighbours (Schultz, 1992).
- Italy was devastated and introverted, was less successful than Germany in creating political stability, and suffered regular changes of government. For the administration of prime minister Alcide de Gasperi (1945–53), European integration offered a means of fostering peace and helping Italy to deal with its internal economic problems, notably unemployment and the underdevelopment of the south.
- Britain was politically stable and wealthier and more powerful than France and Germany, but the war had brought severe physical damage and economic dislocation. The Labour government of Clement Attlee

(1945–51) launched a popular programme of nationalization and welfare provision, and began dismantling Britain's empire, but cooperation with Europe was far from British minds.

- Ireland had remained neutral during the war but was economically tied to Britain, so its attitude towards regional cooperation was determined by that of Britain.
- The three Benelux countries – Belgium, the Netherlands, and Luxembourg – had all been occupied by the Germans, and remained concerned after the war about their inability to protect themselves. They pursued economic cooperation after the war, creating a customs union in 1948 and agreeing the Benelux Economic Union in 1958. Their integrationist tendencies were clear to all.
- The five Nordic states (Denmark, Finland, Iceland, Norway, and Sweden) began work after the war on aligning their national bodies of law, and on taking common positions at international conferences. The Nordic Council, created in 1952, promoted the abolition of passport controls, the free movement of workers, and the development of joint ventures, moving all five countries along the path of international cooperation.
- Spain and Portugal were exceptions to the prevailing rule of democratic stability in western Europe, and were both poor and politically marginalized. Spain had been ruled since 1939 by Francisco Franco, and Portugal since 1928 by Antonio Salazar; neither man was in favour of cooperating with neighbouring countries after the war, and both states remained on the margins of the international community for many years.
- Greece enjoyed economic growth after the war thanks to US financial and military assistance, but remained poor and suffered protracted domestic political tensions that led to military dictatorship in 1967–74.
- Eastern Europe had come under the political control of the Soviet Union after the war, was quickly encouraged along the path of economic centralization and one-party government, and was not interested in meaningful cooperation with the west. Despite democratic movements in countries such as Hungary, the region was kept firmly under the control of Stalinist diktats from Moscow.

While their domestic priorities were occasionally different, west European governments quickly realized that changes taking place at the global level demanded new thinking. In July 1944, representatives from 44 countries – including the United States and all the allied European states – had met at Bretton Woods in New Hampshire to make plans for the postwar global economy. All agreed to an Anglo-American proposal to promote free trade, non-discrimination and stable exchange rates, and supported the view that Europe's economies should be rebuilt and placed on a more stable footing.

Because wartime resistance had been allied with left-wing political ideas, there was a political shift to the left after the war, with socialist and social democratic parties winning power in several European countries. Many of the new governments launched programmes of social welfare and nationalization, emphasizing central economic planning. Fundamental to this approach were the theories of the British economist John Maynard Keynes, who argued for some government control over some aspects of the economy in order to control the cycle of booms and busts. Keynesianism became the basis of postwar economic reconstruction and west European governments increasingly intervened in their economies to control inflation and rebuild industry and agriculture. However, it soon became clear that substantial capital investment was needed if Europe was to rebuild itself. The readiest source of such capital was the United States, which saw European reconstruction as essential to its own economic and security interests, and made a large investment in the future of Europe through the Marshall Plan (see Box 3.1).

As one of the two new postwar superpowers, the United States also found itself playing the role of global policeman, its primary goal being to defend western Europe (and ultimately itself) from the Soviet threat. Its assumptions that Europe had enough people, money and resources to recover from the war, and that the allies would continue to work together, both proved wrong (Urwin, 1995, pp. 13–14). Furthermore, its European allies were divided over the extent to which they felt they could rely on the United States to defend them, and the doubters began to think in terms of greater European cooperation.

Most immediately, the western allies were undecided about what to do with Germany. In June 1948 they united their three zones of occupation into a new West German state with a new currency. The Soviets responded with a blockade around West Berlin, prompting a massive western airlift to supply the beleaguered city. The US Congress was resistant to direct American commitments or entanglements in Europe, but saw the need to counterbalance the Soviets and to ensure the peaceful cooperation of West Germany. In 1949 the North Atlantic Treaty was signed, by which the United States agreed to help its European allies to 'restore and maintain the security of the North Atlantic area'. Canada too signed, along with the Benelux countries, Britain, Denmark, France, Iceland, Italy, Norway, and Portugal. The pact was later given more substance with the creation of the North Atlantic Treaty Organization (NATO), headquartered in Paris until it was moved to Brussels in 1966. The United States was now committed to the security of western Europe.

Box 3.1 The Marshall Plan, 1948–51

US policy after 1945 was to withdraw its military forces as quickly as possible from Europe. However, it soon became clear that Stalin had plans to expand the Soviet sphere of influence, and the US State Department began to realize that it had underestimated the extent of Europe's economic destruction; despite a boom in the late 1940s, sustained growth was not forthcoming. When an economically exhausted Britain ended its financial aid to Greece and Turkey in 1947, President Truman argued the need for the United States to fill the vacuum in order to curb communist influence in the region.

US policy makers also felt that European markets needed to be rebuilt and integrated into a multilateral system of world trade, and that economic and political reconstruction would help forestall Soviet aggression and the rise of domestic communist parties (Hogan, 1987, pp. 26–7). Thus Secretary of State George Marshall argued that the United States should provide Europe with assistance to fight 'hunger, poverty, desperation and chaos'. The original April 1947 State Department proposal for the plan made clear that one of its ultimate goals was the creation of a western European federation (quoted in Gillingham, 1991, pp. 118–19).

The European Recovery Programme (otherwise known as the Marshall Plan) provided just over $12.5 billion in aid to Europe between 1948 and 1951 (Milward, 1984, p. 94), the disbursement of which was coordinated by the Organization for European Economic Cooperation (OEEC), a new body set up in April 1948 with headquarters in Paris. Governed by a Council of Ministers made up of one representative from each member state, the OEEC's goals included the reduction of tariffs and other barriers to trade, and consideration of the possibility of a free trade area or customs union among its members. Opposition from several European governments (notably Britain, France, and Norway) ensured that the OEEC remained a forum for intergovernmental consultation rather than becoming a supranational body with powers of its own (Wexler, 1983, p. 209; Milward, 1984, pp. 209–10).

Although the effects of the Marshall Plan are still debated, there is little question that it helped underpin economic and political recovery in Europe, and helped bind more closely the economic and political interests of the United States and western Europe. It was a profitable investment for the United States, in both political and economic terms, but it also had considerable influence on the idea of European integration – as western Europe's first venture in economic cooperation, it encouraged Europeans to work together and highlighted the mutual dependence among their economies (Urwin, 1995, pp. 20–2). It also helped liberalize intra-European trade, and helped ensure that economic integration would be focused on western Europe.

The NATO members agreed that an attack on one of them would be considered an attack on all of them, but each agreed only to respond with 'such actions as it deems necessary'. The Europeans attempted to take their own defence a step further in 1952 and proposed the creation of a European Defence Community, but this was prevented by political opposition in Britain and France (see below). Nonetheless, Britain was anxious to encourage some kind of military cooperation, and invited France, West Germany, Italy, and the Benelux states to become founding members of the Western European Union (WEU), under which members agreed to give all possible military and other aid to any member that was attacked. The WEU went beyond purely defensive concerns, and the agreement signed by the seven founding members in Paris in October 1954 included the aim 'to promote the unity and to encourage the progressive integration of Europe'. Within days of the launch of the WEU in May 1955 and the coincidental admission of West Germany into NATO, the Soviet bloc created the Warsaw Pact. The lines of the cold war were now defined, and its implications were clearly illustrated by events in Hungary in 1956.

In October the government of Imre Nagy announced the end of one-party rule, the evacuation of Russian troops from Hungary, and Hungary's withdrawal from the Warsaw Pact. Just as Britain and France were invading Egypt to retake the Suez Canal following its nationalization in July 1956 by Gamal Abdel Nasser, the Soviets responded to the Hungarian decision by sending in tanks. The United States wanted to criticize the Soviet use of force and boast to the emerging Third World about the moral superiority of the west, but obviously could not while British and French paratroopers were storming the Suez Canal. Britain and France were ostracized in the UN Security Council, British prime minister Anthony Eden resigned, and the attempt to regain the Suez was abandoned.

The consequences of the French defeat in Indochina in 1954, the Suez crisis and the Hungarian uprising were profound: Britain and France began to reduce the size of their armed forces, finally recognizing that they were no longer world powers capable of significant independent action in the Middle East, or perhaps anywhere; both embarked on a concerted programme of decolonization; Britain looked increasingly to Europe for its economic and security interests; and it became obvious to Europeans that the United States was the dominant partner in the North Atlantic alliance, a fact that particularly concerned the French.

First steps towards integration (1945–58)

The priority for European leaders after the Second World War was to create conditions that would prevent Europeans from ever going to war with each other again. For many, the major threats to peace and security were nationalism and the nation state, both of which had been discredited by the war. For many, Germany was the core problem – peace was impossible, it was argued, unless Germany could be contained and its power diverted to constructive rather than destructive ends. It had to be allowed to rebuild its economic base and its political system in ways that would not threaten European security.

Meanwhile, the growing hostility between the United States and the Soviet Union led Europeans to worry that they were becoming pawns in the cold war. There was clearly a need to protect western Europe from the Soviet threat, but there was concern about the extent to which Europeans and Americans could find common ground, and the extent to which western Europe could rely on US protection. Perhaps Europe would be better advised to take care of its own security. This, however, demanded a greater sense of unity and common purpose than Europe had ever been able to achieve.

The spotlight fell particularly on Britain, which had taken the lead in fighting Nazism and was still the dominant European power. In 1942–3, Winston Churchill had suggested the development of 'a United States of Europe' operating under 'a Council of Europe' with reduced trade barriers, free movement of people, a common military and a High Court to adjudicate disputes (quoted in Palmer, 1968, p. 111). He made the same suggestion in a speech at the University of Zurich in 1946, but it was clear that Churchill felt this new entity should be based around France and Germany and would not necessarily include Britain – before the war he had argued that Britain was 'with Europe but not of it. We are interested and associated, but not absorbed' (Zurcher, 1958, p. 6).

National pro-European groups decided to organize a conference aimed at publicizing the cause of regional unity. The Congress of Europe, held in The Hague in May 1948, was attended by delegates from 16 states and observers from the United States and Canada. Many ambitious ideas were discussed, but the major outcome was the Council of Europe, founded with the signing in London in May 1949 of a statute by ten western European states. The statute noted the need for 'closer unity between all the like-minded countries of Europe' and listed the Council's aims, including 'common action in economic, social, cultural, scientific, legal and administrative matters', but not defence.

The Council, which was headquartered in Strasbourg, had a governing Committee of Ministers, on which each state had one vote, and a 147-member Consultative Assembly made up of representatives nominated from national legislatures. Although membership of the Council expanded, it never became more than a loose intergovernmental organization. It made progress on human rights, cultural issues and even limited economic cooperation, but it was not the kind of body that European federalists wanted.

While the OEEC and the Council of Europe encouraged Europeans to think and work together, opposition from anti-federalists in Britain, Scandinavia and elsewhere ensured that neither would promote significant regional integration. Among those looking for something more substantial were the French entrepreneur and postwar planner Jean Monnet (1888–1979) and Robert Schuman (1886–1963), French foreign minister from 1948 to 1952. Both were enthusiastic Europeanists, felt that practical steps needed to be taken that went beyond the broad statements of organizations such as the Council of Europe, and agreed that the logical starting point should be the resolution of the perennial problem of Franco-German relations.

By 1950 it was clear to many that West Germany had to be allowed to rebuild its industrial base if it was to play a useful role in the western alliance. One way of doing this without allowing Germany to become a threat to its neighbours was for it to rebuild under the auspices of a supranational organization, which would tie Germany into the wider process of European reconstruction. Looking for a starting point that would be meaningful but not too ambitious, Monnet focused on the coal and steel industries, which offered strong potential for common European organization, for several reasons:

- Coal and steel were the building blocks of industry, and the steel industry had a tendency to create cartels. Cooperation would eliminate waste and duplication, break down cartels, make coal and steel production more efficient and competitive, and boost industrial development.
- Because the heavy industries of the Ruhr had been the foundation of Germany's power, and France and Germany had previously fought over coal reserves in Alsace-Lorraine, creating a supranational coal and steel industry might contain German power.
- Integrating coal and steel would make sure that Germany became reliant on trade with the rest of Europe, underpinning its economic reconstruction, and helping the French lose their fear of German industrial domination (Monnet, 1978, p. 292).

Monnet worried that unless France moved quickly, the United States would become the focus of a new transatlantic anti-Soviet alliance, Britain would be pulled closer to the United States, Germany's economic and military growth could not be controlled, and France would be led to its 'eclipse' (Monnet, 1978, p. 294). As head of the French national planning commission, he knew that effective economic planning was beyond the ability of individual states working alone. He also knew from personal experience that intergovernmental organizations had a tendency to be hamstrung by the governments of their member states, and to become bogged down in ministerial meetings. To avoid these problems he proposed a new institution independent of national governments; it would be supranational rather than intergovernmental.

After discussions with Monnet and West German chancellor Konrad Adenauer, Robert Schuman took these ideas a step further at his May 1950 press conference. In what later became known as the Schuman Declaration, he argued that Europe would not be united at once or according to a single plan, but step by step through concrete achievements. This would require the elimination of Franco-German hostility, and Schuman proposed that French and German coal and steel production be placed 'under a common High Authority, within the framework of an organization open to the participation of the other countries of Europe'. This would be 'a first step in the federation of Europe', and would make war between France and Germany 'not merely unthinkable, but materially impossible' (Schuman, quoted in Weigall and Stirk, 1992, pp. 58–9).

The proposal was revolutionary in the sense that France was offering to sacrifice a measure of national sovereignty in the interests of building a new supranational authority that might end an old rivalry and help build a new European peace (Gillingham, 1991, p. 231). Although membership of this new body was open to all western European states, only four accepted: Italy, which wanted respectability and economic and political stability, and the three Benelux countries, which were small and vulnerable, had twice been invaded by Germany, were heavily reliant on exports, and felt that the only way they could gain a significant voice in world affairs and ensure their security was to become part of a bigger regional unit.

The other western European governments had different reasons for not taking part: Portugal and Spain were dictatorships and had little interest in international cooperation; the memories of German occupation were too fresh for Denmark and Norway; Austria, Finland, and Sweden were keen on remaining neutral; Ireland was predominantly agricultural and tied economically to Britain; Britain still had extensive interests outside Europe, exported little of its steel to western Europe, and the new Labour government had just nationalized the coal and steel industries and did not like the supranational character of Schuman's proposal.

The lines of thinking now established, the governments of 'the Six' opened negotiations and on 18 April 1951 signed the Treaty of Paris, creating the European Coal and Steel Community (ECSC). The new organization began work in August 1952 after ratification of the terms of the treaty by each of the member states. It was governed by a nominated nine-member High Authority (with Jean Monnet as its first president), and decisions were taken by a six-member Special Council of Ministers. A nominated 78-member Common Assembly helped Monnet allay the fears of national governments regarding the surrender of powers, and disputes between states were to be settled by a seven-member Court of Justice.

The founding of the ECSC was a small step in itself, but remarkable in that it was the first time that European governments had given up significant powers to a supranational organization. It was allowed to reduce tariff barriers, abolish subsidies, fix prices, and raise money by imposing levies on steel and coal production. It faced national opposition to its work, but its job was made easier by the fact that some of the groundwork had already been laid by the Benelux customs union (founded in 1948). Although the ECSC failed to achieve many of its goals (notably the creation of a single market for coal and steel), it had ultimately been created to prove a point about the feasibility of integration, which it did.

While the ECSC was at least a limited success, two much larger, more ambitious and arguably premature experiments in integration were failures:

- The European Defence Community (EDC) was intended to promote cooperation on defence and bind West Germany into a European defence system. A draft treaty was signed by the six ECSC members in 1952 but it failed to be ratified, mainly because the French were nervous about the idea of German rearmament so soon after the war and did not want to give up control over their armed forces. Also, Britain – still the strongest European military power – was not included, and there could be no workable European defence force without a common foreign policy (Urwin, 1995, p. 63).
- The European Political Community was intended as the first step towards a European federation. A draft plan was completed in 1953 but with the collapse of the EDC all hope of a political community died, at least temporarily.

The failure of these two initiatives was a sobering blow to the integrationists and sent shock waves through the ECSC. Monnet resigned the presidency of the High Authority in 1955, disillusioned by the political resistance to its work and impatient to further the process of integration (Monnet, 1978, pp. 398–404).

The European Economic Community (1958–86)

While the ECSC made modest but solid achievements in its first four years, there were limits to its abilities and Europeanists felt that something more needed to be done to give momentum to the cause of integration. The six ECSC members agreed that coal and steel had been a useful testing ground, but that it was becoming increasingly difficult to develop these two sectors in isolation. A meeting of the ECSC foreign ministers at Messina in Italy in June 1955 resulted in agreement that it was time to 'relaunch' the European idea. They adopted a Benelux proposal 'to work for the establishment of a united Europe by the development of common institutions, the progressive fusion of national economies, the creation of a common market, and the progressive harmonization of their social policies' (Messina Resolution, in Weigall and Stirk, 1992, p. 94).

A committee was set up under the chairmanship of Belgian foreign minister Paul-Henri Spaak to look into the options. Its report led to a new round of negotiations and the signing in March 1957 of the two Treaties of Rome, one creating the European Economic Community (EEC) and the other the European Atomic Energy Community (Euratom), both of which came into force in January 1958. The EEC had a similar administrative structure to the ECSC, with a nine-member quasi-executive Commission, a Council of Ministers with powers over decision making, and a seven-member Court of Justice. A new 142–member Parliamentary Assembly was created to cover the EEC, ECSC and Euratom – in 1962 it was renamed the European Parliament.

The EEC Treaty committed the Six to the creation of a common market within 12 years by gradually removing all restrictions on internal trade, setting a common external tariff for goods coming into the EEC, reducing barriers to the free movement of people, services and capital among the member states, developing common agricultural and transport policies, and creating a European Social Fund and a European Investment Bank. Action would be taken in areas where there was agreement, and disagreements could be set aside for future discussion. The Euratom Treaty, meanwhile, was aimed at creating a common market for atomic energy, but Euratom remained a junior actor in the process of integration and focused primarily on research.

By January 1958 the six founding members of the European Communities had signed three treaties, created a small network of joint institutions, and agreed a number of ambitious goals aimed at integrating many of their economic activities. Problems were encountered along the way, but there were also many achievements:

- Although the 12-year deadline for the removal of barriers to a common market was not met, internal tariffs fell quickly enough to allow the Six to agree a common external tariff in July 1968, and to declare an industrial customs union.
- Bureaucratic bloat and replication were always a possibility, but although critics of European integration pointed accusing fingers at the European Commission, its staff numbers remained low, and decision making was streamlined in April 1965 with the Merger Treaty, which

combined into one the separate councils of ministers and commissions of the three communities. The decision-making process was given both authority and direction by the formalization in 1975 of regular summits of EC leaders coming together as the European Council. The EEC was also made more democratic with the introduction in 1979 of direct elections to the European Parliament.

- Integration brought the removal of the quota restrictions that the member states had used to protect their domestic industries from competition from imported products. Intra-EEC trade between 1958 and 1965 grew three times faster than that with third countries (Urwin, 1995, p. 130), the GNP of the Six grew at an average annual rate of 5.7 per cent, per capita income and consumption grew at 4.5 per cent, and the contribution of agriculture to GNP was halved (Ionescu, 1975, pp. 150–4).
- The free movement of goods across borders would be restricted as long as EEC members had non-tariff barriers such as different standards and regulations on health, safety and consumer protection. Standards were harmonized during the 1960s and 1970s, although it was not until the passage of the 1986 Single European Act that a concerted effort was made to bring all EEC members into line.
- Another priority was to lift restrictions on the free movement of workers. While some limits remained well into the 1990s, progress was made towards easing them during the 1960s and 1970s.
- Agreement on a Common Agricultural Policy (CAP) was achieved in 1968, creating a single market for agricultural products, and assuring EEC farmers of guaranteed prices for their produce. CAP initially encouraged both production and productivity, but it became the single biggest and most controversial item in the EEC budget (see Chapter 8).
- The Six worked more closely together on international trade negotiations and their joint influence was greater than it would have been if they had negotiated individually. The EEC acted as one, for example, in negotiations under the General Agreement on Tariffs and Trade (GATT), and in reaching preferential trade agreements with 18 former African colonies under the 1963 Yaoundé Convention (see Chapter 9).

Despite the achievements, the EEC was still a small, exclusive, and elitist club. The most obvious absentee was Britain, which continued to view itself after the war as a world power. That notion ended with the 1956 Suez crisis, which shook the foundations of Britain's special relationship with the United States, and also made it clear that most of the key decisions on global political and economic issues were being driven by the United States and the USSR. Britain was not opposed to European cooperation, but it was doubtful about the closeness of the ties proposed by Monnet and Schuman, so instead decided to champion a looser exercise in cooperation known as the European Free Trade Association (EFTA).

With a goal of free trade rather than economic and political integration, EFTA was founded in January 1960 with the signing of the Stockholm Convention by Austria, Britain, Denmark, Norway, Portugal, Sweden, and Switzerland. In contrast to the contractual arrangements set up for the EEC by the Treaty of Rome, membership of EFTA was voluntary and involved no institutions beyond a Council of Ministers that met two or three times a year, and a group of permanent representatives serviced by a small secretariat in Geneva.

EFTA helped cut tariffs, but achieved relatively little in the long term, mainly because several of its members did more trade with the EEC than with their EFTA partners. It soon became clear to Britain that political influence in Europe lay not with EFTA but with the EEC, that Britain risked political isolation if it stayed out of the EEC, and that the EEC was actually working – the member states had made impressive economic and political progress and British industry wanted access to the rich EEC market. In August 1961, barely 15 months after the creation of EFTA, Britain applied for EEC membership, as did Denmark and Ireland. They were joined in 1962 by Norway.

Denmark's motive was mainly agricultural: it was producing three times as much food as it needed, and the EEC represented a big market for those agricultural surpluses, as well as a boost for Danish industrial development. Ireland saw EEC membership as way of furthering its industrial plans, reducing its reliance on agriculture, and loosening its ties with Britain. Norway realized the importance of the EEC market. With four of its members apparently trying to defect, EFTA ceased to have much purpose, so Austria, Sweden, and Switzerland all applied for associate membership of the EEC; they were followed in 1962 by Malta, Portugal, and Spain.

Negotiations between Britain and the EEC opened in early 1962, and appeared to be on the verge of a successful conclusion when they fell foul of Charles de Gaulle's Franco-German policy. De Gaulle had plans for an EEC built around a Franco-German axis, saw Britain as a rival to French influence in the Community, was upset that he had not been given equal status at the wartime summits of the allied powers, and resented Britain's lack of enthusiasm for the early integrationist moves of the 1950s. He also felt that British membership would give the United States too much influence in Europe.

Monnet, however, was keen on British membership, and even tried to bring West German chancellor Konrad Adenauer around to his point of view, but the latter shared de Gaulle's anglophobia, and agreed that development of the Franco-German axis was the key. In the space of just ten days in January 1963 de Gaulle signed a new Franco-German treaty and vetoed the British application. He further upset Britain and some of his own EEC partners by reaching the veto decision unilaterally and making the announcement at a press conference in Paris. Since Britain's application was part of a joint package with Denmark and Ireland, their applications were rejected as well.

Britain reapplied in 1967, but de Gaulle again vetoed its application. Following his resignation in 1969 Britain applied for a third time, and this

Map 3.1   *Growth of the EU, 1952–86*

time its application was accepted, along with those of Denmark, Ireland, and Norway. Following membership negotiations in 1970–71, Britain, Denmark, and Ireland finally joined the EEC in January 1973. Norway would have joined as well but a public referendum in September 1972 narrowly went against membership. The Six had now become the Nine.

An additional round of enlargements took place in the 1980s and pushed the borders of the EEC further south and west. Greece had made its first overtures to the EEC in the late 1950s, but had been turned down on the grounds that its economy was too underdeveloped. It was given associate membership in 1961 as a prelude to full accession, which might have come sooner had it not been for the Greek military coup of April 1967. With the return to civilian government in 1974, Greece almost immediately applied for full membership, arguing that EEC membership would help underpin its attempts to rebuild democracy. The Community agreed, negotiations opened in 1976, and Greece joined in 1981.

Spain and Portugal had both requested negotiations for associate membership in 1962, but both were dictatorships. Spain was given a preferential trade agreement in 1970 and Portugal in 1973, but it was only with the overthrow of the Caetano regime in Portugal in 1973 and the death of Franco in Spain in 1975 that EEC membership for the two states was taken seriously. Despite the relative poverty of Portugal and Spain, problems over fishing rights and concern about Portuguese and Spanish workers moving north in search of work, the EEC felt that membership would encourage democracy in the Iberian peninsula and help link the two countries more closely to NATO and western Europe. Negotiations opened in 1978–79 and both states joined in 1986, the Ten thereby becoming the Twelve.

The doubling of membership had several political and economic consequences: it increased the influence of the EEC, it complicated the Community's decision-making processes, it reduced the overall influence of France and Germany, and – by bringing in the poorer Mediterranean states – it altered the internal economic balance of the EEC. Rather than enlarging any further, it was now decided to focus on deepening the relationship among the Twelve. Applications were made by Turkey (1987), Austria (1989), and Cyprus and Malta (1990), and although East Germany entered through the back door with German reunification in 1990, there was to be no further enlargement until 1995.

Economic and social integration (1979–92)

By 1986 the EEC had become known simply as the European Community (EC). Its member states had a combined population of 322 million and accounted for just over one-fifth of all world trade. The EC had its own administrative structure and an independent body of law, and its citizens had direct (but limited) representation through the European Parliament.

However, progress towards integration remained uneven. The creation of a common market was one of the key goals of the Treaty of Rome, but – while the customs union was in place – barriers remained to the free movement of people and capital (including different national technical, health, and quality standards, and varying levels of indirect taxation), European businesses were not competing well on the global market, and scientists and industrialists were failing to collaborate. It was argued that there could never be a true single market without a common European currency, a controversial idea because it would mean a significant loss of national sovereignty and because – in neofunctionalist terms – it would represent a significant move towards political union. These issues had now begun to concern EC leaders, who responded with the three most important steps in the process of integration since the treaties of Paris and Rome: the launch of the European Monetary System, and agreement of the Single European Act and the Treaty on European Union.

The EEC treaty had mentioned the need to 'coordinate' economic policies, but had given the Community no specific powers to ensure this, so in practice coordination had been minimal. New momentum had come in 1969 with a change of leadership in France and West Germany: President Georges Pompidou had been less averse than de Gaulle to strengthening EC ties and Chancellor Willy Brandt had been in favour of monetary union. Turbulence in the international monetary system in the late 1960s gave the idea new urgency and significance, but EEC leaders disagreed about whether economic union or monetary union should come first (Urwin, 1995, p. 155).

The principle of economic and monetary union (EMU) was discussed at a 1969 summit of EEC leaders in The Hague, who agreed to control fluctuations in the value of their currencies and to make more effort to coordinate national economic policies. In August 1971, however, the Nixon administration took the United States off the gold standard, and signalled the end of the Bretton Woods system by imposing domestic wage and price controls and placing a surcharge on imports. This led to international monetary turbulence, which was exacerbated in 1973 by the Arab–Israeli war and the global energy crisis. Because only West Germany, the Benelux countries, and Denmark were able to keep their currencies reasonably stable, the goal of achieving EMU by 1980 was quietly abandoned.

In 1979, a new initiative was launched, known as the European Monetary System (EMS). Using an Exchange Rate Mechanism (ERM) based around an accounting tool known as the European currency unit

Box 3.2 The 1986 Single European Act

The passage of the Single European Act was widely acclaimed as the most important and successful step in the process of European integration since the Treaty of Rome. It had many important consequences:

- It created the single biggest market and trading unit in the world. Many internal passport and customs controls were eased or lifted, banks and companies could do business throughout the Community, there was little to prevent EC residents living, working, opening bank accounts and drawing their pensions anywhere in the Community, protectionism became illegal, and monopolies on everything from electricity supply to telecommunications were broken down.

- It gave Community institutions responsibility over new policy areas that had not been covered in the Treaty of Rome, such as the environment, research and development, and regional policy.

- It gave new powers to the European Court of Justice, and created a Court of First Instance to hear certain kinds of cases and ease the workload of the Court of Justice.

- It gave legal status to meetings of heads of government under the European Council, and gave new powers to the Council of Ministers and the European Parliament.

- It gave legal status to European Political Cooperation (foreign policy coordination) so that member states could work towards a European foreign policy and work more closely on defence and security issues.

- It made economic and monetary union an EC objective and promoted 'cohesion', Eurojargon for the reduction of the gap between rich and poor parts of the EC, thereby avoiding a 'two-speed Europe'.

(ecu) (see Chapter 7 for details), this was designed to create a zone of monetary stability within which governments took action to keep their currencies as stable as possible. The hope was that the ecu would become the normal means of settling debts among Community members, psychologically preparing them for the idea of a single currency. The EMS helped stabilize exchange rates, so in 1989 Commission President Jacques Delors decided to take EMU a step further with the elaboration of a three-stage plan aimed at fixing exchange rates, and then turning the ecu into a single currency. His hopes were dashed, however, by speculation on the world's money markets, causing Britain and Italy to pull out of the ERM, and Ireland, Portugal, and Spain to devalue their currencies. Ironically the crisis deterred speculation and reinforced currency stability, and EMU was back on track by 1994, but there was doubt about how soon Stage Three of the Delors plan could be reached.

Meanwhile there was concern that progress towards the single market was being handicapped by inflation and unemployment, and by the temptation of member states to protect their home industries with non-tariff barriers such as subsidies. Competition from the United States and Japan was also growing. In response, a decision was reached at the 1983 European Council meeting in Stuttgart to revive the original goal outlined in the Treaty of Rome of creating a single market. The result was the signature in Luxembourg in February 1986 of the Single European Act (SEA), which came into force in July 1987. It had several goals (see Box 3.2), the most important of which was to complete all preparations for the single market by midnight on 31 December 1992. This involved agreeing nearly 300 new pieces of law aimed at the removal of all remaining physical barriers (such as customs and passport controls at internal borders), fiscal barriers (mainly in the form of different levels of indirect taxation) and technical barriers (such as conflicting standards, laws, and qualifications). This would create 'an area without internal frontiers in which the free movement of goods, persons, services and capital is assured'. The deadline came and went without all the new laws being adopted, but the single market went into force in January 1993 with the understanding that the backlog of legislation would be cleared as soon as possible.

Despite the signing of the SEA, progress on opening up borders was variable, and there was no common European policy on immigration, visas, and asylum. Impatient to move ahead, the governments of France, Germany, and the Benelux states in 1985 signed the Schengen Agreement, under which all border controls were to be removed. All EU member states except Britain and Ireland have since joined 'Schengenland', along with two non-members: Iceland and Norway. The terms of the agreement allow the signatories to implement controls at any time and not all have introduced truly passport-free travel, but its signature marked a substantial step towards the final removal of border controls.

With all this focus on economic issues, social policy was often over-looked by European leaders. The Treaty of Rome provided for the development of a Community social policy, but this was left in the hands of the member states and was narrowly defined, emphasizing improved working conditions and standards of living for workers, equal pay for equal work among men and women, social security for migrant workers, and increased geographical and occupational mobility for workers. As the economic links among EEC member states tightened, however, so their different levels of wealth and opportunity became more obvious. Even in the mid-1960s, per capita GDP in the Community's ten richest regions was nearly four times greater than in its ten poorest regions. With the accession of Britain, Greece, and Ireland the gap grew to the point where the richest regions were five times richer than the poorest (George, 1996, pp. 143–4).

Social and regional policy has since focused on promoting cohesion by helping the poorer parts of Europe, revitalizing regions affected by serious industrial decline, addressing long-term unemployment, providing youth job training, and helping the development of rural areas. The Commission gives economic assistance in the form of grants from what are collectively known as structural funds. These include the European Social Fund (ESF) (which concentrates on youth unemployment and job creation), the European Regional Development Fund (set up in response to the regional disparities that grew when Britain and Ireland joined the Community), and the Cohesion Fund (which compensates the poorest EU member states for the costs of tightening environmental controls, and provides help for transport projects). The structural funds accounted for 18 per cent of EC expenditure in 1984 but by 2004 represented nearly one-third of EU spending (see Chapter 5).

The SEA made cohesion a central part of economic integration, the assumption being that although the single market would create new jobs, this would not be enough. A boost for social policy came in 1989 with the Charter of Fundamental Social Rights for Workers (the Social Charter), which promoted the free movement of workers, fair pay, better living and working conditions, freedom of association, and protection of children and adolescents. Social issues are now one of the core policy areas for the European Union, with many of the actions taken by the governments of the member states driven by the requirements of EU law. The latter has addressed issues as varied as health and safety at work, parental leave from work, public health, and programmes to help the disabled and the elderly.

Despite the increased focus on cohesion, regional disparities remain; the gap between the highest and lowest income levels in the EU is twice that in the United States, and neither the EU nor the member states have so far been able to deal effectively with unemployment, which was 9 per cent in the euro zone in mid-2004 (and about 10 per cent in France and Germany), compared with 5–6 per cent in the United States and Japan. The Treaty of Amsterdam (see below) not only incorporated the Social Charter into the treaties, but also made the promotion of high employment an EU objective.

From Community to Union (1992–)

The controversial idea of political integration was long left on the back burner because it was felt that there was little hope of political union without economic union. False starts had been made with the European Political Community and an attempt in 1961 to draw up a political charter that would spell out the terms of political union (the Fouchet Plan; see Urwin, 1995, pp. 104–7). A later initiative came out of the 1970 Davignon report, which argued in favour of foreign policy coordination, quarterly meetings among the six foreign ministers, liaison among EC ambassadors in foreign capitals, and common EC instructions on certain matters for those ambassadors.

Meanwhile, foreign policies were coordinated under a process known as European Political Cooperation (EPC), which had some early successes, such as the 1970 joint EC policy declaration on the Middle East and the signature of the Yaoundé Conventions on aid to poor countries. In 1975 Italian prime minister Aldo Moro signed the Final Act of the Conference on Security and Cooperation in Europe (held in Helsinki) 'in the name of the European Community'. EPC was eventually given legal status with the SEA. It worked well in some areas, but was more reactive than proactive and often found European governments at odds with one another. This became clear during the 1990–1 Gulf crisis set off by the Iraqi invasion of Kuwait, when the Community as a whole issued demands to the Iraqi regime, and imposed an embargo on Iraqi oil imports, but few individual member states were actively involved in the allied military response. It became clear once again in 1998 when Britain supported US threats of military action against Iraq, but found little agreement among its EU partners.

Determined to reassert French leadership in the EC, President François Mitterrand had focused on the theme of political union at the Fontainebleu European Council in 1984, with the result that a decision was taken in Milan in June 1985 to convene an intergovernmental conference (IGC) on political union. The outcome was the Treaty on European Union, agreed at the European Council summit in Maastricht in December 1991 and signed by the foreign and economics ministers of the Community in February 1992 (see Box 3.3). The draft treaty had included the goal of federal union, but Britain had balked at this so the wording was changed to 'an ever closer union among the peoples of Europe, in which decisions are taken as closely as possible to the citizen'.

The Maastricht treaty had to be ratified by the 12 member states before it could come into force. There were lengthy political debates in Britain, France, and Germany, but Maastricht received its biggest setback when it was rejected by Danish voters in a referendum in June 1992. It was only narrowly accepted by a referendum in France in September, so its content was further discussed at the European Council meeting in Edinburgh in December 1992. Following agreement that the Danes could opt out of the single currency, common defence arrangements, European citizenship, and cooperation on justice and home affairs, a second referendum was held in Denmark in May 1993, and the treaty was accepted.

Meanwhile, there was further discussion about enlarging the EU. At its June 1993 meeting in Copenhagen, the European Council agreed a formal

Box 3.3 The 1992 Treaty on European Union

Like the Single European Act before it, the Treaty on European Union – usually known as the Maastricht treaty – made some substantial changes to the contract among the member states of the EU:

- Reflecting the lengths to which the member states will occasionally go to reach compromises, a peculiar arrangement was agreed under Maastricht by which – instead of new powers being given to the European Community – three 'pillars' were created, and the whole structure was given the new label 'European Union'. The first pillar consisted of the three preexisting communities (economic, coal and steel, and atomic energy), and the second and third pillars consisted of two areas in which there was to be more formal intergovernmental cooperation: a Common Foreign and Security Policy (CFSP), and home affairs and justice. Final responsibility for the CFSP remained with the individual governments rather than being handed over to the EU. The pillar arrangement is a diplomatic sideshow that is all but irrelevant to an understanding of the EU today.
- A timetable was agreed for the creation of a single European currency by January 1999, confirming the essence of the plan outlined by Commission President Jacques Delors in 1989.
- EU responsibility was extended into new policy areas such as consumer protection, public health policy, transport, education, and (except in Britain) social policy.
- There was to be greater intergovernmental cooperation on immigration and asylum, a European police intelligence agency (Europol) was created to combat organized crime and drug trafficking, a new Committee of the Regions was set up, and regional funds for poorer EU states were increased.
- New rights were provided for European citizens and an ambiguous European Union 'citizenship' was created: this meant, for example, the right of citizens to live wherever they liked in the EU, and to stand or vote in local and European elections.
- New powers were given to the European Parliament, including a 'codecision procedure' under which certain kinds of legislation are subject to a third reading in the European Parliament before they can be adopted by the Council of Ministers.

set of requirements for membership of the EU. Known as the Copenhagen conditions, they formally require that an applicant state must (a) be democratic, with respect for human rights and the rule of law, (b) have a functioning free-market economy and the capacity to cope with the competitive pressures of capitalism, and (c) be able to take on the obligations of the *acquis communitaire* (the body of laws and policies already adopted by the EU). Deciding whether applicants meet these criteria has proved difficult, not least because of the problem of defining 'Europe', as discussed in Chapter 2.

Throughout the 1980s, discussions about enlargement focused on other western European states, if only because they came closest to meeting the criteria for membership. In order to prepare prospective members, negotiations began in 1990 on the creation of a European Economic Area (EEA), under which the terms of the SEA would be extended to the seven EFTA members, in return for which they would accept the rules of the single market. The EEA came into force in January 1994, but had already begun to lose relevance because Austria, Finland, Norway, and Sweden had applied for EC membership. Negotiations with these four applicants were completed in early 1994, and all but Norway (where a referendum once again went against membership) joined the EU in January 1995.

Today, in addition to Norway, there are just two western European countries outside the EU: Iceland and Switzerland. Iceland, with a population of just 300 000, relies largely on the export of fish and does more than half its trade with the EU, and so is finding the logic of joining the EU increasingly difficult to resist. Switzerland, which had considered applying for EC membership in 1992, rejected the EEA and in 1995 found itself completely surrounded by the EU. Demands for the Swiss to open their highways to EU trucks and intra-EU trade increased the pressure for EU membership, but further discussion ended – at least temporarily – in March 2001 when a national referendum went heavily against EU membership, by 77 per cent to 23 per cent.

Partly in preparation for anticipated eastern enlargement, but also to account for the progress of European integration and perhaps move the EU closer to political union, two new treaties were signed in 1997–2000. The first was the Treaty of Amsterdam, which was signed in October 1997 and came into force in May 1999. Much was expected of the treaty, but it fell far short of achieving political union to accompany the economic and monetary union promoted by the SEA and Maastricht, and the 15 leaders were unable to agree anything more than modest changes to the structure of EU institutions in preparation for enlargement. Policies on asylum, visas, external border controls, immigration, employment, social policy, health protection, consumer protection, and the environment were developed, cooperation between national police forces (and the work of Europol) was strengthened, and improvements were made to the arrangements for EU foreign policy. There was also agreement on the goal of a single European currency in January 1999, and on eastern enlargement.

Less radical and headline-making than either the SEA or Maastricht, the key goal of the Treaty of Nice – agreed in December 2000 and signed in February 2001 – was to make the institutional changes needed to prepare for eastward enlargement, and to make the EU more democratic and

Map 3.2 *Growth of the EU, 1990–2004*

transparent. It proved to be a disappointment, though, doing little more than tinkering with the structure of the institutions, including increasing the size of the European Commission and the European Parliament, and redistributing the votes in the Council of Ministers. European leaders were taken by surprise in June 2001 when Irish voters rejected the terms of the treaty, its opponents arguing that it involved the surrender of too much national control, and being particularly concerned about the implications for Irish neutrality. A second vote was taken in Ireland in October 2002, following assurances that Ireland's neutrality on security issues would be respected, and – thanks in part to bigger turnout – the treaty was accepted by a 63 per cent majority.

Meanwhile, the EU took a dramatic step forward on the economic front in early 2002, with the final adoption of the single currency. A decision had been taken in 1995 to call it the euro, and the timetable agreed under Maastricht required participating states to fix their exchange rates in January 1999. Several so-called 'convergence criteria' were considered essential prerequisites: these included placing limits on national budget deficits, public debt, consumer inflation, and long-term interest rates. At a special EU summit in May 1998 it was decided that all but Greece met the four conditions, but public and political opinion in the member states was divided on which should or would fix their exchange rates. While inflation rates were low in the member states in 1998, their unemployment rates were not, and the rate of industrial growth was slowing in several. There was also considerable public resistance to the idea of the single currency in several countries, notably Britain and Germany. In the event, all but Denmark, Sweden, and the UK adopted the euro, banknotes and coins began circulating in January 2002, and the 12 members of the euro zone abolished their national currencies in March. For the first time since the Roman era, most of Europe had a common currency.

The Treaty of Nice came into force in February 2003, but the changes it introduced went largely unnoticed because there had already been broader discussions about the need to make the EU more democratic and to bring it closer to its citizens. At the Laeken European Council in December 2001 it was decided to establish a convention to debate the future of Europe, and to draw up a treaty containing a constitution designed to simplify and replace all the other treaties, to decide how to divide powers between the EU and the member states, to make the EU more democratic and efficient, to determine the role of national parliaments within the EU, and to pave the way for more enlargement.

The Convention on the Future of the European Union met between February 2002 and July 2003 under the presidency of former French president Valéry Giscard d'Estaing, with a total of 105 representatives from the 15 EU member states and the 13 applicant eastern European and Mediterranean countries, as well as representatives from each of the 28 national parliaments, and from the European Parliament. The convention considered numerous proposals, including an elected president of the European Council, a foreign minister for the EU, a limit on the membership of the European Commission, a common EU foreign and security policy, and a legal personality for the EU, whose laws would cancel out those of national parliaments in areas where the EU had been given competence. It took two European Council meetings (December 2003 and June 2004) to reach agreement on the draft treaty, which – at the time of writing – was to be put to public referendums or government votes in most EU member states. Although opinion polls in mid-2004 found large majorities in favour in all EU member states, there was little expectation that the votes would be straightforward.

In May 2004, the EU undertook its most significant enlargement when ten eastern European and Mediterranean states joined: Cyprus, the Czech Republic, Estonia, Hungary, Latvia, Lithuania, Malta, Poland, Slovenia, and Slovakia. Together their economies were smaller than that of the Netherlands, and they increased the population of the EU by less than 20 per cent; the real significance of the 2004 enlargement lay in the fact that the EU was now no longer an exclusive club for wealthy west Europeans. The East was now included, and – for the first time – former Soviet republics (Estonia, Latvia, Lithuania) became part of the European Union. As well as providing an important symbolic confirmation of the end of the cold war division of Europe, the 2004 enlargement also promised to accelerate the process of transforming the economies and democratic structures of eastern European countries. Three out of four Europeans are now residents of the EU, and while it may be some time before Albanians, Bulgarians, Moldovans, Norwegians, Romanians, and other Europeans are brought under the umbrella of the EU, it is impossible for them to resist the economic and political pull of their giant neighbour.

Only one troubling question remains: the matter of Turkey, which has been anxious to join for some time and applied for membership in 1987. While its eligibility has been confirmed and it has been in a customs union with the EU since 1996, Turkey is big (more than 70 million people), poor and predominantly Islamic. In addition to the troubling economic and social questions thus raised, Turkey's human rights record is poor and its application has been opposed by Greece. It was angered by the decision of the European Council in December 1997 not to include it in the next round of enlargement negotiations, particularly as the EU said yes to Cyprus, which has been divided since 1975 into Turkish and Greek zones. In December 2004, the EU finally agreed to open membership negotiations with Turkey.

Conclusions

Europe has travelled a long road since the end of the Second World War. At that time, most European states were physically devastated, the suspicions and hostilities that had led to two world wars in the space of a generation still lingered, western Europe found itself being pulled into a military and economic vacuum as power and influence moved outwards to the United States and the Soviet Union, and eastern Europe came under the political and economic control of the Soviet Union. The balance of power in the west changed as an exhausted Britain and France dismantled their empires and reduced their militaries, while West Germany rapidly rebuilt and became the dominant force in European politics. Intent on avoiding future wars, and concerned about being caught in big-power rivalry, western European leaders began considering new levels of regional cooperation, pooling the interests of their states, and helping give the region new confidence and influence.

Beginning with the limited experiment of integrating their coal and steel industries, and building on an economic foundation and security shield underwritten by the United States, six European states quickly agreed a common agricultural policy, a customs union, and the beginnings of a common market. The accession of new members in the 1970s and 1980s greatly increased the size of the Community's population and market, pushing its borders to the edge of Russia and the Middle East. The global economic instability that followed the end of the Bretton Woods system and the energy crises of the 1970s served to emphasize the need for western European countries to cooperate if they were to have more control over their own future rather than simply to respond to external events.

After several years of relative lethargy the European experiment was given new impetus by completion of the single market, and then by the controversial decision to stabilize exchange rates as a prelude to the abolition of national currencies and the adoption of a single European currency in 2002. At the same time, the European Union increasingly showed a united face to the rest of the world, with more cooperation on foreign and trade policy, and the seeds of a European defence capacity. The effects of integration have been felt in a growing number of policy areas, including agriculture, competition, transport, the environment, energy, telecommunications, research and development, working conditions, culture, consumer affairs, education, and employment.

The short-term future of the EU now depends heavily on what happens to the draft constitution. On the one hand, it promises – after many years during which new treaties have brought regular change – to provide some stability, and a relatively fixed point of reference by which the EU can be better understood. On the other hand, the constitution is both long and uninspiring, and is politically troubling to many of the citizens of the EU. The process of ratification will not be straightforward, and even a single negative vote is likely to pose a hard challenge to the future of European integration.

Chapter 4

The Institutions of the EU

A constitution for Europe
The European Commission
The Council of Ministers
The European Parliament
The European Court of Justice
The European Council
Conclusions

> *... the Union must start adapting its institutions and establishing more coherence in its policies so that it is easier to see what it does and what it stands for.*
>
> European Commission White Paper, 2001

As the European Union has grown, so have the powers and the reach of its institutions. Unfortunately, changes over the years have created a governing structure that is complex and often confusing. Those changes have come mainly as a response to short-term needs and political compromises, without any long-term sense of what the 'government' of the EU should eventually become. The treaties of Amsterdam and Nice were to have included major innovations, but they ended up providing little more than some light tinkering, all of which has now been incorporated into the draft constitutional treaty for the EU, now under deliberation in the member states.

The EU institutions cannot easily be compared with the governing bodies of the member states. The College of Commissioners is something like a cabinet of ministers, but not quite. The European Parliament has some of the powers of a typical legislature, but not all. The European Commission is a bureaucracy, but it is also much more. The European Council and the Council of Ministers are like nothing found in most national governments. The Court of Justice is the only institution to directly parallel those found at the national level – it has most of the features of a typical constitutional court. To complicate matters, the institutions do not amount to a 'government' in the conventional sense of the word, because the member states still hold most of the decision-making powers, and are responsible for implementing EU policies on the ground.

To summarize the work of the major institutions: the European Commission develops proposals for new laws and policies, on which final decisions are taken by the Council of Ministers and the European Parliament. Once a decision is made, the European Commission is responsible for overseeing implementation by the member states. Meanwhile, the Court of Justice works to ensure that laws and policies meet the terms and spirit of the treaties, while the European Council brings the leaders of the member states together at periodic summit meetings to guide the overall direction of European integration.

This brief outline says nothing about the many subtle nuances of European decision making, nor does it convey the many informal aspects of EU government: the different levels of influence exerted by member states; the political and economic pressures that drive the decisions of the member states; the key role played by interest groups, corporations, staff in the Commission, specialized working groups in the Council of Ministers, and the permanent representatives of the member states; and all the muddling through and incremental change that often characterize policy making in the EU, as in national systems of government.

This chapter looks at the five major institutions of the EU, describing how they are structured, showing how they fit into the policy process, and explaining how they relate to each other and to the member states. It paints a picture of a system that is often complicated, occasionally clumsy, and regularly misunderstood. It argues that the EU institutions are caught in a web of competing national interests, and that the conflicting forces of intergovernmentalism and supranationalism are pulling each of them in different directions, but that they are still – to all intents and purposes – a confederal administration of the European Union.

A constitution for Europe

A constitution is typically a written document that describes the structure of a system of government, outlines the powers of the different governing institutions, describes limits on those powers, and lists the rights of citizens relative to government. It is usually fairly short, provisions are made by which it can be amended, and a constitutional court exists with the duty of interpreting the constitution by measuring the laws and actions of government against the content and principles of the constitution. Oddly enough for an entity that has so much influence over the lives of so many people, the European Union has functioned so far without a formal constitution. It has instead been guided by a series of treaties which have had many of the same effects as a constitution, and although studies of EU law have often talked of constitution-building and the 'constitutionalization' of the EU legal order (see Mancini, 1991; Dehousse, 1998, Chapter 2; Shaw, 2000, Chapter 3), many European leaders have been reluctant to give up control, to recognize the EU as a new level of government, and thus to agree that the treaties should be formally recognized in political discussions as a constitution.

When American leaders decided to create the United States of America, they drew up a constitution that had four important features. First, it was a contract between people and government, outlining their relative roles, powers, and rights. Second, it was short and succinct, meaning that it could easily be read and understood by almost anyone. Third, it was ambiguous and provided few details on the specific powers of government, thereby allowing room for evolutionary change. Finally, there was provision for amendments to be made, but – by happy accident – loopholes ensured that the most important changes to the constitution were to come as a result of judicial interpretations provided by the US Supreme Court and new laws passed by the US Congress. These have changed many of the details of the structure of government, allowing the constitution more or less to keep up with prevailing political, economic and social values.

The treaties of the EU have had none of these advantages. Instead of being contracts between people and government, they have been contracts among governments. Instead of being short, they have been long, rambling, and dull, often confusing even the legal experts. Instead of being ambiguous (and thus flexible), the obsession of European leaders with making sure that there is minimal room for misunderstanding has produced documents that have gone into migrainous detail on the specific powers of EU institutions, the policy responsibilities of the EU, and the rights of citizens. And instead of being changed only by formal amendments, by judicial interpretation, or by changes in EU law, wholesale revisions have been introduced as a result of new treaties.

The European constitutional convention that met in 2002–03 might have taken the opportunity to undertake some fundamental spring-cleaning, and to follow the American model by producing a short, readable, and flexible document that would replace the treaties and give Europeans a better sense of what integration meant. It might also have taken the opportunity to introduce some stirring declarations, thereby encouraging Europeans to read it and to learn its key points. But where the authors of the US constitution were drawing up a virtually new political system from scratch, had relatively few opinions to take into account, and were dealing with just 13 largely homogeneous American states, the authors of the EU constitution were faced with the challenge of summarizing an accumulation of fifty years' worth of treaties, and had to take into account not only the views of 15 member states with often different values and priorities, but also of 13 candidate member states from eastern Europe. The result was a document that was long (well over 300 pages), dull, and controversial. It was approved by the leaders of the member states in June 2004, but only after heated debate. All 25 states must ratify the constitution, whether by a national referendum or by a government vote, before it can come into force.

The European Commission

The process by which laws and policies are made in the EU begins with the European Commission, the executive–bureaucratic arm of the EU. It is responsible for developing proposals for new laws and policies (see Box 4.1), for overseeing the execution of those laws and policies once they are adopted, and for promoting the general interests of European integration. Headquartered in Brussels, its staff work in multiple buildings around the city, and in regional cities around the EU and national capitals around the world. It is the most supranational of the EU institutions, and has not only encouraged member states to harmonize their laws, regulations and standards in the interests of removing barriers to trade, but has been the source of some of the most important policy initiatives since the 1960s, including the single market programme and the development of the euro.

Eurosceptics like to scorn the Commission, arguing that it is big, expensive, and powerful, that it meddles in the internal affairs of member states, that its leaders are not elected, and that it has too little public accountability. But the criticism is often misguided:

- Commission leaders are not elected. This is true, but they are appointed by elected national government leaders, and to have them elected would be to give them the kind of independence that national governments fear.
- It sometimes appears secretive and anonymous. Also true, but its record is no worse than that of national bureaucracies and in some ways is better.
- It is small given the size of its task (it has just over 20,000 staff, making it smaller than many national government ministries) and its administrative costs account for just 6 per cent of the EU budget.
- Most importantly, the Commission is not a decision-making body, but simply carries out the wishes of the member states, and makes sure that the general goals of integration are converted into specific actions. Decision-making power rests with the Council of Ministers, which is firmly under the control of the governments of the member states, and with the European Parliament, elected by the voters of the EU.

Box 4.1 European Union law

The key difference between the EU and any other 'international organization' is that the EU has a body of law which is applicable in all its member states, which supersedes national law in areas where the EU has 'competence', and which is backed up by rulings from the Court of Justice. The creation of this body of law has involved the voluntary surrender of powers by the member states in a broad range of policy areas, and the development of a new level of legal authority to which the member states are subject.

The foundation of the EU legal order is provided by the eight treaties: Paris, the two treaties of Rome, the Merger Treaty, the Single European Act, Maastricht, Amsterdam, and Nice. These are the primary rules, out of which have come thousands of secondary rules, taking five main forms:

- *Regulations* are the most powerful, and the most like conventional acts of a national legislature. They are directly applicable in that they do not need to be turned into national law, they are binding in their entirety, and they take immediate effect on a specified date. Usually fairly narrow in intent, regulations are often designed to amend or adjust an existing law.
- *Directives* are binding in terms of goals, but it is left up to the member states to decide what action they need to take to achieve those goals. For example, a 1988 directive on pollution from large industrial plants set targets for the reduction of emissions (how much, and by when), but left it up to the member states to decide individually how to meet those targets. Directives usually include a date by which national action must be taken, and member states must tell the Commission what they are doing.
- *Decisions* are also binding, but are usually fairly specific in their intent, and aimed at one or more member states, at institutions, or even at individuals. Some are aimed at making changes in the powers of EU institutions, some are directed towards internal administrative matters, and others are issued when the Commission has to adjudicate disputes between member states or corporations.
- *Recommendations* and *opinions* have no binding force. They are sometimes used to test reaction to a new EU policy, but they are used mainly to persuade or to provide interpretation on the application of regulations, directives and decisions.

Until the early 1990s the EU was adopting a staggering 6,000–7,000 laws every year, but the number has since fallen to about 1,500–1,800. The fall-off was due in part to a deliberate policy by the Commission to focus more on the implementation of existing laws, and in part to the completion of the single market programme.

The Commission is headed by a College of Commissioners with 25 members (one from each of the member states). This serves a five-year term and functions as something like a European cabinet, making the final decisions on which proposals for new laws and policies to send on for approval. One of the 25 is appointed president, and each commissioner has a portfolio for which he or she is responsible, the subjects of the portfolios reflecting the policy responsibilities of the EU (see Table 4.1). Under the constitutional treaty, membership will be reduced in 2014 to no more than two-thirds of the number of member states, with members chosen on a rotation from among the states.

Commissioners are appointed by their national governments, but they are not national representatives, and they must swear an oath of office saying that they will renounce any defence of national interests. There are no formal rules on appointments, but nominees are discussed with the nominee for president, and must be acceptable to other governments and to the European Parliament (for details on the process, see Nugent, 2001, pp. 82–8). As the powers of the Commission have increased, and the EU has become a more significant political force, postings to the Commission have become more desirable and more important, and commissioners are becoming both younger and more technocratic.

The dominant figure in the Commission is the president, the person who comes closest to being the leader of the EU. The word 'leader' should be treated with some caution, though, because the president does not have the same political status as a head of government, and is more the Chief Bureaucrat of the EU. However, the president has considerable authority within the Commission: he or she can influence the appointment of other commissioners, has sole power over distributing portfolios, sets the agenda for the Commission, can launch major new policy initiatives, can take over new responsibilities, chairs meetings of the College, and represents the Commission in dealings with other EU institutions and national governments. From 2005, the president will be able to reshuffle portfolios mid-term (with College approval), giving the office even more influence over the Commission.

As with all such positions, the powers of the office depend to some extent on the personality of the office holder. Following several early presidents who in the main did not make much of an impression, the administration of former French economics minister Jacques Delors in 1985–94 changed everything. Delors centralized authority, had firm ideas about a strong, federal Europe asserting itself internationally, and used this vision to push the EU in many new directions; his name is associated particularly with the single market and single currency programmes. He was succeeded in January 1995 by Jacques Santer, former prime minister of Luxembourg, who avoided bold new initiatives, and focused instead on improving the implementation of existing laws and policies. The Santer College resigned en masse in January 1999 following charges of nepotism and incompetence against some of its members. Santer was replaced by

Table 4.1   *The European commissioners, January 2005*

Name	Country	Key portfolios
José Manuel Barroso	Portugal	President
Siim Kallas	Estonia	Vice President; Administrative Affairs, Audit, Anti-Fraud
Jacques Barrot	France	Vice President; Transport
Günter Verheugen	Germany	Vice President; Enterprise and Industry
Franco Frattini	Italy	Vice President; Justice, Freedom, Security
Margot Wallström	Sweden	Vice President; Institutional Relations, Communication Strategy
Benita Ferrero-Waldner	Austria	External Relations
Louis Michel	Belgium	Development and Humanitarian Aid
Markos Kyprianou	Cyprus	Health and Consumer Protection
Valdimir Špidla	Czech Rep	Employment, Social Affairs, Equal Opportunities
Mariann Fischer Boel	Denmark	Agriculture and Rural Development
Olli Rehn	Finland	Enlargement
Stavros Dimas	Greece	Environment
László Kovács	Hungary	Taxation and Customs Union
Charlie McCreevy	Ireland	Internal Market and Services
Andris Piebalgs	Latvia	Energy
Dalia Grybauskaité	Lithuania	Financial Programming and Budget
Viviane Reding	Luxembourg	Information Society and Media
Joe Borg	Malta	Fisheries and Maritime Affairs
Neelie Kroes	Netherlands	Competition
Danuta Hübner	Poland	Regional Policy
Ján Figel	Slovakia	Education, Training, Culture, Multilingualism
Janez Potocnik	Slovenia	Science and Research
Joaquin Almunia	Spain	Economic and Monetary Affairs
Peter Mandelson	UK	Trade

Table 4.2   *Presidents of the European Commission*

1958–67	Walter Hallstein (West Germany)
1967–70	Jean Rey (Belgium)
1970–72	Franco Maria Malfatti (Italy)
1972	Sicco Mansholt (Netherlands) (interim)
1973–76	Francois-Xavier Ortoli (France)
1977–80	Roy Jenkins (Britain)
1981–84	Gaston Thorn (Luxembourg)
1985–94	Jacques Delors (France)
1995–99	Jacques Santer (Luxembourg)
1999	Mario Monti (Spain) (interim)
1999–2004	Romano Prodi (Italy)
2004–	José Manuel Barroso (Portugal)

former Italian prime minister Romano Prodi, whose presidency saw the passage of the treaties of Amsterdam and Nice, the holding of the constitutional convention, the arrival of the euro, and the 2004 enlargement. Prodi was replaced in 2005 by José Manuel Durão Barroso, the incumbent prime minister of Portugal (see Table 4.2).

There are few formal rules regarding how the president is appointed (for details on recent appointments, see Nugent, 2001, pp. 63–8). It has become normal for the leaders of the member states to decide the appointment at the European Council held in the June before the term of the incumbent Commission ends, settling on someone acceptable to all of them and to the European Parliament. Appointed for renewable five-year terms, the president will usually be someone with a strong political reputation, a strong character, proven leadership abilities, and a philosophy toward the EU that is acceptable to all major EU leaders.

Below the College, the Commission is divided into 26 directorates-general (DGs) – which are equivalent to national government ministries – and nine services (see Table 4.3). Every DG is responsible for a particular policy area, has its own director-general, and is tied to a commissioner. Some DGs are bigger, wealthier, busier, and more important than others, the ranking being a reflection of the extent to which the EU is active in different policy areas; those dealing with external affairs, industry, and agriculture are more powerful and more prominent, while those dealing with fisheries, energy, and education are smaller and less influential. For their part, the services deal with a variety of external matters, such as emergency aid and relief, and the EU's external development aid programme, and internal administrative matters, including fraud and corruption within EU institutions, and providing legal advice to the Commission.

Table 4.3 *Directorates-general and Services of the European Commission*

Directorates-general

Agriculture	Health and Consumer Protection
Budget	Information Society
Competition	Internal Market
Development	Interpretation
Economic and Financial Affairs	Joint Research Center
Education and Culture	Justice and Home Affairs
Employment and Social Affairs	Personnel and Administration
Energy and Transport	Press and Communication
Enlargement	Regional Policy
Enterprise	Research
Environment	Taxation and Customs Union
External Relations	Trade
Fisheries	Translation

Services

EuropeAid Cooperation Office	Internal Audit Service
European Anti-Fraud Office	Legal Service
Eurostat	Publications Office
Group of Policy Advisers	Secretariat General
Humanitarian Aid Office	

The general task of the Commission is to ensure that EU policies are advanced in light of the treaties (for details, see Edwards and Spence, 1997, Chapter 1). It does this in five ways.

- *Powers of initiation.* The Commission makes sure that the principles of the treaties are turned into laws and policies. It has a monopoly over drafting new laws, and can draw up proposals for new policy areas, as it did with the Single European Act and the Delors package for economic and monetary union. Proposals can come from a commissioner or a staff member of one of the DGs, may be a response to a ruling by the Court of Justice, may flow out of the requirements of the treaties, or may come out of pressure exerted by member state governments, interest groups, the European Council, the European Parliament, and even private corporations.

  A new piece of EU legislation will begin life as a draft written by middle-ranking officials in one of the DGs. It will then work its way up through the different levels of the DG, being discussed with outside parties (such as interest groups or corporations), and with other DGs, being amended along the way. The draft will finally reach the College of Commissioners, which can accept a proposal, reject it, send it back down the line for redrafting, or defer making a decision. Once accepted, it will be sent to the European Parliament and the Council of Ministers for a decision. The process can take anything from months to years, and Commission staff will be involved at every stage.

- *Powers of implementation.* Once a law or policy is accepted, the Commission is responsible for making sure that it is implemented by the member states. It has no power to do this directly, but instead works through national bureaucracies, using its power to collect information from member states, to take to the Court of Justice any member state, corporation, or individual that does not conform to the spirit of the treaties or follow subsequent EU law, and to impose sanctions or fines if a law is not being implemented.

  The Commission has its own monitoring teams, but they do not have the personnel to police every member state, so it usually has to rely on reports from member states, or whistle-blowing by governments, individuals, corporations, or interest groups. The Commission adds to the pressure by publicizing the progress on implementation, hoping to embarrass the laggards into action. Until 1993, compliance was based on goodwill and an agreement to 'play the game'; Maastricht gave the Commission new powers to take a state to the Court of Justice, which can then impose a fine. Most cases of non-compliance arise not so much out of a deliberate avoidance by a member state as out of differences over interpretation or differences in the levels of efficiency of national bureaucracies.

- *Acting as the conscience of the EU.* The Commission is expected to rise above competing national interests and to represent and promote the general interest of the EU. It is also expected to help smooth the flow of decision making by mediating disagreements between or among member states and other EU institutions.

- *Management of EU finances.* The Commission makes sure that all EU revenues are collected, plays a key role in drafting and guiding the annual budget through the Council of Ministers and Parliament, and administers EU spending.

- *External relations.* The Commission has been given the authority by the member states to represent the EU in dealings with international organizations such as the United Nations and the World Trade Organization. It is also a key point of contact between the EU and the rest of the world; more than 140 governments have opened diplomatic missions in Brussels accredited to the EU, while the EU has opened more than 130 offices in other parts of the world, staffed by Commission employees. The Commission also vets applications for full or associate membership from aspirant member states. If the EU decides to open negotiations with an applicant, the Commission oversees the process.

The Commission has been a productive source of initiatives for new laws and policies, and is much more accessible and open than, say, the Council of Ministers. It has been at the core of European integration since the beginning, and while it has not always made the best use of the resources it has available, its staff on the whole is professional and hard-working, and the criticisms made against the Commission by Eurosceptic media and politicians are often unfair and misinformed.

The Council of Ministers

The Council of Ministers is the major decision-making branch of the EU, the primary champion of national interests, and arguably the most powerful of the EU institutions. Yet it is the institution about which most Europeans know the least: its meetings are held in secret, it attracts little media coverage, and it has been the subject of much less academic study than the Commission or Parliament. When Europeans think about the activities of the EU, they tend to first think of (and blame) the Commission, forgetting that the Council of Ministers actually makes the final decisions. In many ways, its powers make the Council more like the legislature of the EU than the European Parliament, although new powers for Parliament in recent years have made the two bodies into 'co-legislatures'.

Once the Commission has proposed a new law or policy, it is discussed and amended by the Council of Ministers and the European Parliament. Headquartered in the Justus Lipsius Building in Brussels, the Council (formally the Council of the European Union) is one of the most intergovernmental of EU institutions. It consists of national government ministers, who meet in one of nine so-called technical councils, the membership depending on the topic under discussion. The most important of these is the General Affairs and External Relations Council (GAERC), which brings together the EU foreign ministers to deal broadly with internal and external relations, and to discuss politically sensitive policies and proposals for new laws. Economics and finance ministers meet together as Ecofin, agriculture ministers as the Agriculture and Fisheries Council, and so on. The relevant European commissioner will also attend in order to make sure that the Council does not lose sight of broader EU interests. How often each council meets depends on the importance of its area. The GAERC, Ecofin and the Agriculture and Fisheries Council meet monthly because of the amount of work on their agendas, but the councils dealing with other issues meet perhaps only two to four times each year. Most meetings last no more than one or two days, and are held in Brussels.

Between meetings of ministers, national interests in the Council are protected and promoted by permanent representations, or national delegations of about 30–40 professional diplomats, which are much like embassies to the EU. The heads of delegations – the Permanent Representatives – meet every week in the powerful Committee of Permanent Representatives (COREPER), whose critical role in EU policy making is routinely overlooked. COREPER acts as a link between Brussels and the member states, conveys the views of the national governments, and keeps capitals in touch with developments in Brussels. Most importantly, it makes decisions. It prepares Council agendas, oversees the committees and working parties set up to sift through proposals, decides which proposals go to which council, and makes many of the decisions about which proposals will be accepted and which will be left for debate by ministers. In many cases, the hard decisions have already been made before the ministers meet.

Direction is given to the deliberations of the Council and COREPER by the presidency of the Council of Ministers, which is held not by a person, but by a member state. Every EU member state has a turn at holding the presidency for a spell of six months, the baton being passed in January and July each year. The state holding the presidency sets the agenda for European Council meetings (and for the EU as a whole), arranges and chairs meetings of the Council of Ministers, chairs at least one meeting of the European Council, promotes cooperation among member states, runs EU foreign policy for six months, acts as the main voice of the EU on the global stage, coordinates member state positions at international conferences and negotiations in which the EU is involved, and (along with the president of the Commission) represents the EU at meetings with the president of the United States, and at the annual meetings of the G8 group of major industrialized countries. The success of a presidency is measured according to the extent to which the incumbent member state is able to encourage compromise and agreement among the EU members, as well as by what is delayed, opposed, or promoted (Brewin and McAllister, 1991). (For details on recent presidencies, see Elgström, 2003.)

There are both advantages and disadvantages to the rotating presidency. Among the advantages: it allows the leaders of the member states to convene meetings and launch initiatives on issues of national interest, to bring those issues to the top of the EU agenda, and – if they do a good job – to earn prestige and credibility. It also allows the leaders of smaller states to negotiate directly with other world leaders and helps the process of European integration by making the EU more real to the citizens of the country holding the presidency. Among the disadvantages: as the EU has grown, so has the workload of the presidency, and some of the smaller states have found themselves struggling to find the necessary leadership. As membership of the EU has expanded, so has the cycle of the presidency.

Figure 4.1   *The European policy process*

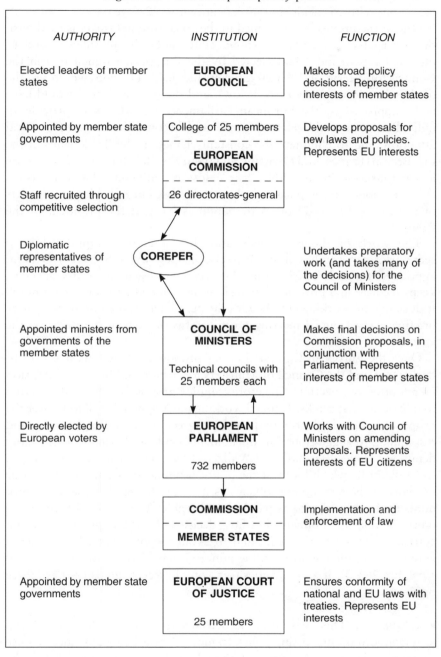

With 15 member states, each had a turn at the helm only once every 7½ years, but with 25 members that has grown to 12½ years.

One of the provisions contained in the constitutional treaty is to abolish the arrangement by which member states hold the presidency, and to instead have an individual elected by the European Council to run the Council for a term of 2½ years, renewable once. The vote would use the qualified majority system (see below), and the person elected would have to be approved by the European Parliament. The idea is to provide an individual who could set the agenda and become the focus of political attention, and to eliminate the constant change in the 'leadership' of the EU. Britain, France, and Germany all favour the idea, but smaller states are less enthusiastic because they fear a loss of influence. There is also a concern about the complications that could arise out of having two leaders of the EU – the president of the Commission and the president of the Council.

The work of the presidency and the Council is supported by a secretariat-general based in Brussels, headed by a Secretary-General appointed for a five-year term. The secretariat-general drafts agendas, keeps records, and provides the work of the Council with some continuity. It does this by working closely with the permanent representatives, and by briefing every Council meeting on the status of each of the items on the agenda.

Once the European Commission has proposed a new law, it is sent to Parliament and the Council of Ministers for debate and for a final decision on adoption or rejection. The more complex proposals will usually go first to one or more specialist Council working parties, which will look over the proposal in detail, identifying points of agreement and disagreement, and responding to suggestions for amendments made by Parliament (for more detail, see Hayes-Renshaw and Wallace, 1997). The proposal will then go to COREPER, which looks at the political implications, and tries to clear as many of the remaining problems as it can, ensuring that the meeting of ministers is as quick and as painless as possible. The proposal then moves on to the relevant Council for a final decision. Ministers prefer to reach a consensus whenever they can, and to avoid a formal vote. Even when a vote is called, the countries in the minority may simply acquiesce (Dinan, 1999, pp. 262–3). If an issue goes to a vote, however, ministers have three options:

- *Unanimity*. This was once needed where a new policy was being introduced or an existing policy framework was being amended. Its use has been increasingly restricted, though, and it is now needed only if the Council is looking at a new law in selected policy areas, including foreign and security policy, asylum, immigration, economic policy, and taxation. The use of unanimity gives each member state the power of veto, but the Amsterdam treaty introduced a 'constructive abstention' procedure by which a member state would not be obliged to apply a particular decision, but would recognize that the EU was committed.

- *A simple majority.* This is used mainly if the Council is dealing with a procedural issue or working under treaty articles, but as the SEA and Maastricht broadened the number of issues and areas in which a qualified majority vote could be used, the use of majority voting declined.

- *A qualified majority vote (QMV).* This is needed for almost every other kind of decision where ministers have failed to reach a consensus. Instead of each minister having one vote, each is given several votes roughly in proportion to the population of his or her member state (see Table 4.4). To be successful, a proposal must win 232 out of a possible 321 votes (72.3 per cent of the votes), a majority of states must be in favour, and the votes in favour must represent states with a combined population that is at least 62 per cent of the EU total. Under the new constitution, the formula will change slightly from 2009: the votes must represent 55 per cent of the member states and 65 per cent of the population. A proposal will also be defeated by a blocking minority of at least four member states representing 35 per cent of the population. QMV will become the general rule, with unanimity needed only on issues dealing with taxation and some elements of foreign and social policy.

Because the Council of Ministers is a meeting place for national interests, the keys to understanding how it works are terms such as compromise, bargaining, and diplomacy. The ministers are often leading political figures at home, so they are motivated by national political interests. They are also ideologically driven, and their authority will

Table 4.4   *Votes in the Council of Ministers*

Germany	29	Belgium	12	Lithuania	7
UK	29	Hungary	12	Latvia	4
France	29	Portugal	12	Slovenia	4
Italy	29	Austria	10	Estonia	4
Spain	27	Sweden	10	Cyprus	4
Poland	27	Slovakia	7	Luxembourg	4
Netherlands	13	Denmark	7	Malta	3
Greece	12	Finland	7		
Czech Republic	12	Ireland	7	Total	321

depend to some extent on the stability of the governing party or coalition at home. All these factors combine to pull ministers in many different directions, and to deny the Council the kind of structural regularity enjoyed by the Commission.

The European Parliament

The European Parliament (EP) has long been a junior member in the EU decision-making system, mainly because (unlike conventional legislatures) it cannot introduce laws or raise revenues (these are powers of the Commission), and it shares the powers of amendment and decision with the Council of Ministers. Parliament also has a credibility problem: it is the most democratic of EU institutions, because it is the only one that is directly elected by voters in the member states, but few EU citizens know what it does, and they have not yet developed the same kinds of psychological ties to the EP as they have to their national legislatures.

Despite its handicaps, Parliament has shrewdly used its powers to play a more active role in running the EU, and has been entrepreneurial in suggesting new laws and policies to the Commission. It has also used arguments about democratic accountability to force the other institutions to take it more seriously. Where it once mainly reacted to Commission proposals and Council votes, it has become much more aggressive in launching its own initiatives and making the other institutions pay more attention to its opinions. It has won more powers to amend laws and to check the activities of the other institutions, with the result that it now has equal standing with the Council of Ministers on deciding which proposals for new laws will be enacted and which will not.

The European Parliament is the only directly elected international legislature in the world. It has a single chamber, and the 732 members of the European Parliament (MEPs) are elected by universal suffrage by all eligible voters in the EU for fixed, renewable five-year terms. The number of seats is divided up among the member states very roughly on the basis of population, so that Germany has 99 while Malta has just five (see Table 4.5). This formula means that bigger countries are under-represented and smaller countries over-represented; thus, again roughly speaking, Germany, Britain, France, and Italy each have one MEP per 800,000 citizens, while the ratio for Belgium, the Czech Republic, Hungary, and Portugal is 1:425,000 citizens, for Malta it is 1:80,000, and for Luxembourg it is 1:67,000.

Absurdly, Parliament's buildings are divided among three cities: while the administrative headquarters are in Luxembourg, and parliamentary committees meet in Brussels for about two to three weeks every month

Box 4.2 Specialized EU institutions

As the work of the EU has grown, so has the number of specialized agencies created to deal with specific aspects of its work. They now include the following:

- *Committee of the Regions (created in 1994, based in Brussels)*. This allows representatives of local units of government to meet and discuss matters relating to regional and local issues. Most of its 317 members are elected local government officials.
- *Court of Auditors (1977, Luxembourg)*. The EU's financial watchdog, with 25 auditors appointed for six-year renewable terms, who carry out annual audits of the accounts of EU institutions.
- *Economic and Social Committee (1958, Brussels)*. This allows employers, workers and other sectional interests to meet and express their views. Most of its 317 members come from industry, agriculture, and the professions.
- *European Agency for the Evaluation of Medicinal Products (EMEA) (1995, London)*. Harmonizes the work of national drug regulatory bodies, helps reduce costs that drug companies incur by having to win separate approvals from each member state, and helps overcome the protectionist tendencies of states unwilling to approve new drugs that might compete with those already produced by domestic drug companies.
- *European Central Bank (1998, Frankfurt)*. Created to replace the European Monetary Institute set up in 1994. The main job of the Bank is to ensure monetary stability by setting interest rates in the euro zone (see Box 7.3 on p. 174).
- *European Centre for Disease Prevention and Control (2004, Stockholm)*. Identifies, assesses and communicates information on current and emerging threats to human health from communicable diseases.
- *European Environment Agency (1993, Copenhagen)*. The Agency collects information from the member states and neighbouring non-EU states, which is used to help develop environmental protection policies, and to measure the results.
- *European Investment Bank (1958, Luxembourg)*. The bank is an autonomous institution created to encourage 'balanced and steady development' by granting loans and giving guarantees, its projects help poorer regions, support the modernization and improved competitiveness of industry, and must be of common interest to several member states or to the EU as a whole. Its single biggest project was the Channel Tunnel. It is managed by a Board of Governors consisting of the finance ministers of the member states.
- *European Police Office (Europol) (1999, The Hague)*. Europol promotes police cooperation within the EU by managing a system of information exchange targeted against terrorism, drug-trafficking, and other serious forms of international crime.

Table 4.5   *Seats in the European Parliament, 2004–09*

Germany	99	Portugal	24	Lithuania	13
United Kingdom	78	Czech Republic	24	Latvia	9
France	78	Hungary	24	Slovenia	7
Italy	78	Sweden	19	Estonia	6
Spain	54	Austria	18	Cyprus	6
Poland	54	Slovakia	14	Luxembourg	6
Netherlands	27	Denmark	14	Malta	5
Greece	24	Finland	14		
Belgium	24	Ireland	13	Total	732

(except August), the Parliamentary chamber is situated in Strasbourg, and MEPs are expected to meet there in plenary sessions (meetings of the whole) for about three or four days each month except August. Since committees are where most of the real bargaining and revising takes place, and since 'additional' plenaries can be held in Brussels, few MEPs actually attend the Strasbourg plenaries, preferring to spend most of their time in Brussels. This arrangement comes courtesy of the French government, which stubbornly insists that Strasbourg must remain the site for plenary sessions. This not only undermines the credibility of the EP, but inflates its budget.

The EP is chaired by a president, who presides over debates during plenary sessions, decides which proposals go to which committees, and represents Parliament in relations with other institutions. The president must be an MEP, and is elected by other MEPs for 2½-year renewable terms (half the life of a Parliamentary term). The president would probably come out of the majority party group if there were one, but since no one party has ever had a majority, he or she is chosen as a result of inter-party bargaining. To help with the work of dealing with many different party groups in Parliament, the president works with the chairs of the different party groups in the Conference of Presidents, which draws up the agenda for plenary sessions and oversees the work of parliamentary committees.

Like most national legislatures, the EP has standing and ad hoc committees which meet in Brussels to consider legislation relevant to their area or to carry out parliamentary inquiries (see Judge and Earnshaw, 2003, pp. 177–96). The committees have their own hierarchy, which reflects the varying levels of Parliamentary influence over different policy areas: among the most powerful are those dealing with the environment and the budget. Seats on committees are distributed on the basis of a mixture of the balance of party groups, the seniority of MEPs, and national interests. For example, there are more Irish and Danish MEPs on the agriculture committee than on committees dealing with foreign and defence matters.

Elections to the European Parliament are held on a fixed five-year rotation, and all MEPs stand for reelection at the same time. Every member state uses multi-member districts and variations on the theme of proportional representation (PR), either treating their entire territory as a single electoral district or dividing it up into several large Euro-constituencies. Seats are then divided among parties according to their share of the vote. France, for example, has 78 seats, so if French party A wins 50 per cent of the vote, it will be given 50 per cent of the French seats (39), and if party B wins 40 per cent of the vote, it will be given 40 per cent of the seats (31), and so on.

As noted in Chapter 2, PR has the advantage of reflecting more accurately the proportion of the vote given to different parties, but it also results in many small parties being elected to Parliament, spreading the distribution of seats thinly (but also obliging parties to form multinational groups – see Box 4.3). Also, PR leads to voters being represented by a group of MEPs of different parties, and constituents may never get to know or develop ties with a particular MEP.

Although it cannot introduce legislation, Parliament's powers to influence and amend EU law have grown. As well as the advisory and supervisory powers set out in the treaties, Parliament has several essentially negative powers: the Commission tries to anticipate the EP's position while drawing up a proposal, Parliament can delay or kill a proposal by sitting on it, and it also has the power to dismiss the Commission (for details, see Westlake, 1994, Chapter 3). Unfortunately, the concern of member states with preserving their powers over decision making in the Council of Ministers has created a complex legislative process:

- By the Treaty of Rome, Parliament was given a *consultation procedure* under which it was allowed to give a non-binding opinion to the Council of Ministers before the latter adopted a new law in selected areas, such as aspects of transport policy, citizenship issues, the EC budget, and amendments to the treaties. The Council could then ask the Commission to amend the draft, but the Commission had no obligation to respond.
- The SEA introduced a *cooperation procedure* which gave Parliament the right to a second reading for certain laws being considered by the Council of Ministers, notably those relating to aspects of economic and monetary policy.
- Maastricht created a *codecision procedure* under which Parliament was given the right to a third reading on bills in selected areas, thereby sharing powers with the Council in these areas. Maastricht also

extended Parliament's powers over foreign policy issues by obliging the presidency of the European Council to consult with the EP on the development of a common foreign and security policy.

Box 4.3 Parties in the European Parliament

MEPs are not national representatives, so they do not sit in national blocks. Instead, they come together in cross-national ideological groups with roughly similar goals and values. The 2004 European elections brought 160 different parties to the EP, many of which consisted of as few as one or two members; since there is little that these parties can achieve alone, it is in their interests to build alliances with other parties. Some of these have been marriages of convenience, and while there is still much changeability in the EP, groups have built more consistency and focus with time (for details, see Hix and Lord, 1997).

Moving from left to right on the ideological spectrum, the party groups after the 2004 elections were as follows:

- *European United Left/Nordic Green Left (EUL/NGL)*. One of the least consistent of the party groups, it is made up mainly of German, Italian, Greek, and Czech leftists.
- *Party of European Socialists (PES)*. For a long time the biggest group in Parliament, with a few ex-communists on the left but dominated by more moderate social democrats. It has members from almost every EU country, with France, Spain, and Germany sending the biggest contingents.
- *European Liberal Democrat and Reform Group (ELDR)*. Consistently the third largest group in the EP, the ELDR contains members from 17 member states. Difficult to pinpoint in ideological terms, most of its members sit in or around the centre, and its biggest national blocs are from Britain, Italy, and Germany.
- *Greens/European Free Alliance (Greens/EFA)*. Has seen substantial growth in recent years, with new additions to its numbers after the 2004 elections making it the fourth biggest party group in the EP. Pursues a variety of issues related to social justice.
- *European People's Party and European Democrats (EPP–ED)*. Long the second largest group in Parliament, the EPP became the biggest after the 1999 elections. Right of centre, it contains MEPs from every EU member state, with the delegations from Germany, Britain, Italy, and Spain being the largest.
- *Union for Europe of the Nations (UEN)*. A small group of right-wing MEPs born out of French Gaullism, but who have more recently been driven by opposition to Maastricht and federalism, and have so far refused to link up with their most natural ally, the EPP.
- *Europe of Democracies and Diversities (EDD)*. With little to differentiate it from the UEN, the EDD is an unlikely association of small right-wing and/ or anti-federalist parties from Britain, the Netherlands, and Denmark.

- Under the *assent procedure*, Parliament has equal power with the Council over decisions on allowing new members to join the EU, giving other countries associate status, and on the EU's international agreements; decisions on all these must win the support of a parliamentary majority.

The Treaty of Amsterdam significantly increased the powers of Parliament by abolishing the cooperation procedure on everything except certain issues related to economic and monetary union (over which the member states wanted to retain control), and increasing the number of areas to which the codecision procedure applied from 15 to 38; these now include public health, movement of workers, vocational training, the structural funds, transport policy, education, customs cooperation, consumer protection, and the environment.

In addition to these legislative powers, Parliament also has joint powers with the Council of Ministers over fixing the EU budget, so that the two institutions between them constitute the 'budgetary authority' of the EU – they meet biannually to adopt a draft and to discuss amendments. The EP can ask for changes to the budget, ask for new appropriations for areas not covered (but cannot make decisions on how to raise money), and ultimately – with a two-thirds majority – can reject the budget.

Finally, Parliament has several supervisory powers over other EU institutions, including the right to debate the annual programme of the Commission, to put written or oral questions to the Commission, and to approve the appointment of the College of Commissioners. The most potentially disruptive of Parliament's powers is its ability – with a two-thirds majority – to force the resignation of the entire College of Commissioners through a vote of censure. While this power has never been used, Parliament came close in January 1999 after charges of mismanagement and nepotism were directed at two members of the College. Instead of firing the entire College, the EP opted for an investigation into the charges. Anticipating a vote of censure, the Santer Commission resigned just before the findings of the investigation were published in March. In October 2004, Parliament was able to block the appointment of the new Italian Commissioner Rocco Buttiglione, who had expressed controversial views on homosexuality and women.

The European Court of Justice

The Court of Justice is the most underrated (and perhaps the most overworked) of the five major institutions of the EU. While the Commission and Parliament attract most of the media and public attention, and become embroiled in the biggest political controversies, the Court has quietly gone about its business of clarifying the meaning of European law. Its activities have been critical to the progress of European integration, and its role just as significant as that of the Commission or Parliament, yet few Europeans know what it does.

The job of the Court is to make sure that national and European laws – and international agreements being considered by the European Union – meet the terms and the spirit of the treaties, and that EU law is equally, fairly, and consistently applied throughout the member states. It does this by ruling on the 'constitutionality' of EU law, giving opinions to national courts in cases where there are questions about the meaning of EU law, and making judgements in disputes involving EU institutions, member states, individuals, and corporations. In so doing, the Court gives the EU authority and makes sure that its decisions and policies are consistent and fit with the agreements inherent in the treaties.

EU law takes precedence over the national laws of member states where the two come into conflict, but only in areas of EU 'competence': where the EU is active and where the member states have given up powers to the EU. Hence the Court does not have powers over criminal law or family law, but has instead made most of its decisions on the kind of economic issues in which the EU has been most actively involved. It has had less to do with policy areas where the EU has been less active, such as education and health.

Based in the Palais de Justice, part of a cluster of EU institutions which make up the Centre Européen on a plateau above the city of Luxembourg, the Court is the supreme legal authority of the EU, and the final court of appeal on all EU laws. It made its most basic contribution to the process of integration in 1963 and 1964 when it declared that the Treaty of Rome was not just a treaty, but was a constitutional instrument that imposed direct and common obligations on member states, and took precedence over national law.

The Court has also established important additional precedents through decisions such as *Costa* v. *ENEL* [1964], which confirmed the primacy of EU law, and the *Cassis de Dijon* case of 1979, which greatly simplified completion of the single market by establishing the principle of mutual recognition: a product made and sold legally in one member state cannot be barred from another (see Chapter 7). Other Court rulings have helped increase the powers of Parliament, strengthened individual rights, promoted the free movement of workers, reduced gender discrimination, and helped the Commission break down the barriers to competition.

The Court of Justice has 25 judges, each appointed for a six-year renewable term of office. In order to keep the work of the Court running smoothly, the terms are staggered, so about half the judges come up for renewal every three years. The judges are theoretically appointed by common agreement among the governments of the member states, so there is technically no national quota. However, because every member state has the right to make one nomination, all 25 are effectively national appointees. The persistence of the quota emphasizes once again the role of national interests in EU decision making.

Apart from being acceptable to the other member states, judges must be independent, must be legally competent, and must avoid promoting the national interests of their home states. Some judges have come to the Court with experience as government ministers, some have held elective office, and others have had careers as lawyers or as academics; whatever they have done in their previous lives, they are not allowed to hold administrative or political office while they are on the Court. They can resign from the Court, but they can only be removed by the other judges (not by member states or other EU institutions), and then only by unanimous agreement that they are no longer doing their job adequately.

The judges elect one of their own to be president by majority vote for a three-year renewable term. The president presides over Court meetings, is responsible for distributing cases among the judges and deciding the dates for hearings, and has considerable influence over the political direction of the Court. Despite his or her critical role in furthering European integration, the president – Vassilios Skouris of Greece since 2003 – never becomes a major public figure in the same mould as the president of the Commission.

To speed up its work, the Court is divided into chambers of between three and six judges, which make the final decisions on cases unless a member state or an institution asks for a hearing before the full Court. (Since the 2004 enlargement, hearings before the full Court have been replaced by hearings before a Grand Chamber of 13 judges.) To further ease the workload, the judges are assisted by eight advocates-general, advisers who review each of the cases as they come in, and deliver a preliminary opinion on what action should be taken and on which EU law applies. The judges are not required to agree with the opinion, or even to refer to it, but it gives them a point of reference from which to reach a decision. Although advocates-general are again appointed in theory by common accord, one is appointed by each of the Big Five member states, and the other four are appointed by the smaller states. One of the advocates-general is appointed First Advocate-General on a one-year rotation.

The Court of Justice has become busier as the reach of the EU has widened and deepened. In the 1960s it was hearing about 50 cases per year and making about 15–20 judgements, but now it hears about 600 cases per year, and completes about 500–600 per year. As the volume of work grew during the 1970s and 1980s, it was taking the Court up to two years to reach a decision on more complex cases. To move matters along, a subsidiary Court of First Instance was created in 1989, to be the first point of decision on less complicated cases. If cases are lost at this level, the parties involved may appeal to the Court of Justice. There are 25 judges on the lower Court – one from each member state – and it uses the same basic procedures as the Court of Justice.

The work of the Court falls under two main headings:

- *Direct actions*. These are cases (all heard by the Court of First Instance) where an individual, company, member state, or EU institution brings proceedings against an EU institution or a member state. For example, a member state might have failed to meet its obligations under EU law, so a case can be brought by the Commission or by another member state. The Commission has often taken member states to Court charging that they have not met their single market obligations. Private companies can also bring actions if they think a member state is discriminating against their products.

  Direct actions can also be brought against the Commission or the Council to make sure that EU laws conform to the treaties, and to attempt to cancel those that do not. The defendant is almost always the Commission or the Council because proceedings are usually brought against an act they have adopted. Others can be brought against an EU institution that has failed to act in accordance with the terms of the treaties. The European Parliament brought one such action against the Council of Ministers in 1983 (Case 13/83), charging that the Council had failed to agree a Common Transport Policy, as required under the Treaty of Rome. The Court ruled that while there was an obligation on the Council, no timetable had been agreed, so it was up to the member states to decide how to proceed.

- *Preliminary rulings*. These make up the most important part of the Court's work, are now heard exclusively by the Court of Justice, and account for about 25–30 per cent of the cases it considers. If a matter of EU law arises in a national court case, the national court can ask for a ruling from the European Court on the interpretation or validity of that law. Members of EU institutions can also ask for preliminary rulings, but most are made on behalf of a national court, and are binding on the court in the case concerned.

Unlike all the other EU institutions, where English is becoming the working language, the Court works mainly in French, although a case can be heard in any official EU language at the request of the plaintiff or defendant. Court proceedings usually begin with a written application, describing the dispute and the grounds on which the application is based.

The President assigns the case to a chamber, and the defendant is given one month to lodge a statement of defence, the plaintiff a month to reply, and the defendant a further month to reply to the plaintiff. The case is then argued by the parties at a public hearing before a chamber of judges. Once the hearing is over, the judges retire to deliberate, and – having reached a conclusion – return to Court to deliver their judgement.

Court decisions are supposed to be unanimous, but votes are usually taken by a simple majority. All decisions are secret, so it is never publicly known who – if anyone – dissented. The Court has no direct powers to enforce its judgements, so implementation is left mainly to national courts or the governments of the member states, with the Commission keeping a close watch. Maastricht gave the Court of Justice new powers by allowing it to impose fines, but the question of how the fines would be collected was left open, and the implications of this new power are still unclear.

The European Council

The European Council is often described as an extension of the Council of Ministers, but it is actually very different both in terms of its powers and its composition. More a process or a forum than a formal institution (although it will become a full institution under the new constitution), it consists of the heads of government of the EU member states, their foreign ministers, and the president and vice-presidents of the Commission. This group meets at least twice each year at two-day summits, and provides strategic policy direction for the EU. The Council is something like a steering committee or a board of directors: it discusses the broad issues and goals of the EU, leaving it to the other EU institutions to work out the details.

The Council was created in 1974 in response to a feeling among some European leaders that the Community needed better leadership, and a body that could take a more long-term view of where the Community was headed. It immediately became an informal part of the Community decision-making structure, although its existence was only finally given legal recognition with the Single European Act. Maastricht elaborated on its role, but did not provide much clarity beyond noting that the Council would 'provide the Union with the necessary impetus for its development and shall define the general political guidelines thereof'.

The Council has been an important force for integration, with many of the most important initiatives of recent years coming out of Council discussions – these have included the launch of the European Monetary System in 1978, and the discussions that led to the Maastricht, Amsterdam and Nice treaties. Council summits have also issued major declarations on international crises, reached key decisions on institutional changes (such as the 1974 decision to begin direct elections to the European Parliament), and given new clarity to EU foreign policy. But the Council has also had its failures, including its inability to speed up agricultural or budgetary reform, or to agree common EU responses to crises in Iraq and the Balkans.

The European Council makes the key decisions on the overall direction of political and economic integration, internal economic issues, foreign policy issues, budget disputes, treaty revisions, new member applications, and institutional reforms (such as the changes that were made under the Treaty of Nice). The summits achieve all this through a combination of brainstorming, intensive bilateral and multilateral discussions, and bargaining. The mechanics of decision making depend on a combination of the quality of organization and preparation, the leadership skills of the presidency (which convenes and chairs each summit), and the ideological and personal agendas of individual leaders. The interpersonal dynamics of the participants is also important: for example, the political significance of the Franco-German axis has long been important (although less so since eastward enlargement has diluted the voting and political power of the Big Two). Leaders who have been in office a long time or who have a solid base of political support at home will be in a very different negotiating position from those who do not.

Regular summits of the Council are held in June and December every year, with additional meetings held whenever necessary. The meetings are hosted by the country holding the presidency of the Council of Ministers, and in the past have taken place either in the capital of that country, or in a regional city or town, such as Cardiff, Bonn, or Goteborg (but almost all meetings are now held in Brussels). Organization is left largely to the leadership of the member state holding the presidency, which usually sees the summits as an opportunity to showcase the priorities of that member state. The agenda is driven in part by the ongoing priorities of the EU, but also by the particular priorities of the member state. The goal is to agree a set of Conclusions of the Presidency, an advanced draft of which is usually awaiting the leaders at the beginning of the summit, and provides the focus for discussions.

Officially, the Council has no set agenda, but there has to be some direction, so it is usual for senior officials from the country holding the presidency to work with the Council of Ministers to develop an agenda. The items on the agenda depend on circumstances: national delegations normally have issues they want to raise, there must be some continuity from previous summits, and leaders will often have to deal with a breaking problem or an emergency that needs a decision. Some issues (especially economic issues) are routinely discussed at every summit. The Commission may also promote issues it would like to see discussed, and an active presidency might use the summit to bring items of national or regional interest to the attention of the heads of government.

Preparations for each summit begin as soon as a member state takes over the presidency in January or July, monthly meetings of the foreign ministers try to resolve potential disagreements, and as the date for the summit approaches, the prime minister and foreign minister of the state holding the presidency become increasingly involved. About ten days before the summit, the foreign ministers meet to finalize the agenda and to iron out any remaining problems and disputes. The more agreements they can broker in advance, the less likely the summit itself will end in failure (Johnston, 1994, pp. 27–31). Some summits are routine, and result in general agreement among leaders; others see deep differences in opinion, with some member states perhaps refusing to agree a common set of conclusions.

The summits themselves usually run over a period of two days, beginning with informal discussions over breakfast, and moving into details at plenary sessions held in the morning, afternoon, and – if necessary – evening. Overnight, officials from the presidency and the Secretariat of the Council of Ministers will work on the draft Conclusions, which will be discussed at another plenary on the morning of the second day, and – if necessary – at a final session in the afternoon. The summit then normally ends with the public release of the Conclusions.

In order to keep them manageable, plenaries are usually restricted to the leaders of the member states, their foreign ministers and two officials from the Commission, including the president. Even with just one adviser per country, interpreters, two officials from the presidency, one from the Council of Ministers secretariat, and three from the Commission, there may be more than a hundred people in the room. The Council tries to take its decisions on the basis of unanimity, or at least of consensus, but the occasional lack of unanimity may force a formal vote, and some member states may want to attach conditions or reservations to the Conclusions. As well as the formal plenary sessions, summits usually break out into subsidiary meetings, including those between foreign ministers, and regular bilateral meetings between prime ministers over breakfast or coffee.

The summits are always major media events, and are surrounded by extensive security, a need that became particularly obvious with the street demonstrations against globalization during the June 2001 summit in Goteborg, Sweden. Enormous symbolism is attached to the outcomes of the summits, which are measured according to the extent to which they represent breakthroughs, or show EU leaders to be bogged down in disagreement. Failure and success reflect not only on the presidency, but on the whole process of European integration. The media attention devoted to summits is often enough in itself to concentrate the minds of participants and to encourage them to agree, although this did not apply to the December 2003 summit in Brussels: intended to reach agreement on the draft constitution, its failure was seen in part as a reflection on the erratic Italian presidency and the leadership of prime minister Silvio Berlusconi.

Because the European Council obviously has more power over decision making than any other EU institution, it has tended to take power away from those institutions. It can, in effect, set the agenda for the Commission, override decisions reached by the Council of Ministers, and largely ignore Parliament altogether. Any hopes that the Commission might have once had that it could develop an independent sphere of action and power has largely disappeared with the rise of the European Council. Certainty about the present and potential future role of the Council is clouded by its ambiguities, and opinion remains divided over whether it is an integrative or a disintegrative body (Johnston, 1994, pp. 41–8).

Conclusions

The European Union has built a substantial family of administrative bodies since its inception. Among them, they are responsible for making general and detailed policy decisions, developing and adopting laws, overseeing the implementation of laws and policies by the member states, ensuring that those laws and policies meet the spirit and the letter of the treaties, and overseeing activities in a variety of areas, from environmental management to transport, consumer protection, drug regulation, and police cooperation.

Although European leaders have never said as much, these institutions amount to a confederal government of Europe. They fit the standard definition of confederalism: a general system of government coexisting with local units of government, each with shared and independent powers, but with the balance in favour of the local units (in this case, the member states). Except for the European Parliament, EU citizens do not have a direct relationship with any of the EU institutions, instead relating to them through their national governments.

Despite concerns in some of the member states about the federalization of Europe, the institutions still lack many of the features of a conventional federal government. For example, there is no European army or air force, no elected European president, no European tax system, no European foreign and defence policy, and no single postal system. Furthermore, the focus of decision making still rests with the European Council and the Council of Ministers, both of which are intergovernmental rather than supranational. Finally, the European Union is still ultimately a voluntary arrangement, and lacks the powers to force its member states to implement European law and policy. The withdrawal of one of its members would not be regarded as secession.

Nonetheless, while debates rage about the finer points of the decisions reached by the EU institutions, the national governments of the member states have transferred significant powers to these institutions. Particularly since the passage of the Single European Act, the activities of the Commission, the Council of Ministers, Parliament, and the Court of Justice have had a more direct impact on the lives of Europeans, and government in Europe is no longer just about what happens in national capitals and regional cities, but also about what happens in Brussels, Luxembourg and Strasbourg.

The relationships among the five major institutions, and between them and the governments of the member states, is constantly changing as the balance of power is adjusted and fine-tuned. Out of a combination of internal convenience and external pressure is emerging a new layer of government that is winning more powers as the member states cautiously transfer sovereignty from the local and national levels to the regional level. In the two chapters that follow, we will see what this has meant for the member states and for the citizens of Europe.

Chapter 5

The EU and the Member States

The changing identities of the member states
Understanding the policy process
The politics of the budget
The changing character of the EU
Conclusions

We have not successfully rolled back the frontiers of the state in Britain, only to see them reimposed at a European level, with a European superstate exercising a new dominance from Brussels.
Margaret Thatcher, British prime minister, 1988

One of the most enduring debates about European integration centres on the relationship between the EU and its member states. Should we still think of Estonia, Germany, Hungary, Italy, and Sweden as independent sovereign states, or should we think of them now as actors within a larger Europe? Can integration proceed at the macro level while European states preserve their separate identities at the micro level? How much can the states still do alone, and how much has been subsumed into the powers of a European superstate? Is there, in fact, a European superstate? Many Europeans are deeply critical of what the EU has meant for their home states, and continue to champion the cause of separate national identities and residual powers for their home governments. But there are others who argue that the pooling of powers is not only beneficial but has gone beyond the point of no return, and that national identities can be retained even in the face of common policies and joint institutions.

There is no question that the relationship among the member states has changed substantially, and that however we now describe the EU, its member states relate to each other quite differently from the way they did before the EU was created. As the member states have integrated their economies, agreed universal standards and regulations, and developed common policies on such issues as trade, foreign relations, environmental protection, transport, and working conditions, so the differences among them have declined, the relationships among them have changed, and the integrative pressures they have experienced have become deeper and more complex.

This not only poses a puzzle for Europeans themselves, but – as we shall see in Chapter 9 – it also puzzles outsiders. For the most part, the outside world still looks on Europe as a region of sovereign states, and is only slowly waking up to the fact that those states will often act as one in their dealings with the rest of the world. They may have individual seats in the United Nations and the World Trade Organization, but they typically work out joint positions on important foreign policy issues, and vote together. Internally, though, they will often be fighting rearguard actions in the interests of preserving their distinctive national identities. At their most cynical, the member states choose to put Europe first when it suits them (as when they can achieve the most by working together), and choose to play up their national identity when that works better. More broadly, though, they have found themselves increasingly the subject of internal and external pressures that have pushed them irresistibly towards joint policy making on a broad variety of issues. The result is that they are coming to realize that they are European more quickly than the rest of the world.

The list of the effects of integration on the EU member states is lengthy and complex. In order to illustrate these effects, this chapter looks first at some of the constitutional and legal issues raised by integration, and at what integration has meant for the relationship among the member states. It then looks at the way that policies are made at the European level, and at how the policy process has changed the relationship between the parts and the whole. It then looks at the politics surrounding the EU budget, before ending with some general conclusions about the impact of integration on the member states of the EU.

The changing identities of the member states

Human society is in a constant state of change, and Europe is no exception. Political, economic, and social relationships among Europeans have undergone continuous alteration over time, generated in large part by changes in communications and economic activity. As noted in Chapter 1, the state system with which we are all familiar today dates back barely two centuries, and was preceded by political arrangements that were themselves constantly changing, and that led routinely to the redrawing of the political boundaries between different communities. A quick flick through an historical atlas of Europe shows the boundaries of states constantly changing, even as recently as the late 1980s and 1990s, which saw – for example – the reunification of Germany, and the break-up of Czechoslovakia, Yugoslavia, and the Soviet Union.

Before the Second World War, Europe held the balance of global political, military, and economic power, and the major actors in international relations included Britain, Germany, and France. The international system was defined in large part by the competition among European powers for political, economic, and military advantage. This all changed after 1945, when Europe found itself squeezed militarily and ideologically between the two superpowers and saw the focus of economic power shifting to new centres, notably the United States and Japan. As discussed in Chapter 3, the need to save Europe from itself combined with the need to build economic and military security in the postwar world to encourage western European elites to call for a new sense of regional community, and for cooperation rather than competition. Where the relationship among European states before the war had been driven by competition, now it was driven by cooperation.

As late as the 1960s and 1970s, European states still related to each other as sovereign states with strong and independent national identities. They had their own bodies of law, they pursued their own distinctive sets of policies, and travellers were reminded of the differences between countries when they crossed national borders and had to show their passports. There were controls and limits on the movement of people, money, goods, and services, and citizens of one state who travelled to another felt very much that they were 'going abroad'. The nation state was dominant, and was both the focus of mass public loyalty and the source of primary political and administrative authority. Italians were clearly Italians, the Dutch were clearly Dutch, and Poles were clearly Poles – at least this is what most Europeans wanted to believe, and were encouraged to believe by circumstances.

The situation today is quite different, and the relationship between the EU and its member states has been transformed. There has been a shift of authority from the member states to the European Union, and an agreement to share or pool the exercise of power over a large number of policy areas. The member states have remained the essential building blocks in this process, but they have moved far beyond the simple cooperation normally associated with international organizations, and have built a new layer of institutions underwritten by a common body of laws. Whether the member states have actually *surrendered* authority, however, and thereby created a superstate with its own sovereign powers, is a debatable and contentious point (see Box 1.2, page 10).

In those policy areas where the governments of the member states have agreed to shift 'competence' (that is, responsibility) to the EU, national leaders now reach most key decisions through negotiation with their counterparts in the other member states, typically in the meeting rooms of the Council of Ministers and the European Council. Debates on the effects and the meaning of the treaties have combined with day-to-day discussions within the Commission and the Council of Ministers to encourage national leaders to work towards multinational compromises, and towards a European consensus. As this has happened, it has become increasingly difficult for leaders to define and pursue 'national interests', because they have had to think more in terms of European interests. Increasingly, national and European interests have become indistinguishable from one another. At the same time, ordinary Europeans are reminded less often of their national differences, and the borders that once divided the member states have become so porous that in some places they have almost disappeared.

Spillover of different kinds has led to the development of complex networks of cooperation at almost every level: trade, transport, communications, labour relations, policing, agriculture, research and development, financial services, the environment, and so on. The result, argues Wallace (1996, p. 452), has been that governments have had to decide 'which issues they choose to define as key to the preservation of sovereignty, autonomy, or national idiosyncrasy, conscious of the political costs of defining too many issues in the symbolic terminology of high politics'.

At the core of these changes in recent years has been an ongoing debate about subsidiarity, the principle that decisions should be taken at the lowest level possible for effective action. It was first raised in the European context in 1975 when the European Commission – in its response to the Tindemans report (see Chapter 6) – argued that the Community should be given responsibility only for those matters that the member states were no longer capable of dealing with efficiently. There was little further discussion until the mid-1980s, when member states opposed to increasing the power of the Commission began quoting the principle. It was finally brought into the mainstream of discussions about the EU by Article 3b of Maastricht:

> In areas which do not fall within its exclusive competence, the Community shall take action, in accordance with the principle of subsidiarity, only if and in so far as the objectives of the proposed action cannot be sufficiently achieved by the Member States and can therefore, by reason of the scale or effects of the proposed action, be better achieved by the Community.

There are at least three problems with the concept of subsidiarity. First, it cannot be used to reduce EU powers in areas that have already been defined as being within its competence. Second, there are no absolutes in the debate about whether or not an action can be better achieved by the member states acting alone or the EU acting as a whole. Third, subsidiarity is aimed at limiting the powers of the EU through a political–judicial discussion about competence rather than through a clarification of the relative powers of European citizens, member states, and EU institutions.

European integration has been accompanied by a growth in the body of European law and a reduction in the ability of national governments independently to make policy and law, according to national interests and priorities. Simultaneously, national legislatures have become weaker and more marginalized in a process that has been described (pejoratively) as 'creeping federalism'. National legislatures once had almost complete authority to make laws as their members saw fit, within the limitations created by constitutions, public opinion, the powers of other government institutions, and the international community. They now find themselves focusing increasingly on those policy areas in which the EU is not yet so active, and reacting in other areas to the requirements of EU law and the pressures of regional integration.

It is debatable just how responsibilities are now divided up between the EU and the member states (see Box 5.1). In the realm of 'high politics' (a concept rarely defined, but usually understood to mean the universal, the persistent, or the most pressing concerns of government, such as economic and foreign policy) the member states have less freedom of movement than before. The adoption of the euro, for example, has ensured that there are now few elements of economic and monetary policy that are not primarily driven by Europe rather than by the member states, at least within the euro zone (see Chapter 7). On international issues, even though the EU still has some way to go before it can claim a common policy, and the member states still have much individual freedom in their relationships outside Europe and in the way they define and express their defence interests, the EU is becoming a more distinctive and assertive actor on the world stage. The EU takes common positions on most trade issues and on relations with specific regions of the world, but the waters have been muddied by the extent to which member states such as Britain and France still pursue distinctive national interests, particularly in their former colonies.

In the realm of 'low politics' (matters that are both more sectional and further down the agendas of most governments, such as the environment, culture, and transport) there are still distinctions between issues that (a) come under EU jurisdiction, (b) are shared by the EU and the member states, or (c) are the preserve of member states. However, these distinctions have become less clear with time. There is little question that agricultural policy is now almost entirely made at the European level, the loosening of internal border controls has been accompanied by a tightening of external controls that has seen more pan-European cooperation, and environmental quality standards are now set almost entirely by EU law. Decisions on social matters such as employment and residence are increasingly being made at the European level as personal mobility moves up the policy agenda. Member states still make most of their own decisions on internal

Box 5.1 The division of policy authority

One of the more important pieces of Eurojargon is 'competence', meaning policy authority. Over time, the competence of the EU institutions has grown at the expense of the member states. It began modestly, being limited to the powers transferred under the terms of the European Coal and Steel Community. Even within those powers, however, there was the promise of the changes to come; the treaty, for example, gave the ECSC the power to ensure the rational use of coal resources (a precursor to environmental policy), to promote improved working conditions (a precursor to social policy), and to promote international trade (a precursor to trade and foreign policy). The EU institutions have since been given competence over a broader set of policy issues, and as its authority has grown, the authority of the member states has declined.

The policy areas for which the EU has competence today are outlined in the treaties, the assumption being that all other policy areas remain the responsibility of the member states. But there is much ambiguity built in to the system, and there is no clear distinction between exclusive and nonexclusive competence, with the result that authority in most areas is divided, the balance of power in some areas tending towards the EU, and in other areas towards the member states:

Areas in which the balance lies with the EU	Areas in which authority is shared	Areas in which the balance lies with the member states
agriculture	culture	broadcasting
competition	employment	citizenship
consumer protection	energy	criminal justice
cross-border banking	export promotion	defence
cross-border crime	foreign relations	education
customs	information networks	elections
environment	overseas aid	health care
EU transport networks	regional development	land use
monetary policy	small and medium	local transport
(euro zone)	enterprises	policing
fisheries	social issues	postal services
immigration	vocational training	
trade	tax policy	
working conditions		

Thanks to a combination of formal agreements, expediency, and the often irresistible effects of policy spillover, it is safe to say that almost all policy areas are now influenced in some fashion by decisions taken both at the level of the EU and of the member states.

transport, but are working together on the development of trans-European highways and railways, and on the administration of airline systems and air transport. They still have national policies on investment in poorer rural areas and urban regeneration, but these are increasingly influenced by European regional policy.

There have also been important psychological changes in the relationship among the member states. There are still many reminders of the differences among Europeans – most obviously language – but those differences have become less distinct as Europeans have become more mobile. Nationalism remains an issue, especially among minorities and those most actively opposed to integration, but increased individual mobility has allowed Europeans not just to visit other member states on vacation, but to live in – and even 'emigrate' to – those states. Europeans are slowly transferring their loyalty from individual states to a more broadly defined European identity, and are thinking of themselves less as Germans or Belgians or Slovaks and more as Europeans.

Critics of integration have long argued that one of the greatest dangers posed by integration is the homogenization that comes as member states lose their individuality in the move towards Europe-wide standards and regulations. They argue that authority is shifting from national governments mandated by the people towards a European super-state that lacks such a mandate. However, while much still needs to be done to strengthen the ties between the EU and its citizens (see Chapter 6), the EU is still at heart a confederation, in which citizens have the closest ties to their home states, and national governments set the pace of regional integration. And rather than lead to a homogenized Europe, integration has actually helped promote a reassertion of cultural differences as Europeans have grown to understand and appreciate the variety of the regions in which they live (see Box 5.2).

Indeed it is often argued that a Europe of the regions may come to rival or even replace a Europe of the states. In the interests of correcting economic imbalances, and prompted by growing demands for greater decentralization, European states began to regionalize their administrative systems in the 1960s, and as a result regions have emerged as important actors in politics and policy (Keating and Hooghe, 1996). Regions have come to see the EU as an important source of investment and of support for minority cultures, and in some cases this has given more confidence to nationalist movements (such as those in Scotland and Catalonia), as they feel less dependent on the support of the state governments. The logical conclusion is that forces of this kind will lead to Europe integrating and decentralizing at the same time, with the member states as we know them today squeezed in the middle.

Box 5.2 The rise of regional identity

Ironically, as the nation states of Europe have been busy cooperating on the construction of the European Union, so national minorities within these states have become more visible, more vocal, and more demanding of greater independence. In other words, as there has been macro-level integration, so there has been a degree of micro-level disintegration. The effect has been to remind us that Europe is not just a region divided into three dozen nation states, but into more than 100 different nationalities. They run the gamut from the Dutch and English in the maritime north, to Portuguese and Cantabrians on the Atlantic coast, Alsatians and Franconians in the northwest, Bavarians, Swiss, and Styrians in the Alpine regions, Castilians, Andalusians, and Lugurians in the west-central Mediterranean, Serbs and Croats in the Balkans, Czechs, Slovaks, and Ruthenians in the east, Poles and Lithuanians in the northern plains, and Lapps, Finns, and Karelians in the northern Baltic (see Fernández-Armesto, 1997, for more details).

In some cases — such as the Cornish in England, Galicians in Spain and Lombards in Italy — these nations have been fully integrated into the larger states of which they are part. In others, integration has never been complete, secessionist movements have been active, and there have been calls for greater self-determination and even independence. This is particularly true in Britain, where the Scots and the Welsh have had regional assemblies since 1999, and a large segment of public opinion in Scotland is in favour of independence. There are similar demands for independence or devolution from Bretons and Corsicans in France, Basques in the Spanish-French borderland, Catalans in Spain, and Walloons in Belgium.

The status of national minorities has traditionally been a domestic matter for individual national governments, but European integration has helped redefine the relationship between the parts and the whole. As the member states lose their distinctive political identity, so the cultural identity of minorities is strengthened and the pressure for disintegration grows. It is possible that greater self-determination will lessen the demand among nationalists for complete independence, and that we will simply see a reassertion of cultural differences within the member states. It is also possible, however, that self-determination will lead to independence for minorities within the European Union, and a redrawing of administrative lines along cultural lines.

Understanding the policy process

Public policies are the deliberate actions (or inactions) of government in response to the needs of society. When governments come to power, they are faced with a set of problems and challenges, and the responses they adopt (or avoid) are their policies. Another way of thinking about policies is to describe them as the outputs of government. The various different pressures on government – such as public opinion, economic changes, and external pressures – can be described as the inputs, and policies can be described as the end results, or the outputs of government.

Policies exist at many different levels, from the local community to towns, cities, counties, states, the national level, and – in the case of the EU – the multinational level. Policies are adopted and pursued not just by governments, but by bureaucracies, political parties, lobbies, and individual government institutions. Within the EU there are multiple different communities with their own separate and often conflicting policy interests, ranging from the major institutions (such as the Commission, Parliament, and the Council of Ministers), to the directorates-general within the Commission, to the regional and national policy interests pursued by member states, to the cross-national policies pursued by groups with shared interests, such as the environmental lobby, farmers, corporations, workers, labour unions, and parties within the European Parliament.

The pressures that create and impact policies at the national level are many and complex, but at the level of the EU those complexities are compounded. Influences on the policy process are both internal and external to the EU institutions, formal and informal, predictable and unpredictable, anticipated and opportunistic, and structured and unstructured. They include the following:

- *Treaty obligations.* The treaties outline both the general goals and principles of European integration, as well as some of the more specific tasks of the EU institutions. So, for example, Maastricht said that the general goals of the EU were (among others) to 'promote economic and social progress ... the strengthening of economic and social cohesion ... [and] to assert its identity on the international scene'. These are broad and ambiguous goals, but they set the foundations for policy, which must be turned into specific actions, mainly in the form of new laws.
- *Pressures to harmonize national laws and policies in order to avoid economic or social differences among the member states, and to ensure the smooth functioning of the single market.* These accounted, for example, for most of the early laws on environmental policy, which were designed to remove the barriers to the single market created by different environmental standards.
- *Legislative pressures.* Many new proposals for policy and law come out of requirements or assumptions built into past laws. This is certainly the case with laws that include within them an obligation for amendment or review after a specified period of time, and is particularly true of the EU's framework directives, which set general goals with the assumption

that more laws – known as daughter directives – will be developed later that provide more detail and focus.

- *Policy evolution and spillover*. Policy is rarely static, and the principles and goals of EU policy are constantly redefined as greater understanding emerges about the causes and effects of problems, as technological developments offer new options for addressing old problems, as the failure of existing policies demands new approaches, as the balance of interests changes within the member states, and as the political, economic, and social priorities of European integration evolve.
- *Pressures from EU institutions*. While the Commission has a monopoly over the development of new proposals for law, it is subject to various formal and informal pressures, including suggestions from the European Council regarding the broad goals of EU policy, 'invitations' from the European Parliament (EP) and the Council of Ministers to develop new proposals, suggestions or demands from the EP or the Council of Ministers for changes in Commission proposals, and the impact of rulings by the Court of Justice on the content and nature of EU law.
- *The requirements of international law*. The EU as a unit has signed numerous international treaties on behalf of the member states, most of which impose specific obligations on the EU. This means the development of new laws and policies to respond to those obligations, and the development of common positions taken during negotiations on the progress of implementation.
- *Initiatives by individual national leaders, or groups of leaders*. For example, much of the headway on security policy has been made in recent years because of initiatives taken by Tony Blair of Britain and Jacques Chirac of France (see Chapter 9).
- *The pressures of public opinion*. These have been increasingly important, for example, in the development and agreement of new treaties and in the debate over the new constitution.
- *Internal pressures*, such as ongoing concerns about unemployment, or the need to monitor the movement of criminals around the EU.
- *External pressures*, such as economic problems in other parts of the world, trade problems and disputes, or disagreements with other countries.
- *Emergencies or crises*, such as the 2003 fallout with the United States over Iraq, or the Danish rejection of Maastricht and the Irish rejection of Nice.

The member states have their own sets of priorities and values, and their own approach to dealing with policy needs. In an ideal world, policy agendas would be developed rationally, problems would be prioritized, options would be carefully researched and weighed, and the best solutions would be implemented, monitored, and evaluated. But modern society is too complex to make such an ideal possible, and studies of policy routinely emphasize the scarcity of real organization. The result is that policy is often driven by compromise, opportunism, and unpredictable political pressures. This is certainly true of the EU, where the challenge of identifying and addressing the needs of more than 450 million people, who have their own ideas about their priorities and the best way of dealing with their problems, results in a policy system that is coloured by six main characteristics.

Compromise and bargaining. In a democratic society, all politics is a matter of compromise. Individuals cannot all have things their own way, because there are always others who will disagree with their analysis of a problem and their suggested prescriptions. The fewest compromises are needed in unitary systems of government with majoritarian political parties (such as Britain and Spain), where the focus of political power rests with a national government made up of a single political party. More compromises are needed in federal systems such as Belgium and Germany, where there is a division of powers between national and sub-national government, or in member states governed by coalitions (such as Austria, Ireland, or Portugal). With a political system such as the EU, however, where the power structure is still not clearly defined, where political relationships are still evolving, and where the 'government' is effectively a coalition of the representatives of the member states, the entire policy process revolves around compromise.

Some policy initiatives, such as the single market, have been less difficult to address than others because they have enjoyed a high degree of political support. The costs to national sovereignty were relatively low, while the potential benefits to national economies were relatively high. But in other areas, the member states have fought hard to protect national interests, forcing sometimes unhappy compromises. The creation of the Common Agricultural Policy, for example, was based around compromise, with France winning concessions on agriculture in return for concessions given to German industry. Similarly, the negotiations leading up to Maastricht were riddled with compromises and package deals, notably over the timetable for the development of the euro. The adoption of the euro was itself a compromise, with every member state given the option of either joining or not.

Political games. In the process of seeking compromises, politics is typically reduced to a struggle for power and influence, with one person or group trying to win concessions from – or pressing their views on – others. Such struggles take place even in the smallest and most local of communities in human society, but they are magnified in the EU by its sheer size and by the extent to which member states and institutions compete with each other, unconstrained (so far) by the presence of a constitution. Guy Peters (1992, pp. 106–7) describes three sets of interconnected games in the EU:

- A national game among member states, which are trying to extract as much as possible from the EU while giving up as little as possible. This was the case even with the six founding members, all of which had relatively similar ideas about the value of integration, and were relatively homogeneous. As the EU has since expanded in size, so the game has become more intense, because both the stakes and the pay-offs have been much greater, while the EU has at the same time become more politically, economically, and socially diverse.
- A game played out among EU institutions, which are trying to win more power and influence relative to each other. Not only have the stakes been raised with time, but the significance of European integration has changed. Once just an experiment in combining coal and steel industries, it grew to become a single market, and has since grown to cover almost all of Europe, and to develop policy responsibilities in a wide variety of areas. As the changes have occurred, so the EU institutions have jockeyed with each other for a greater role. Keohane and Hoffmann (1991, pp. 13–14) even conclude that the EU has become a network of institutions that prefer – out of self-interest – to interact with each other rather than with outsiders.
- A bureaucratic game in which the directorates-general in the Commission have their own organizational cultures and are competing for policy space. Again, this has been driven in large part by the growing policy responsibilities of the EU, the new resources available to the Commission, and the natural inclination within bureaucracies to compete for influence.

Multi-speed integration. The old 'Community method', by which all the member states were obliged to proceed at the same pace and to adopt and implement the same laws and policies, has been replaced by what has been variously known as 'multi-speed' integration, Europe *à la carte*, a Europe of 'variable geometry', or 'enhanced cooperation'. These are all terms for an arrangement that allows different member states to adopt different elements of European policy. For example, Britain was allowed to opt out of the Social Charter (see Chapter 6), only 12 member states made the switch to the single currency in 2002, not all member states have removed border controls as planned under the Schengen Agreement, and traditionally neutral states such as Ireland and Finland have decided not to participate in a common European defence policy. The Treaty of

Amsterdam imposed conditions that limited the scope of the application of 'enhanced cooperation', while Nice required a minimum of eight member states to take part, removed the right of each member state to veto the plan, and provided for the possibility of enhanced cooperation in foreign policy.

Formal versus informal. The EU has found itself subject to a combination of policy pressures that have been formal and informal. William Wallace defines formal integration as the deliberate actions taken by policy makers to create and adjust rules, to establish and work through common institutions, to regulate, encourage or inhibit social and economic flows, and to pursue common policies. He defines informal integration as patterns of interaction that develop without the intervention of deliberate government decisions, following the dynamic of markets, technology, communications, and social exchange, or the influence of mass movements. Wallace also distinguishes between proactive and responsive integration, the former having deliberate and explicit political aims, while the latter reacts to economic and social change (Wallace, 1990, pp. 54–5).

If all EU member states had similar political agendas, similar economic and social structures, similar levels of wealth and productivity, and the same sets of standards and regulations, integration would be relatively straightforward and would lean towards the formal and the proactive. However, the member states have different structures, policies, values and levels of wealth, so they approach integration from different perspectives. Concerned with avoiding a multi-speed Europe, national leaders have often had to react to the unforeseen effects of integration, and so have found themselves being driven by informal pressures. For example, while the process of integration has been focused on harmonizing standards, laws and regulations, it has also obliged European leaders in some areas simply to agree to proceed through 'mutual recognition' (if something is good enough for one state, it is good enough for them all).

Incrementalism. Policy making in a democratic society is inevitably cautious, because neither public nor political opinion will typically tolerate radical change. Policy tends to build on precedent, adjusting and fine-tuning what has gone before rather than bringing about wholesale change. This has been particularly true at the European level, because of concerns over the loss of national sovereignty, the absence of a consensus about the wisdom of European integration, and the need for constant compromise. The EU has occasionally agreed relatively dramatic policy initiatives (such as the Single European Act, Maastricht, the launch of the euro, and eastern enlargement), but none of these changes have come without considerable deliberation and debate, and most EU policy making is based on gradualism and incrementalism. Because there are so many counterweights and counterbalances in the policy process, member states and EU institutions can rarely take the initiative without conferring first with other member states or EU institutions. The process has sometimes slowed to the point where critics of integration have complained about inertia.

Spillover. Critics of the EU have also charged that it has tried to become involved in too many policy areas, and that institutions such as the Commission have become too powerful and even imperial. What they often fail to realize, though, is that the EU institutions have usually had little choice: the launch of a new initiative can reveal or create new problems or opportunities, which in turn can lead to a demand for additional supporting initiatives. This policy spillover has been one of the enduring features of policy making in the EU, the prime example coming from efforts to complete the single market. The task of removing barriers to the free movement of people, money, goods, and services could not be achieved either easily or quickly, and involved making many of the adjustments – anticipated or not – that opened up the European market. This meant moving into new areas of policy that were never anticipated by the founding treaties, including social issues, working conditions, and the environment.

All these characteristics have created a policy process that is complex, constantly changing, and still not yet fully understood. It is revealing that while there has been a growth in the number of published studies of the different institutions of the EU, and of the relationship between individual member states and the EU, there are still very few studies of the broader policy process and of the ways in which policy making at the European level has changed the relationship both among member states, and between member states and Europe as a whole. This suggests that we still have some way to go before we can achieve an understanding of the European policy process.

The politics of the budget

An example of the kinds of pressures that have come to bear on the relationship between the EU and its member states can be found in budgetary politics. The budget is one of the biggest influences on policy at any level of government, because the choices that a government makes regarding how and where to raise and spend money affect both the policy choices it makes and the effectiveness of the policies it pursues. It is typically less a question of how *much* is raised and spent than of *how* and *where* that money is raised and spent. The revenue and spending of the

Table 5.1   *The European Union budget*

Revenue	Billion €	Expenditure	Billion €
GNP own resources	73.2	Agriculture	45.7
VAT own resources	14.3	Structural	30.8
Duties and levies	11.4	Internal policies*	7.5
Miscellaneous	0.8	External action**	5.0
		Administration	6.0
		Preaccession aid[†]	2.9
		Compensation[‡]	1.4
		Reserves	0.4
Total	99.7	Total	99.7

* Includes transport, energy, environment, consumer policy, education, research and development.
** Includes the CFSP and humanitarian aid.
[†] Provided for the A-10.
[‡] Transfers to A-10 to help them with their budgets.
Figures are for 2004.

European Union is no exception, and the budget has frequently set off controversies that have resulted in member states being at odds with one another and with the EU institutions. The level of controversy is surprising considering the relatively small size of the EU budget: just under €100 billion ($120 billion) in 2004, or less than 1.3 per cent of the combined GDPs of the member states. Some of the biggest battles have concerned the relative amounts given and received by each member state, and the balance between national contributions and the EU's own sources of revenue. To the extent that the EU has had to rely on national contributions, it has been more subject to political leverage by the member states. To the extent that it has been able to develop its own sources of revenue, the EU institutions have been able to build more independence.

The European Economic Community – like most international organizations – was originally funded by national contributions. Each member state made a payment roughly in proportion to the size of its population, thus France, Germany, and Italy each contributed 28 per cent of the budget, Belgium and the Netherlands 7.9 per cent, and Luxembourg 0.2 per cent. In an attempt to win more independence for itself, the Commission in 1965 suggested that the revenue from tariffs placed on imports from outside the EC should go directly to the Community, thereby providing it with its 'own resources'. At the same time, Parliament began pushing for more control over the budget as a means of gaining more influence over policy. Charles de Gaulle thought that the Commission already had too much power, and it was these proposals (combined with France's opposition to reform of the Common Agricultural Policy) that led to the 1965 empty-chair crisis (see Dinan, 2004, pp. 104–5).

Pressure for budgetary reform persisted regardless, and changes in the early 1970s led to an increase in the proportion of revenues derived from the Community's own resources: customs duties, levies on agricultural imports, and a small proportion of value-added tax (VAT). But there were two problems with this formula: it took no account of the relative size of the economies of member states, and the amounts raised were insufficient to meet the needs of the Community, which was not allowed to run a deficit or to borrow to meet shortfalls. To make matters worse, two-thirds of all spending went to agricultural price supports, which grew as European farmers produced more crops (see Chapter 7). Meanwhile, revenue from customs duties fell because the Community's external tariffs were reduced, revenue from agricultural levies fell as the EC's self-sufficiency in food production grew, income from VAT failed to grow quickly enough because consumption was falling as a percentage of the Community's GNP (Shackleton, 1990, pp. 10–11), and several member states were unwilling to raise the limit on the EC's own resources.

By the early 1980s, the Community was nearly bankrupt, and it was obvious that either revenues had to be increased or spending had to be restructured or cut. Matters came to a head over the insistence by the new British prime minister, Margaret Thatcher, that Britain's contributions be recalculated. Arguing that Britain bore an unfair share of the Community budget, and received an inadequate amount in return, she caused shudders at her first European Council appearance in 1979 by bluntly telling her Community partners: 'I want my money back'. Her campaign continued through the early 1980s, tied to her demands for a reform of the Common Agricultural Policy. After much acrimonious debate, a complex deal was reached at the 1984 Fontainebleau European Council by which Britain's contributions were cut, its rebates were increased, and the overall budget was recalculated in preparation for the accession of Spain and Portugal, which, as poor countries, were to be net recipients of Community funds. More reforms agreed by the European Council in 1988 resulted in the system of revenue raising we find today:

- The budget cannot be greater than 1.27 per cent of the combined GNP of the member states.
- About 73 per cent of revenues come from national contributions based on national GNP levels, with each member state paying a set amount in proportion to its GNP.
- Revenues from VAT account for just over 14 per cent of revenues.
- Just over 11 per cent of revenues come from customs duties on imports from non-member states and from agricultural levies.

The effect of the changes was to make the richer states the biggest net contributors, while the poorer states have the biggest net receipts. As the wealthiest European member state, Germany was willing to accept this formula in 1988, but as its economy has gone through a downturn in recent years, so it has become the leading discontent on budgetary matters, arguing that the deal Britain received in 1984 should be extended to all 'overburdened' member states. When the Commission published its Agenda 2000 proposals in 1997, aimed at preparing for eastward enlargement and reform of the Common Agricultural Policy and the regional funds, it stirred up a hornet's nest of debate about the future of the budget. Several countries that were net contributors – including Austria, Germany, the Netherlands, and Sweden – began pressing for a reexamination of the budget, suggesting that contributions be capped at 0.3 per cent of national income. This caused particular nervousness among net recipients such as Greece and Spain, which were concerned that they would have to take on a greater burden of funding rebates.

In fact, most member states today are making contributions that are almost exactly in proportion to the relative sizes of their national economies. One of the notable exceptions is Britain, whose healthy economic growth in recent years (its economy recently overtook that of France to become the second biggest in the EU) has led to a significant gap between its budget contribution (14 per cent of the EU-15 total) and its GNP (18 per cent of the EU-15 total).

In terms of spending, the EU budget has raised a separate set of political problems. Like almost every budget, EU expenses consist of a combination of mandatory payments over which it has little or no choice (such as agricultural price supports) and discretionary payments (such as spending on regional or energy policy) regarding which there is more flexibility. EU spending is about equally divided between the two:

- About 46 per cent in 2004 went to agricultural subsidies and supports to fisheries. These guarantee minimum prices to farmers for their produce, regardless of volume. Thanks to reforms in agricultural policy (see Chapter 7), the proportion of EU spending that goes to agriculture has fallen substantially from its peak during the 1970s, when it accounted for nearly 75 per cent of the budget. But it is still substantial, and the EU is committed to making these payments.
- About 31 per cent of spending went to the structural funds: development spending on poorer regions of the EU, including spending under the European Social Fund aimed at helping offset the effects of unemployment, and investments in agriculture. The proportion of EU expenditures in this area has almost tripled since the mid-1970s. Another 2.9 per cent (€2.8 billion) was spent on aid to the ten mainly Eastern European countries that joined the EU in 2004.

- About 6 per cent went to administrative costs for the EU institutions.
- Most of the balance (about €12.5 billion) went to all the other policy areas in which the EU was active, including transport, energy, the environment, consumer policy, education, research and development, and foreign policy activities.

The EU budget is only partly a reflection of the policy areas in which the member states have agreed to transfer competence to the EU institutions. Looking at the figures, one could easily conclude that Europe was not much more than an exercise in agricultural and regional development. But it must be remembered that much of the work of the EU involves little or no operational cost; for example, the entire single market programme has been based largely on the development of new laws and policies. The same is true of competition policy, environmental protection (where most of the costs are borne by national and local government or private business), trade matters, and fiscal policy.

It must also be remembered that the member states have their own domestic budgets to invest in agriculture and in the kind of development supported by the structural funds. So, in this sense, the EU budget is little more than a modest compliment to the work of the member states. Although battles have been fought over the years over the question of relative national contributions and payments, one of the characteristics of the EU budget today is its relative peace and stability (Laffan, 1997, p. 245). This is reflective of a growing sense that income and spending – by amount, source, and target – have achieved a balance that most member states can live with.

The changing character of the EU

Changes in the relationship among the member states of the EU have complicated discussions about the character and effects of international relations, because the EU only partly fits with conventional ideas about the ways in which societies organize and govern themselves. As noted in Chapter 1, the EU is not a 'state' because it lacks many of the typical features of a state, including a strong and separate legal identity, political unity and sovereignty, powers of coercion, and significant financial independence. And while it has some of the features of an international organization, it has developed unprecedented levels of power and influence over its members. This has led some scholars to argue that the EU is not really an institution, but is better understood as an ideal, a process, a regime, or even a network that has involved not so much a transfer of powers as a pooling of sovereignty (Keohane and Hoffmann, 1991, p. 10).

Jean Monnet commented in 1975 that he saw no point in trying to imagine what political form the United States of Europe would take, and that 'the words about which people argue – federation or confederation – are inadequate and imprecise' (Monnet, 1978, p. 523). He might have been able to ignore the question thirty years ago, but if we are to understand the relationship between the EU and the member states today, and to develop a clearer sense of where European integration is headed, then we need to try and reach some kind of agreement on the nature and character of the EU. The process of integration has gone beyond the point of no return, and European political union is now spoken of less in terms of 'if' than in terms of 'when' and 'how'. So we must think more actively about the form that 'union' might take, and what it will mean for the member states.

There have been at least three different sets of forces at work in European integration, pulling the member states in several directions:

- *Intergovernmental versus supranational.* One of the most basic questions about European integration concerns the extent to which the decisions reached by the governments of the member states are driven by the protection of national interests rather than the promotion of the interests of the EU as a whole (see Box 5.3). Are the governments of the member states trying to preserve their sovereignty by relating to each other as equals, or are they transferring sovereignty to a new supranational authority? In some respects the European Union remains a pact among independent states, but in other respects the balance of power has shifted to European institutions.
- *Independence versus dependence.* Western Europe consists of a network of legally independent states, but they are bound more closely together than some of their citizens care to admit, by history, culture, and shared political and economic interests. The pressures of integration have strengthened their mutual ties, and the member states have moved along a path from independence to mutual dependence. This is particularly true in the sphere of economic policy, with the growth in investment, trade flows, and movement of workers, and the creation of pan-European industries and corporations.
- *Competition versus cooperation.* Until the Second World War the history of Europe was one of competition, conflict, and changing alliances and balances of power. The balance of power continues to change, but it does so inclusively rather than exclusively, and instead of being driven by conflict, it is driven by the need to cooperate. The competing goals of separate states have been replaced by the promotion of mutual interests, and the EU member states work increasingly closely together in a variety of policy areas.

Where the member states now sit on these three different continua is debatable, but there is little doubt that integration has moved them more

Box 5.3 Intergovernmental conferences

The extent to which decision making in the EU is still intergovernmental rather than supranational is reflected in the way that many of the big decisions of recent years have come out of intergovernmental conferences (IGCs), convened outside the formal framework of the EU's institutions to allow negotiations among the governments of the member states. Even as the powers of those institutions have grown, so the IGC has become an increasingly common event on the EU calendar; there have been eight IGCs since 1950, but six of them have been held since 1985.

The first IGC was opened in May 1950, was chaired by Jean Monnet, and led to the creation of the ECSC and the signing of the Treaty of Paris. The second was opened at Messina in April 1955, and led to the creation of the EEC and Euratom and the signing of the Treaties of Rome. Perhaps because national leaders were focused on building the three Communities and the common market, because of the intergovernmental nature of Community decision making in the early years, and because of the fallout from the energy crises of the 1970s, it was to be another 27 years before another IGC was convened. Concerned about the lack of progress on integration and Europe's declining economic performance in relation to the United States and Japan, the third IGC was launched in September 1985, and by December had outlined the framework of what was eventually to become the Single European Act.

Two more IGCs met during 1991 to look at political union and monetary union, their work resulting in the Treaty on European Union. A sixth IGC was launched in 1996 with institutional reform and preparations for eastward enlargement at the top of its agenda, the product of which was the Treaty of Amsterdam. Institutional reform was also on the agenda of the IGC that led to the 2000 Treaty of Nice, widely regarded as a disappointment. The eighth IGC in 2003 reviewed the draft of the new European constitution, which was itself designed to 'promote new forms of European governance'.

The IGCs since 1985 have been negotiated by a combination of national government ministers and permanent representatives, and have continued to symbolize the extent to which decision making on the big initiatives of the EU still rests with the member states. While there is nothing in the founding treaties about IGCs, they have become a normal part of the calendar of European integration, and most have resulted in important decisions on the development of the EU.

towards supranationalism, dependence, and cooperation. What has this meant for the member states?

First, the EU has more authority over its members than any international organization that has ever existed. It is not yet a government in itself, but is instead a melange of national governments and supranational institutions, whose links have created a confederation with federalizing tendencies.

While supranationalism may describe the political process of the EU, it has been argued that the EU has always rested ultimately on a set of intergovernmental bargains (Keohane and Hoffmann, 1991, p. 10). Opinion is divided about the extent to which it has moved beyond such bargains; realists argue that the member states are still the key actors, and that integration is driven by their decisions, while neofunctionalists argue that integration has taken on a life and momentum of its own.

Second, the EU has its own budget and bureaucracy, a large body of treaties and laws to which the member states are subject, and a court that can adjudicate disputes between member states, or between member states and the EU. But its institutions lack the power to raise taxes, have neither the power nor the personnel directly to enforce the law, and must rely almost entirely on the voluntary compliance of the member states. The most powerful of the EU institutions – the European Council, the Council of Ministers, and COREPER – are part of the structure of the European Union, but they are the meeting place for governments and do not have a life of their own above and beyond the member states. The most supranational of the institutions – the Commission, the Court of Justice, and the European Parliament – still have relatively fewer powers.

Finally, as noted earlier in this chapter, the extent to which the EU has responsibility over making public policy varies from one area to another. On agricultural and economic issues, the balance is in favour of the EU. On social and environmental issues, the trend is in favour of the EU. On matters relating to education, policing, and criminal law, the balance of power still rests with the member states. Recent amendments to the treaties have resulted in the accelerated transfer (or pooling) of policy responsibility, and the introduction of the euro has meant a final, irrevocable step in the integration of economic policy, which will in turn provide irresistible pressure to complete the integration of other internal policy issues.

Most people like to use labels to help them understand their environment, but there are no such easy labels for the EU, or at least none on which most people can agree. Europeans are well aware of the dangers of the divisions they are leaving behind, but are much less clear about the features of the unity towards which they are moving. As Benjamin Franklin argued after trying to find a model upon which the new American republic could be based, history consists only of beacon lights 'which give warning of the course to be shunned, without pointing out that which ought to be pursued' (Franklin, in *Federalist*, no. 37).

'Boundaries are difficult to draw in a world of complex interdependence', argue Keohane and Hoffmann (1991, p. 12); 'because relationships cross boundaries and coalitional patterns vary from issue to issue, it is never possible to classify all actors neatly into mutually exclusive categories'. The EU has many intergovernmental characteristics, but over time they have given way to a growing emphasis on supranationalism. The member states are increasingly answering to a higher authority, with many of the features of confederalism and some of the features of federalism. Both these concepts take many different forms, and for Eurosceptics to talk about federalism as some kind of hell towards which Europe should not travel is too simple. The European brand of federalism already has several unique features, and once it achieves some kind of regularity, those features will look very different from most of the characteristics we usually associate with federalism.

Conclusions

While debates rage about the powers and nature of the European Union, with both support for and resistance to the expansion of EU powers and responsibilities, there is no question that its member states have lost powers to the EU and now have less political and economic independence than they did even twenty years ago. Integration has changed the relationship among EU member states at several levels: there has been a reduction in social differences, a harmonization of standards, laws and regulations, and removal of the physical and fiscal barriers that have differentiated the member states from one another.

There is also an emerging consensus that cooperation in a variety of other areas makes better sense than independent action, which can lead to unnecessary competition and duplication of effort. It is still too early to talk about a federal relationship among the member states, and between them and the EU institutions, but the trend is undoubtedly in that direction. Several levels of government are being created, all with independent powers. How far European cooperation will go depends on how we choose to define subsidiarity, but while this is moving higher up the agenda of EU negotiations, the definition of which issues are best dealt with at the level of the member state and which at the level of Europe remains fluid.

The member states still have a large measure of control over domestic policy, in a wide variety of important areas, from foreign policy to defence policy, tax policy, education, criminal justice, and health care. Compared, for example, to the American case, where the states now have only residual responsibilities in a modest selection of areas, and whose independence from national government in Washington DC is largely symbolic, the member states of the EU are still powerful, independent actors. This is unlikely to last indefinitely, however. Internal political and economic pressures have meant a gradual surrender of powers by the member states, a steady accumulation of responsibilities by the EU institutions, and –

increasingly – the sense that Europe is governed both from Brussels and from 25 national capitals.

External pressures are also bound to continue to tighten the definition of Europe. Most of the rest of the world has not yet woken up to the implications of European integration, and to the idea that the 25 member states of the EU can and should be seen as a political and economic unit, that is exerting its global influence ever more effectively. Non-Europeans still treat Europeans mainly as citizens of individual member states, but this is slowly changing. As it does, it will give Europeans themselves a greater sense that they can be both European *and* British or Italian or Greek or Czech or Lithuanian. This in turn will give a tighter definition to the concept of Europe.

Chapter 6

The EU and its Citizens

The democratic deficit
The people's Europe
Participation and representation
Improving accountability
Conclusions

I have never understood why public opinion about European ideas should be taken into account.
                    Raymond Barre, French prime minister (1976–81)

The Maastricht treaty famously claims that the goal of European integration is to create 'an ever closer union among the peoples of Europe, in which decisions are taken as closely as possible to the citizen'. But even the most enthusiastic supporters of the EU admit that it has always been less a popular movement for change than a process begun and sustained by elites. The average European has few opportunities directly to influence the work of the EU, a problem that has become serious enough to earn its own label: the democratic deficit.

'What about us?' the European public might reasonably ask. 'Does anyone in Brussels or our national capitals care what we think?' It sometimes seems as though the work of the EU goes on despite public opinion, which is often confused, sometimes doubtful, and in some cases actively hostile. Many of the big decisions are taken as a result of negotiations among political leaders, and ordinary voters are only sporadically asked what they think. They can tell their national governments, but this is only an indirect form of representation, and the governments often take decisions without referring back to the people. Voter interests are directly represented in the European Parliament, but it is one of the weaker European institutions. The Commission and the Court of Justice promote the interests of 'Europe', but citizens have no direct influence on senior appointments to either body.

To make matters worse, most Europeans are mystified by the European Union. Journalists often misrepresent the way it works, the Commission has done a bad job of explaining what it does, and most academic writing makes it sound dull and legalistic. The result is confusion and apathy (as reflected, for example, in the poor turnout at European elections). The European Council decided in 1984 to begin promoting 'a people's Europe' in an attempt to make Europe more 'real' to its people, and changes have been made to the treaties in order to promote 'transparency' (making the deliberations of the EU institutions more open to scrutiny), but the argument that popular enthusiasm can somehow be generated by public policy is fundamentally flawed.

The evolution of the European Union has changed the way that Europeans relate to each other, in many different ways. Some of the changes have come as a direct result of policy decisions, such as the removal of border controls and the expansion of opportunities through the single market. Other changes have been an indirect consequence, growing out of the realization among Europeans that they are involved in a joint exercise with implications for them all. Under the circumstances it is essential that more attention is paid to public opinion, that the Commission, the Council of Ministers, and the European Council do a better job of explaining what they are doing, that national leaders pay more attention to public opinion, and that citizens make more of an effort to understand what is being done in their name and play a more active role in letting their leaders know how they feel.

This chapter asks what integration has meant for Europeans, and for the nature of democracy in the European Union. It begins with an assessment of the problems arising from the democratic deficit, examining the relationship between public opinion and the decisions taken by national leaders. It then looks at the channels through which Europeans can express their opinions on EU policy – including elections, referenda, and working through interest groups – and ends with a discussion about the kinds of changes that still need to be made to bring Europe closer to its citizens.

The democratic deficit

The EU has a survey research programme known as Eurobarometer, which regularly measures public opinion on a wide variety of issues relating to European integration, ranging from views on the entire process to those on specific policies. Surveys over the last twenty years have found that enthusiasm for the EU has waxed and waned: support grew from 50 per cent in 1980 to a peak of 71 per cent in 1990, but fell in Germany after reunification, and then more widely throughout the EU in the wake of the controversy over Maastricht. By 2000–4, only 48–50 per cent of Europeans thought that membership was a 'good thing' (Eurobarometer 54, April 2001; Eurobarometer 61, July 2004). Meanwhile, opinion in the A-10 was not favourable; only 40 per cent of respondents had a positive image of the EU, and only 43 per cent thought that membership of the EU would be a good thing.

There has also been a decline in the number of people who think that their country has benefited from membership, from 58 per cent in 1990 to 47 per cent today. In the A-10, the number of people who thought their country would benefit fell from 57 per cent to 52 per cent in 2003–4. Among those most enthusiastic about membership are poorer member states such as Greece, Ireland, Portugal, and Spain, while the doubters include several newer and/or wealthier member states such as Austria, Britain, Denmark, and Sweden (see Figure 6.1).

These mixed feelings are probably the result of four major factors. First, integration is a relatively new issue for the average European. True, the Treaty of Rome was signed back in 1957, but it has only been since the early 1990s that the effects of integration have begun to be felt more broadly and to impact the lives of Europeans more directly. One result is that most Europeans have only recently begun to think with any substance about the costs and benefits of integration, or to learn more about how it works.

Second, the actions of national leaders are often at odds with the balance of public opinion. Take the issue of enlargement, for example: only 44 per cent of EU citizens supported the idea in 2000 while 35 per cent were opposed, and only 26 per cent saw it as a priority for the EU while 62 per cent did not. Undeterred, the Commission negotiated with aspirant members, and ten of them joined in May 2004. Policy on the euro provides another example: support strengthened in the lead-up to its adoption in 2002, but it was still lukewarm, with only 55 per cent in favour, 37 per cent against, and 8 per cent undecided. Equally undeterred, the leaders of 12 member states gave up their national currencies and switched to the euro, in every case failing to put the issue to a public referendum. Two years after the adoption of the euro, Europeans still had mixed views: just 47 per cent were happy with it, while 44 per cent were unhappy (Eurobarometer, Flash EB 153, November 2003). This mismatch between public and political opinion inevitably promotes cynicism about European integration, and dulls enthusiasm.

The Danish people's rejection of Maastricht in June 1992 should have been a salutary lesson; it came as a shock not just to the Danish government, but to all European governments. It was much the same with the Irish people's rejection of the Treaty of Nice in June 2001. The results raised questions about just how many other initiatives might have been rejected – or passed by small majorities – if put to national referenda in member states. For example, the euro was rejected by national referenda in Denmark and Sweden, and would almost certainly have been rejected by German voters if put to the test in the mid-1990s, because polls found that more than 60 per cent were opposed to the idea, and unwilling to surrender the Deutschmark. Given the essential role of Germany in the

Figure 6.1 *Public opinion on EU membership*

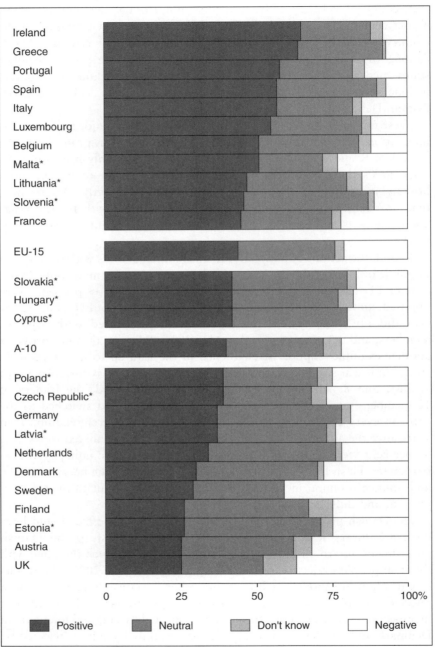

* The A-10 (the 10 'accession' states who joined the EU in 2004).
Source: Eurobarometer 61 (July 2004 – fieldwork undertaken Feb/March 2004).

single currency, such a result would have dealt a crippling blow to the programme.

The third problem is that national leaders, European institutions, the media and academic experts have done a poor job of explaining the implications and the costs and benefits of integration. To be fair, integration is a complex process that is constantly changing, and the implications of the changes have not always been fully understood, even by policy makers – every new step has produced unanticipated effects (the single market programme being a prime example) and the switch to the euro was a leap into the unknown. But there has been no constitution to which citizens can refer for clarification, the treaties confuse more than they illuminate, the growing volume of information on the EU tends to focus on the minutiae of the treaties and European law, media coverage in the Eurosceptical media misleads by emphasizing the negative at the expense of the positive, and the average European remains confused (see Box 6.1). This is particularly true in the A-10.

Finally, and perhaps most fundamentally, there is the democratic deficit. This has been defined by Williams (1991, p. 162) as 'the gap between the powers transferred to the Community level and the control of the elected Parliament over them', and by Archer (2000, p. 58) as 'the shift in decision-making powers from the national to the EU level, without accompanying strengthening of parliamentary control of executive bodies'. These definitions imply that the democratic deficit could be narrowed by giving Parliament greater powers, or by giving national legislatures greater control over EU institutions, but the problem is much broader, and a better definition of the democratic deficit would be as follows: the gap between the powers of European institutions and the ability of European citizens to influence their work and decisions.

The deficit takes several forms:

- The leaders of the member states, meeting as the European Council, reach decisions on important policy matters without always referring to their electorates. Less than half the EU-15 member states asked their citizens whether they even wanted to join the European Community or the European Union. The Maastricht treaty was negotiated largely behind closed doors, poorly explained to the European public and – despite the important changes it made to the structure and goals of the EU – was put to the test of a referendum in only three member states (Denmark, France, and Ireland), one of which (Denmark) said no. Amsterdam and Nice were equally poorly explained, and equally poorly tested.
- Despite its powers over proposing and developing new European laws, the Commission is subject to little direct or even indirect public

Box 6.1 The knowledge deficit

No matter how much the European Commission tries to make Europe seem more real to its citizens, and no matter how often the European Council talks about the importance of transparency, one critical problem remains: the average European knows little about how the EU works. This has been made clear by the results of recent Eurobarometer surveys, in which respondents are asked how much they know about the EU, its policies, and its institutions, and to give themselves a score out of 10, with 10 meaning they know a great deal and 1 meaning they know little. While 6 per cent admitted that they knew nothing at all in 2004, no less than 70 per cent of respondents gave themselves (failing) scores of 5 or less, and the average for the sample worked out at 4.48. Just 7 per cent gave themselves scores of 8 or higher (Eurobarometer 61, July 2004).

Those who felt they knew the most included managers, university graduates, people who used the media regularly, and those in the age range of 25–54. Those with the lowest levels of knowledge included manual workers, retirees, and people with a high school education or lower. In descending order, Austrians, Germans, Greeks, Danes, and the Dutch felt they knew the most, while Belgians, the Irish, Spaniards, Britons, and Portuguese knew the least. Interestingly, levels of knowledge about the EU were roughly the same in the A-10 as in the EU-15, perhaps because of the extensive media coverage of the EU in those countries as they prepared for membership.

When tested on their knowledge of the EU, 55 per cent of respondents incorrectly thought that it was created just after the First World War, 50 per cent did not know that Members of the European Parliament were directly elected by voters, 48 per cent incorrectly thought that the president of the European Commission was elected, and one-third thought that there were only 12 member states in the EU. Meanwhile, nearly one in three Europeans in 2004 had never even *heard* of the Council of Ministers, and about one in five had never heard of the European Commission, the Court of Justice, or the European Central Bank. Meanwhile, reflecting popular prejudices, one in four Europeans think that the biggest item on the EU budget is the cost for officials, meetings, and buildings. (As we saw in Chapter 5, it actually accounts for just 6 per cent of EU spending, while agriculture accounts for 46 per cent.) (All results from Eurobarometer 61.)

These are not encouraging figures. It will be difficult for Europeans to develop a sense of belonging to the European Union if they continue to know so little about it, and as long as they know so little, they will not make their views known about its work. This will perpetuate the democratic deficit, and decisions will continue to be taken by a policy elite of national leaders and Eurocrats. Ironically, the lack of public knowledge persists despite attempts by the Commission to make its work more accessible through printed and audiovisual media and the internet. Unfortunately, the latter are heavy on rhetoric and light on substance.

accountability. Appointments to the College must be approved by Parliament, but otherwise they are made without reference to the people. The president of the Commission is appointed as a result of a strange and informal little power dance among the leaders of the member states, represents the views of the EU in several international fora without a mandate from the people, and has tenure that is subject to the whims of national leaders rather than the opinions of European citizens. Furthermore, there is little opportunity for citizens to take part in or contribute to the deliberations of the Commission, and only limited (albeit improving) opportunity for the European Parliament to hold it accountable for its initiatives and decisions.

- Meetings of the Council of Ministers and the permanent representatives in Brussels are closed, despite the fact that many of the most important decisions on the content of new laws and policies, and on their acceptance or rejection, are taken there. Ministers and representatives take the kinds of decisions that – at the national level – are taken by members of elected assemblies, who are held accountable for their actions at elections and in the court of public opinion.

- The European Parliament – the only democratically elected institution in the EU system – lacks several of the powers of a true legislature: it cannot raise revenues or introduce new laws, and it has only a limited ability to hold the Commission accountable for its decisions. It has worked hard to win new powers for itself, but most of the important decisions on EU law and policy are still taken elsewhere.

- The Court of Justice is the institution that best champions the cause of individual Europeans, being the final court of appeal for anyone who feels they have been hurt by European law, by its non-appliance, or by contradictions between European and national law. However, Europeans have no say in appointments to the Court, nor will they until the kind of legislative confirmation that is used for courts in many member states is adopted by the EU, and nominees to the Court of Justice and the Court of First Instance are investigated and confirmed by the European Parliament.

- The formal rights of Europeans relative to the EU institutions are modest: they have the right to vote in European elections, to petition Parliament or the European ombudsman (see below) if they feel their rights or interests have been violated, to access the documents of EU institutions (within certain limits), and to diplomatic representation outside the EU by any member state, provided their own country has no local representation.

The biggest problem with the democratic deficit is that it is a damaging psychological barrier between Europeans and the EU, preventing the development of the ties that must exist between leaders and citizens in order for a system of government to work. Under the circumstances it is hardly surprising that Europeans feel so little attachment to the EU institutions. It is also hardly surprising that the anti-European media are able to generate so much public distrust and resentment towards these institutions, which often appear distant and mysterious. This is most obvious in the case of the Commission. Although it is a small and productive institution, and can only propose and oversee the implementation of new laws, it is often portrayed as powerful, overpaid, unaccountable, and secretive. It is helped little by the fact that most of its staff occupy a series of anonymous buildings spread around the suburbs of Brussels, and that access to those buildings by ordinary Europeans is heavily restricted.

The European Commission is well aware of the problems, and made some candid admissions in a White Paper published in 2001 on the issue of governance:

> Europeans ... increasingly distrust institutions and politics or are simply not interested in them. The problem ... is particularly acute at the level of the European Union. Many people are losing confidence in a poorly understood and complex system to deliver the policies that they want. The Union is often seen as remote and at the same time too intrusive ... [The EU] must start adapting its institutions and establishing more coherence in its policies so that it is easier to see what it does and what it stands for. A more coherent Union will be stronger at home and a better leader in the world ... Reform must be started now.

The paper also defended the work of EU institutions, noting that there is a perception that the EU cannot act effectively where a clear case exists (such as on unemployment, food safety scares, and security concerns on EU borders), that even where the EU acts effectively it does not get fair credit for its actions, that people do not see that improvements in their quality of life often come from European rather than national initiatives, that ' "Brussels" is too easily blamed by Member States for difficult decisions that they themselves have agreed or even requested', and that many Europeans 'do not know the difference between the [EU institutions, and do not] understand who takes the decisions that effect them and do not feel the Institutions act as an effective channel for their views and concerns' (Commission of the European Communities, 2001, pp. 3, 7). Unfortunately, rather than making specific suggestions for change, the paper made the usual mistake of talking in generalities and employing bureaucratic notions of better involvement, more openness, greater flexibility, 'partnership arrangements', 'a more systematic dialogue', and 'policy coherence' – whatever these mean.

While there is little question that fundamental reforms are needed to make the EU institutions more efficient, accountable and democratic, moves in this direction usually come up against the resistance of national governments: to make these institutions more democratic would be to reduce the control that national governments currently exert over them. The Treaty of Amsterdam emphasized the need to make the work of the EU comprehensible and 'transparent', but while it established the right of Europeans to greater access to European documents, this is not the same as affording them a greater opportunity to influence the content of those documents.

Franklin (1996, p. 197) describes the lack of proper democratic accountability in the EU as 'a crisis of legitimacy'. It is unlikely that the essential psychological link between EU institutions and EU citizens will be made until the European Parliament becomes a true legislature, national political parties form pan-European federations and run for election as such, and the outcome of European elections has a direct effect on the content and performance of the Commission and the Council of Ministers. But this will not happen as long as the governments of the member states feel the need to use the Council of Ministers as the guarantor of national interests.

The people's Europe

It took more than thirty years for political leaders to begin asking Europeans what they thought about the process of integration. A report was drawn up in 1975 at the request of the European Council by Leo Tindemans, prime minister of Belgium, looking into the steps that might be taken to achieve a more integrated Europe that was 'closer' to its citizens. But nothing more was done until June 1984, when the EEC heads of government, meeting in Fontainebleu and spending most of their time agreeing reforms to the Community budget, briefly turned their attention to the idea of a 'people's Europe'. Pietro Adonnino, a former Italian MEP, was hired to chair a committee to put forward suggestions on how the EEC could be brought more closely in touch with its citizens.

The committee endorsed arrangements that had already been made for a European passport and a European flag. All national passports have since been replaced by a standardized burgundy-coloured 'European' passport bearing the words 'European Union' in the appropriate national language, and the name and coat of arms of the holder's home state. This ensures that Europeans are given equal treatment by the customs and immigration authorities of other countries, and also helps give them a sense of belonging to the EU. But these passports do not make their holders European citizens – see below.

Meanwhile the European Commission created an annual 'Europe Day' (9 May, the anniversary of the Schuman Declaration), adopted as the official European anthem the 'Ode to Joy' by Friedrich von Schiller, sung to the final movement of Beethoven's Ninth Symphony, and, most importantly, adopted as its own the flag that had been used by the Council of Europe since 1955 – a circle of 12 gold stars on a blue background. The European flag, which was designed by Paul Levy, director of information for the Council of Europe, was chosen in preference to several other designs (Bainbridge and Teasdale, 1995, pp. 188–9) and has since become a potent symbol of Europe – it can be seen flying on public buildings and hotels throughout the EU, and is omnipresent at meetings of EU leaders. (It was popularly thought until the early 1990s that the 12 stars represented the 12 member states but the number was coincidental and the design has not been changed as membership of the EU has grown.)

The Single European Act incorporated more of the Adonnino recommendations, the most important of which was the easing of restrictions on the free movement of people. At the time of the Treaty of Rome it was understood that an open labour market would be an essential part of a single market, but while all Community citizens were given the right to 'move and reside freely' within all the member states, this was subject to 'limitations justified on grounds of public policy, public security or public health'. Since integration in the early days was economically driven, priority was given to making it easier for people who were economically active to move from one state to another. Limits were placed on migration, initially because governments wanted to protect themselves against the possibility of a shortage of skilled workers, and then because of the lack of opportunities in the target states (Barnes and Barnes, 1995, p. 108).

Changes under the SEA allowed residents of the EU-15 to move and live anywhere in the EU, provided they are covered by health insurance and have enough income to avoid being a 'burden' on the welfare system of the country to which they move. The governments of the member states have been anxious to control the effects of the economic pressures that encourage workers to leave the poorer parts of the EU for the richer parts, thereby increasing welfare spending and making unemployment worse in those richer parts, and to control the movement of non-EU citizens, particularly Turks, North Africans, and refugees from the Balkans. At the heart of the free movement debate has been a concern about differences in welfare laws, which is why agreement of common social policies has been given high priority (see Chapter 8), and why there has been a focus on meeting the needs of younger and older people.

The removal of the barriers to free movement has helped make Europeans more mobile in the last 10–15 years, and the number of non-nationals living in member states has risen. There were five million immigrants in 1950, ten million in 1970, and there are probably close to 15 million today, although the removal of the barriers to movement has made it difficult to be sure. The flow of immigration was initially from the south to the north, and most of those moving were workers from Mediterranean states looking for higher-paying jobs, and then sending for their families to join them. Immigration flows today are more complex because there has been an increase in the movement of professionals and managers. Where Europeans once moved involuntarily for economic reasons, more are now moving voluntarily and for a variety of different reasons – they may be looking for a different environment in which to live, retiring to warmer parts of the EU, or looking for a new start in a new country.

Tourism has played an important role in making Europeans more mobile. Most Europeans could once afford to travel only within their own countries, but the advent of cheap mass tourism since the late 1960s has led to a marked increase in the numbers of people taking holidays in other member states. Day trips, weekend breaks, stays of one or two weeks, timeshares, the purchase of holiday homes and extended visits for those who can afford the time have all combined to increase the ease and comfort with which Europeans travel around the continent. Language differences still pose a psychological barrier, but the easing of restrictions on movement has combined with the introduction of the euro to make other member states seem less 'foreign' to Europeans.

All these demographic shifts have been helped by another element of the Adonnino report that was formalized by the SEA: arrangements for the mutual recognition of professional qualifications. Although the basic training for most health workers (doctors, nurses, dentists, and so on) was standardized relatively early and they were quickly given the right to work in any member state, progress in other areas was slower. The Commission at first tried to work on each profession in turn, to reach agreement on the requirements, and then propose a new law. But this was time-consuming, which is why it took 17 years to harmonize the requirements for architects and 16 years for pharmacists. Progress was made in 1988 with the general systems directive, under which the member states agreed (effective 1991) to trust the adequacy of qualifications that required at least three years of professional training in other member states. The list of mutually recognized professions has since grown, and now includes accountants, librarians, architects, engineers, and lawyers. The Commission has meanwhile published a comparative guide to national qualifications for more than 200 occupations, helping employers work out equivalencies across the member states.

An important element in worker mobility is education and youth training, in which the EU has become more involved since Maastricht by

Box 6.2 Promoting European culture

A common history and culture are important elements in the identity of a nation state. Where they exist, strong states tend to enjoy a high degree of legitimacy (public acceptance), which breeds stability and longevity. Where they do not exist, and where there are significant social divisions, there is more likely to be instability and a weaker sense of common identity. France is an example of a state with a high level of cultural legitimacy, while British national identity is weakened by divisions among the English, the Scots, the Welsh, and the Northern Irish, and Belgium is weakened by divisions between its Flemish and Wallonian communities.

When Europeans think of their history and culture they are more likely to think of what divides them than of what unites them. The EU has tried to address this problem by promoting the idea of a common European culture (even though such promotion may be anathema to some – how can culture be legislated or 'promoted'?). Despite the fact that Eurobarometer polls show a majority in favour of cultural policy being left to the member states, Maastricht introduced a commitment that the EU would 'contribute to the flowering of the culture of the Member States' with a view to improving knowledge about the culture and history of Europe, conserving European cultural heritage, and supporting and supplementing non-commercial cultural exchanges and 'artistic and literary creation'.

What this has so far meant in practice has been spending money on restoring historic buildings, supporting training schemes in conservation and restoration, preserving regional and minority languages, subsidising the translation of works by European authors (particularly into less widely spoken languages), and supporting cultural events. For example, the EU has funded a Youth Orchestra and a Baroque Orchestra to bring young musicians together, declared since 1985 European 'Capitals of Culture' (including Graz in Austria, Genoa in Italy, and Cork in Ireland) and established a European Cultural Month in cities in non-member states (such as Basel, Cracow, and St Petersburg).

While the sentiments behind these projects are laudable, it is difficult to see how cultural exchanges and the development of a European cultural identity can really work unless they are driven by Europeans themselves. It is easy to argue that Shakespeare, Michelangelo, Voltaire, Goethe, Picasso and Mozart are all part of the heritage of Europe, but it is more difficult to promote the idea of a modern pan-European popular culture or a European identity. Even the most mobile of art forms – film and rock music – come up against the barrier of national preferences, and little that is not produced in English has had commercial success outside its home market.

encouraging educational exchanges and addressing the critical issue of language training. The inability to speak other languages poses a barrier to the free movement of workers, and stands as a reminder of the differences among Europeans, so the EU has set up a host of programmes to help promote cooperation. These include the Leonardo da Vinci programme, which promotes international vocational training exchanges, and the Socrates programme, which promotes education. Under Socrates is the Erasmus programme (which focuses on student and faculty exchanges among colleges and universities, and makes it easier for students to transfer credits) and Erasmus Mundus (which encourages cross-border master's programmes involving at least three universities in at least three countries).

The EU now has 21 official languages: Czech, Danish, Dutch, English, Estonian, Finnish, French, German, Greek, Hungarian, Irish, Italian, Latvian, Lithuanian, Maltese, Polish, Portuguese, Slovak, Slovene, Spanish, and Swedish. Almost all secondary school pupils in the EU learn at least one foreign language, although some have a better record than others at becoming bilingual or multilingual. The Dutch and the Scandinavians do best, while the British do worst, having been spoiled by the growth of English as the international language of commerce and entertainment, and by the large number of continental Europeans who speak English: more than 90 per cent of secondary school pupils in Germany, Spain, the Netherlands, and Denmark learn it as a second language. Meanwhile fewer than one in three Italian and German pupils are learning French (Eurostat Web page, 2001).

The issue of language cuts to the core of national pride, and particularly concerns the French, who have gone to great lengths to stop the spread of 'franglais' – the use of English words in French, for example 'le jumbo jet' (officially *le gros porteur*) and 'le fast food' (officially *pret-à-manger*) (overlooking the fact that many French words and phrases have infiltrated the English language, from *amateur* to *brochure*, *cliché*, *dossier*, *souvenir*, and *vogue*). In an attempt to prevent any one language dominating the others it has been suggested that all Europeans should learn Esperanto, an artificial international language developed in 1887, or even that Latin should be revived. Despite the number of EU employees who work as translators, the publication of EU documents in all 21 official languages, and the attempts by France to stave off the threats posed by Anglo-American culture, it is inevitable that English – with the help of international business, telecommunications, entertainment, and sport – will become the common language of Europe.

While tourism, the removal of technical barriers to movement and the promotion of language training all contribute to free movement, integration will never be able to do much about the social and psychological barriers posed by differences in the routine of daily existence. Americans can readily travel from one state to another in search of jobs or to improve the quality of their lives, and will find their daily routine changing little; they will find the same shops, the same banking system, the same money, the same programmes on television, and so on. By contrast, Europeans not only face different languages, but must also deal with a host of new norms and rules, including everything from new social customs to new sets of road signs and traffic regulations, different procedures for renting or buying a home, taking out car insurance or opening a bank account, and a new array of products on the shelves of local supermarkets. It is psychologically difficult enough for an American family to uproot itself and move hundreds of miles away, but while an Italian moving to Denmark or a Swede moving to Hungary can eventually learn how things are done locally, the challenge of acculturation is much greater. New EU laws cannot address this kind of problem.

Another of the changes introduced by Maastricht was the promotion of European citizenship, although this is not what it seems. 'Citizenship' in democracies is usually defined as full and responsible membership of a state, and has been described by some social scientists as including the right to equality before the law, the right to own property, the right to freedom of speech, and the right to a minimum standard of economic and social welfare. But these are all rights that legal non-citizens of democracies also enjoy. What makes a citizen different from a non-citizen in practical terms is that a citizen can vote and run for elective office in his or her home state, can serve on a jury in that state, is eligible to serve in the armed forces of that state (although some countries allow non-citizens to serve), cannot be forcibly removed from that state to another, has the right to receive protection from the state when outside its borders, is recognized as a subject of that state by other governments, and must usually obtain the permission of other governments to travel through or live in their territory. More intangibly, citizens feel a sense of 'belonging' to their home state.

According to Maastricht 'every person holding the nationality of a Member State shall be a citizen of the Union', but this is much less than it sounds. A step in the direction or real citizenship was taken with the agreement that citizens of a member state finding themselves in need in a non-EU country where their home state has no diplomatic representation can receive protection from the diplomatic and consular authorities of any EU state that has a local office. Another step was taken with the easing of restrictions on voting and running for elective office, but citizens of one state living in another can only vote and stand for municipal and European Parliament elections, not for national elections.

Another change introduced by Maastricht under the 'People's Europe' initiative was the creation of a European ombudsman. If a legal resident of the EU feels that any of the EU institutions (other than the Court of Justice and the Court of First Instance) is guilty of 'maladministration', and can make a compelling case, the European Parliament must ask the ombudsman to review the complaint, and if necessary carry out an investigation. Appointed for a five-year term that runs concurrently with the term of Parliament, the ombudsman is expected to be both impartial and independent of any government. Since the first ombudsman was appointed in 1995, the Commission has been the target of most of the complaints, which have included charges that it has failed to carry out its responsibilities as guardian of the treaties, that it lacks sufficient transparency, and that it has abused its power. The number of complaints has grown over the years, which is probably less a sign that things are getting worse than a sign that more people are becoming aware of the work of the ombudsman.

Participation and representation

Although well-meaning, the People's Europe project is ultimately superficial. Making Europe more 'real' to Europeans is one thing, but giving them a real say in how it makes its decisions – and so creating a real connection – is quite another. The realization by the citizens of the member states that they belong to a larger communal entity is something that ultimately must come from them. They need to understand the implications of integration, they must see and directly experience its benefits, and they must feel that they can have a real impact on the way it evolves. Of course, if the EU is a confederation (as this book argues) then direct links between EU institutions and Europeans are unnecessary: the people hold their national governments accountable, which in turn represent their interests at the European level. But this is no more than an ideal, because not only do Europe's national leaders often pursue narrow political interests, but they often reach agreements on European policy in the face of public opposition.

Giving Europeans a direct stake in the work of the EU, and encouraging them to take the EU as seriously as they take their national governments, means closing the democratic deficit. As 'Europe' becomes a more important issue in national politics, and as voters figure policies on Europe into their calculations about competing national political parties and leaders, so Europeans will have more influence on policies and positions adopted in the meeting rooms and hallways of the Commission, the Council of Ministers, and the European Council. Until this happens, there are three other channels through which they can influence the outcome of

European policy decisions: voting in European elections, taking part in referenda, and supporting the work of interest groups.

European elections

Held every five years since 1979, elections to the European Parliament (EP) give Europeans the opportunity to decide the make-up of the EP, which has an increasingly effective role in making European law. Voters must be 18 years of age and must be citizens of one of the EU member states. Since Maastricht, they have been allowed to vote in whichever country they have residence, and even to run for the EP wherever they live, regardless of citizenship. To vote they must make a declaration to the local electoral authority and meet local qualifications; to run for office they must meet qualifications in their home state. The minimum age for candidates varies from 18 to 25 years, depending on the country of residence, and there are also different rules on how candidates qualify; some member states do not allow independent candidates, some require candidates to pay deposits, others require them to collect signatures, and so on (Westlake, 1994, pp. 84–5).

Unfortunately, turnout at EP elections is low, undermining the credibility and political influence of Parliament. From a modest peak of 63 per cent in 1979, figures fell to just under 57 per cent in 1994, then took a relatively sharp fall to just over 49 per cent in 1999, tailing off to just under 46 per cent in 2004. Belgium and Luxembourg usually have the best turnout (85–92 per cent), but in most member states fewer than half of all voters now turn out. Several countries started out on a high note upon joining the EU, only to see their voters lose enthusiasm: for example, Portugal fell from 72 to 39 per cent, Austria from nearly 70 to 42 per cent, and Finland from 60 to 40 per cent. Optimists expected that the figures in 2004 for the A-10, in their first flush of membership, would be high – in the event, they were among the worst ever: less than 42 per cent turned out in most countries, and just one in five in Poland and Slovakia (see Figure 6.2).

There are several explanations for this state of affairs, the most compelling of which is the relative significance of 'first-order' and 'second-order' elections (Reiff and Schmitt, 1980; Hix, 1999, pp. 180–4). Voters give priority to national elections, because they determine who controls the national executive and legislatures, which in turn make the decisions that are most immediate and relevant in the lives of citizens. National elections are also hard-fought and attract the most media attention. By contrast, European elections are seen as second-order elections because there is less at stake; there is no potential change of government involved, and most Europeans either know very little about what Parliament does, or are confused or badly informed about European issues.

Figure 6.2   *Turnout at European Parliament elections, 2004*

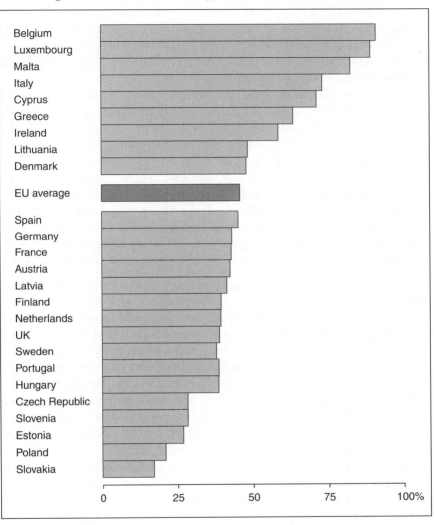

Among the other explanations for low turnout:

• There is the novelty of European elections, which have been on the electoral calendar only since 1979. Where most voters have been socialized into appreciating the importance of national elections, they have not always yet taken to the idea that EP elections are worth their attention.

• MEPs do not become well-known political figures, so there is little of the personality politics that often sparks voter interest in national elections.

- EU voters have developed few psychological ties to the European Parliament, which may be the best known of all the EU institutions, but still seems anonymous and distant to most. As noted in Box 6.1, only 50 per cent of Europeans even know that its members are elected.
- The media and national politicians pay relatively little attention to European elections, so they generate less voter interest.
- Low turnout mirrors a general downward trend in national elections in many EU member states. Where turnout at EP elections fell by 13 per cent between 1979 and 1999, it fell by 10–14 per cent over roughly the same period in (for example) France, Germany, Ireland, and the Netherlands (Corbett, 2001).
- Turnout is often a reflection of how voters view their home governments and national political issues, and many will use their vote to send a message to national politicians. This is exacerbated by the way most political parties run as national parties, rather than as members of genuine Europe-wide party groups. So if voters are not interested by national politics, they are less likely to turn out at European elections.

Not only is turnout low, but there are structural problems with European elections that undermine their impact and significance: they are not held on the same day in all member states, countries such as Germany use different electoral systems for national and European elections, and member states use different forms of proportional representation (PR). For example, while Belgium, Ireland, and Italy use regional lists and divide their countries into multiple constituencies, Denmark, France, Portugal, and Spain use national lists and treat their countries as one constituency. Britain long used the same first-past-the-post system used for national and local elections, but adopted PR for EP elections in 1999 in order to fall into line with the rest of the EU.

One of the suggestions made by the Adonnino committee that has not yet been implemented was for the establishment of a uniform electoral procedure for European elections. The idea was first outlined in the Treaty of Paris, repeated in the Treaty of Rome and raised again on several subsequent occasions, but little has been achieved in practical terms. Even the definition of the word 'uniform' in this context is debatable, and while a decision was taken at the 1974 Paris summit that the goal would be met if European elections were secret, direct, based on universal suffrage and held on the same day, this has not been the end of the story.

Referenda

National referenda allow European voters to express their opinions on narrow (but usually important) topics. Not every country uses them, and they have only been used for selected issues, but they have come to play an increasingly important role in the process of European integration, and there has been increased moral and political pressure for their use. Some have been little more than tools for political manipulation, as when Britain held a referendum in 1975 that was ostensibly about whether or not Britain should stay in the Community following renegotiation of the terms, but was actually designed to settle a division of opinion about Europe within the government (Nugent, 2002, p. 483). Others have had a significant impact on the course of European integration, as when the terms of Maastricht and Nice were amended following their rejection in referenda in, respectively, Denmark and Ireland. Voters are so rarely given the opportunity to express their views on EU matters that referenda are often used to express opinions on the EU and European integration more generally, rather than just the issue at hand.

Most referenda have fallen into one of two major categories:

- *Whether or not to join the EU.* These have been held only by newer members of the EU, beginning with the votes held in Denmark, Ireland, and Norway in 1972. A majority of Danes and Irish approved, but a majority of Norwegians disapproved, and said no in a second referendum in 1994. The Swiss also said no to EU membership in a referendum in 2001. All three countries that joined the EU in 1995 held referenda, as did nine of the ten countries that joined in 2004 (the exception was Cyprus). The results were all positive for membership, but levels of enthusiasm varied: the Slovaks, Lithuanians, and Slovenians were the most supportive, with 90–92 per cent majorities in favour, while in Finland, Sweden, and Malta, bare majorities of just over 50 per cent said yes. The only example of a territory leaving the EU came in 1982, when the 53,000 voters of Greenland – which had joined in 1973 as part of Denmark – opted to leave.
- *Whether or not to accept a new treaty.* This has only been a recent phenomenon, and only in a select few countries. Denmark held a vote on the Single European Act in 1986, mainly because the government wanted to outmanoeuvre parliament, which had voted against ratification. Most Danes (56.2 per cent) said yes on that occasion, but a bare majority of 50.7 per cent turned down Maastricht in 1992, and 54 per cent of Irish voters turned down the Treaty of Nice in 2001. The negative votes gave Europeans pause for thought, and resulted in changes to the treaties. New referenda in both countries subsequently went in favour of the treaties. The Danish vote on Maastricht also drew attention to the elitist nature of EU decision making, and obliged European leaders to think more about public opinion. Referenda were also held in 1998 in Denmark and Ireland on the terms of the Amsterdam treaty, and both were positive.

Just as important as the result of some of these referenda has been the symbolism often attached to the *absence* of referenda. The issue of adopting the euro was particularly controversial, and was put to a vote in just two countries, Denmark and Sweden, where the outcomes were both negative. Meanwhile, none of the 12 governments that opted to join the euro held a referendum, typically for fear of a similar result. The Blair administration in Britain has promised a referendum when the time is right, but has so far demurred, again mainly for fear of a negative vote; the Eurobarometer 61 poll (2004) found 61 per cent of Britons opposed to adopting the euro.

The next few years promise to be busy on the referendum front, with many of the 25 member states (including Britain, the Czech Republic, France, Ireland, Portugal, and Spain) holding national votes on whether or not to ratify the draft constitution. It promises to be a bumpy road, with the real possibility of more than one country voting no. How long the constitution will be able to hold up in the face of public opposition remains to be seen.

Interest groups

While national leaders promote national agendas, non-governmental organizations – or interest groups – have cut across national frontiers to promote the shared sectional interests of groups of people in multiple member states. In addition to the EU bodies that represent these interests, such as the Economic and Social Committee and the Committee of the Regions (see Box 4.2, page 95), the last 20–25 years have seen the growth of hundreds of non-governmental organizations that represent the views of a large number of groups of people with a stake in EU policy and law. Many are an outgrowth of preexisting national groups, others have been set up specifically to respond to European issues, and many have opened offices in Brussels in order to be close to the Commission and the Council of Ministers. Studies in the 1990s indicated that there were nearly 700 groups working to influence decisions taken at the European level, about two-thirds of which had existed since 1980 or earlier. Just over 60 per cent were business groups, 21 per cent dealt with public interest issues and 16 per cent were professional organizations (Aspinwall and Greenwood, 1998).

The growth in interest group activity at the European level has paralleled the growth in the power and influence of the EU institutions, or the 'Europeanization' of policy areas that were once the reserve of national governments (Mazey and Richardson, 1996, p. 200). The groups have not always simply followed the evolution of the EU, going wherever new opportunities for influence have presented themselves, but have often been actively involved in pushing the EU in new directions. Business leaders, for example, were champions of the single market, arguing that competition among European corporations was a handicap to their ability to take on the Americans and the Japanese. At the same time, the European Commission has encouraged interest group activity; it uses groups as a source of expert knowledge and to test the viability of new laws, and also uses them to monitor the compliance records of member states: most groups are only too happy to blow the whistle on their home governments if they are not implementing EU law.

Historically, business and labour groups have been the most active, mainly because the process of integration was for so long driven by economic issues (Greenwood, 2003). As the EU won new powers over competition policy, mergers, and the movement of workers, so business and labour groups made greater efforts to influence the Commission and the Council of Ministers. Not only are individual corporations represented either directly or through lobbying firms in Brussels, but several cross-sectoral federations have been created to represent the interests of a broader membership. These include the Union of Industrial and Employers' Confederations of Europe (UNICE, which represents 32 national business federations from 22 countries), the European Round Table of Industrialists (which brings together the chief executives of major European corporations such as Fiat, Philips, ICI and Siemens), and the EU Committee of the American Chamber of Commerce (which represents American firms active in Europe).

Labour is also represented in Brussels, notably through groups such as the European Trade Union Confederation (ETUC), whose membership consists of European-level industry federations, and national labour federations, such as Britain's TUC or Germany's DGB. Professional interests are represented by groups such as the Council of European Professional and Managerial Staff (EUROCADRES), and by associations representing everything from architects to dentists, journalists, opticians and vets. Several Brussels-based interest groups include member organizations from outside the EU, a reflection of how much the EU has come to matter to business and labour throughout Europe.

Groups representing public interests, such as consumer issues and the environment, have also become more active as the EU has become more involved in matters about which they care. Until the 1970s, environmental groups focused their attentions on national governments, because they had different priorities, and because most environmental policy in western Europe was still made at the national level. As the Community became more active on the environment in the mid-1980s, it became a more profitable target for interest group pressure. The new emphasis given to EU-level activities was reflected in the opening of offices in Brussels in the second half of the 1980s by such groups as Friends of the Earth,

Greenpeace, and the World Wide Fund for Nature, while many other groups employed full-time lobbyists. As environmental groups became more active, so did groups representing the industrial perspective on environmental issues, such as the European Chemical Industry Council, Eurelectric, and the European Crop Protection Association.

Increased access to EU policy makers led in turn to a more systematic approach among environmental groups to Euro-lobbying, and a clear trend towards approaching domestic environmental problems as EU-wide problems. The complexity of those problems encouraged domestic groups to work more closely together and to form transnational coalitions, the best known of which is the European Environmental Bureau (EEB). Founded in 1974 with the encouragement of the Commission, the EEB is an umbrella body for national interest groups in the EU, and acts as a conduit for the representation of those groups in the EU institutions, particularly the Commission. The Bureau now claims to represent more than 130 national environmental groups with a combined membership of 23 million (for more information, see McCormick, 2001, pp. 116–22).

The methods that Euro-groups use are similar to those used by groups at any level: promoting public awareness in support of their cause, building membership numbers in order to increase their influence and credibility, representing the views of their members, forming networks with other interest groups, providing information to the EU institutions, meeting with EU lawmakers in an attempt to influence the content of law, and monitoring the implementation of EU law at the national level.

Aspinwall and Greenwood (1998) argue that the representation of interests at the European level has become more diversified and specialized, and that Euro-groups are becoming protagonists – they now try to influence policy rather than simply to monitor events, using increasingly sophisticated means to attract allegiance. A symbiotic relationship has developed between the Commission and interest groups, with the former actively supporting the work of many groups and giving them access to its advisory committee meetings, and the latter doing what they can to influence the content and development of policy and legislative proposals as they work their way through the Commission.

The activities of interest groups have helped offset the problem of the democratic deficit by offering Europeans channels outside the formal structure of EU institutions through which they can influence EU policy. They have also helped focus the attention of the members of interest groups on how the EU influences the policies that affect their lives, have helped draw them more actively into the process by which the EU makes its decisions, and have encouraged them to bypass their national governments and to focus their attention on European responses to shared and common problems.

Improving accountability

European integration began as an agreement among government leaders to cooperate in selected policy areas, all the key decisions being taken by those leaders or their representatives. Even as its impact broadened, it remained an elite-driven process, and although citizens now have more influence over the decisions taken by the EU, public opinion is still marginalized. National leaders are held accountable through national elections, party competition, and media comment, but voters have little direct impact on the decisions those leaders take in their name at the European level. EU institutions continue to use a decision-making structure that is out of step with new realities, a problem that undermines the credibility and effectiveness of the European Union. As Featherstone (1994, p. 168) puts it, the elitist and technocratic character of institution-building might have served its purpose in the 1950s, but its continuation 'threatens instability and an increasing lack of legitimacy in the system'.

The reform of European institutions has been on the agenda of several European Council meetings, but progress to date has been limited by the desire of the governments of the member states to keep as much control as possible over the decisions taken in the name of European integration. The discussions leading up to the Amsterdam treaty were an opportunity to address the problem, but they resulted in little substantial change: the equal roles of Parliament and the Council of Ministers in the legislative process were recognized, the legislative process in Parliament was simplified, the powers of the Court of Justice were extended over such issues as asylum, immigration and cooperation in police and judicial matters, and the powers of the Court of Auditors and the Committee of the Regions were increased. The Treaty of Nice was another opportunity to look at how the institutions worked, but produced only changes to the numbers instead of fundamental structural change. The draft constitution does little more than build on the ideas introduced by Amsterdam and Nice.

Given that integration is now having so much more impact on the lives of Europeans, it is time for a new effort to be made to improve public understanding of the structure of the EU, and to improve the public accountability of the EU institutions. To date, the powers of EU institutions have been allowed to grow in response to the evolving interests of the EU, but the EU has now become active in so many areas, and is having an impact on so many aspects of the lives of Europeans, that the links between the EU institutions and European voters need to be strengthened. Possible reforms might include the following:

- The European Parliament should become a true legislature. For this to happen the power to initiate the law-making process would have to shift from the Commission to Parliament, and Parliament would have to be given greater power over decisions on the EU budget. It should also be sited exclusively and permanently in Brussels, so that it is close to the Commission and the Council of Ministers.

- The Council of Ministers should be replaced by a second, upper chamber of Parliament, providing a different level of representation from that offered by the present chamber. It might be something like the United States Senate, where every state has the same number of representatives, irrespective of size, or the German Bundesrat, where the number of representatives varies roughly according the population of each state. Alternatively, because it would be difficult to justify giving 400,000 Maltese the same representation as 82 million Germans, the upper chamber might be based instead on the internal regions of the member states, or on sectoral interests such as industry and the professions. The former have already been given advisory powers through the Committee of the Regions, and the latter through the Economic and Social Committee, so the new chamber might evolve out of one or both of these committees. However the upper chamber is structured, it should have the same powers over legislation as the lower – all proposals would have to go through the same process of introduction, discussion, amendment, and adoption before they could become law.

- The president of the European Commission should be directly elected by all eligible voters for a limited number of terms, and should have the right to appoint his or her own commissioners (either from inside Parliament or – with Parliamentary approval – from outside). The Amsterdam treaty included an agreement that the president be given greater powers over selecting commissioners and exercising policy leadership, and changes made under Nice will allow the president to reshuffle the membership of the College. Given the growing executive powers of the presidency, however, the time is fast approaching when the decision regarding who becomes president will be taken out of the hands of national government leaders and given to European voters.

- The powers of the European Commission should be focused on policy implementation. In other words, it should have the same role as a conventional bureaucracy, and be charged with ensuring the execution of laws developed and adopted by Parliament.

- Key appointments – including those to the Court of Justice, the Court of First Instance, the College of Commissioners, the European Central Bank, and other EU institutions – should be made subject to Parliamentary approval. Similarly, commissioners and directors-general should be called more often before Parliamentary committees to answer for their policy decisions and the performance of their departments.

The Amsterdam and Nice treaties fell short of meeting their primary objective of overhauling EU institutions in preparation for an expansion of membership. Much now rests with the constitution. Even if it is adopted, questions will still remain about the relationship between Europeans and the EU institutions.

Conclusions

The European Union has helped redefine the relationship among Europeans. Where they have long identified themselves in national terms, and have been tied economically, legally and culturally to one nation state or another, the reduction of the barriers to trade and to the movement of individuals over the past decade has encouraged Europeans to think of themselves as part of a larger entity with broader interests. Common policies have resulted in key powers over the lives of individual Europeans shifting to Brussels, so that an increasing number of Europeans feel the effect of decisions made at the EU level. Personal mobility has increased and, cultural barriers aside, Europeans have taken more interest in neighbours who have long been considered as 'foreign' rivals and occasionally a direct threat to their own national interests.

However, while this horizontal integration has been taking place, the vertical ability of Europeans directly to influence the European Union has lagged. Integration has been driven by the priorities and the values of the leaders of the member states, who have made most of their decisions with limited reference to their citizens. The result has been the creation of a European governing structure that is only indirectly accountable to the views of the people who live within it. European law is proposed and implemented by a European Commission whose leadership is not accountable to European voters. Key decisions on the adoption of new laws and policies are taken by national representatives meeting secretly as the Council of Ministers. The only institution that directly represents European citizens – the European Parliament – is denied the power to propose new laws, and must share the power to adopt new laws with the Council of Ministers.

Europeans are divided about the wisdom of integration, with only half of them agreeing that membership has been a 'good thing' for their country, and most of them admitting that they do not understand how the EU works. As European institutions struggle to sell the concept of integration to the citizens of the member states, they are handicapped by the absence of effective channels of accountability, and by the perpetuation of the democratic deficit. Changes made under the People's Europe programme and as a result of new treaties have made Europe more real to its citizens, but uniform passports, a European flag, and student exchange programmes fall far short of the kinds of changes needed to make Europeans feel as though they are truly connected to the EU. The democratic deficit can only be addressed by a wholesale reform of the EU institutions aimed at making them accountable to the citizens of Europe instead of to the leaders of the member states. But this is something that few national leaders would willingly contemplate even if their citizens were more enthusiastic than they appear to date.

Chapter 7

Economic Policy

The single market
Effects of the single market
Inside the euro zone
Conclusions

The single market was the theme of the Eighties. The single currency was the theme of the Nineties. We must now face the difficult task of moving towards a single economy, a single political unity.
Romano Prodi, European Commission president, 1999

Economic issues have dominated the life and work of the European Union. Beginning with the experiment in pooling coal and steel production, and moving through the customs union, the Common Agricultural Policy, exchange rate stability, the single market, and the single currency, the EU agenda has been driven in large part by matters involving trade, tariffs, markets, currencies, competition, and labour mobility. It has only been relatively recently that the agenda of integration has broadened to include a wider variety of policy issues, from social affairs to the environment.

The priority given to economic integration was made clear from the outset in three of the primary goals of the Treaty of Rome:

- A customs union in which all tariff barriers and other obstacles to trade among EEC members would be removed, and agreement reached on a common external tariff so that all goods coming into the EEC – no matter where their point of entry – would be subject to the same costs and controls. A related goal was the agreement of a common commercial policy towards third countries (see Chapter 9).
- A European single (or common) market in which there was free movement of people, money, goods, and services. In order to set the groundwork for this, the member states had to develop a common competition policy by minimizing or abolishing state assistance to national industries so as to avoid economic distortions, breaking down monopolies and cartels, and harmonizing national health and safety standards.
- A common agricultural policy by which farmers were paid guaranteed prices for their produce, and agricultural markets were stabilized and food supplies assured.

The customs union was completed without much fanfare in 1968 with the agreement of a common external tariff, but non-tariff barriers to trade among the member states persisted, including variations in technical standards and quality controls, different health and safety standards, and different rates of indirect taxation. Prospects for the single market seemed to move beyond reach in the mid-1970s as recession encouraged member states to protect their national markets. Meanwhile, the Common Agricultural Policy soaked up Community spending, and led to massive overproduction by European farmers (see next chapter).

By the 1980s it had become clear that urgent action was needed to reverse the EC's relative economic decline, and a boost had to be given to the single market programme in order to respond to foreign competition. If duplication of effort could be reduced, joint research encouraged, trans-European corporate mergers promoted, and the final barriers to trans-European business removed (went the argument), Europe's economies could become more efficient and competitive, and its businesses more profitable. It was this change of thinking that produced the 1985 Schengen Agreement to remove border controls, the 1986 Single European Act aimed at completing the single market, the ongoing attempts to build exchange rate stability, and – in 2002 – the most important step towards the final construction of an integrated regional economy: the replacement by 12 member states of their national currencies with a single European currency, the euro.

The single market

At its summit in Brussels in February 1985, the European Council agreed that it was time to refocus on one of the original goals of the European Community: the completion of a single market in which there would be no barriers to trade. This had been so central to the identity and the purpose of the Community that throughout the 1960s and 1970s it was known interchangeably as the Common Market. The dream was to promote freedom of access and movement in four key areas:

- *People*: legal residents of EU member states would be allowed to live and work in any other member state, and have their professional qualifications recognized.
- *Money*: currency and capital would be allowed to flow freely across borders, and EU residents could use financial services in any EU country.
- *Goods*: businesses could sell their products throughout the EU, and consumers would be free to buy those products in any member state without incurring costs or penalties.

- *Services*: every kind of service – from architecture to banking, insurance, legal aid, medicine and beyond – could be offered in any member state, regardless of the home base of the provider.

However, worryingly little progress had been made, mainly because the member states continued to go their own ways on economic strategy, protecting national markets and corporations, and wrestling independently to deal with high unemployment, low investment, and slow growth. National monopolies in transport and communications largely bought services and products from national sources rather than seeking more competitive options outside their borders. Technical standards varied across the Community, adding a potent block to trade in merchandise. Member states had laws requiring foreign firms active within their borders to buy goods with local content. And a host of border and customs controls persisted, along with varying rates of value-added tax (see Neal and Barbezat, 1998, pp. 9–11).

As Community leaders sat down to meet in February 1985, Jacques Delors had just taken over as president of the Commission and was keen to see movement on the single market. Trade and industry commissioner Lord Cockfield oversaw the drawing up of a White Paper outlining the changes that needed to be made (Commission of the European Communities, 1985). This in turn became the basis of the Single European Act (SEA), the first significant change to the Treaty of Rome signed nearly thirty years before. It was discussed at an IGC between September 1985 and January 1986, signed in February 1986, and came into force in July 1987. Unlike the debates that were later to surround the development of the treaties of Maastricht, Nice, and Amsterdam, the SEA was a relatively uncontroversial document. Even the arch-Eurosceptic Margaret Thatcher was supportive: 'At last, I felt, we were going to get the Community back on course, concentrating on its role as a huge market, with all the opportunities that would bring to our industries' (Thatcher, 1993, p. 556). (She was later to change her mind.)

The fundamental goal of the SEA was to remove the remaining non-tariff barriers to the free movement of people, money, goods, and services by the end of 1992. These barriers took three main forms: physical, fiscal, and technical.

Physical barriers

The most obvious of the physical barriers to the single market were customs and border checks, which persisted at the EC's internal borders despite the agreement of the customs union in 1968. Member states still controlled the movement of people (they were particularly concerned about illegal immigrants – see Box 7.1), collected value-added tax and excise taxes on alcohol, tobacco, and luxury goods, enforced different health standards, controlled banned products, and tried to prevent the spread of animal and plant diseases. Not only were these checks expensive, inconsistent, and time-consuming, but they interfered with the free flow of people, goods, and services. They were also a psychological barrier to integration, reminding Europeans that they still lived in a region of independent nation states.

In 1984 France and Germany decided to accelerate the reduction of border checks, and in June 1985 joined the Benelux countries in signing the Schengen Agreement. Named for the town in Luxembourg near which it was signed, the Agreement set off a series of meetings among the five countries aimed at agreeing and implementing the measures needed to end internal border controls. It was to have come into effect in January 1990, but plans were delayed because of concerns in Germany about the status of East Germans following reunification in October, and because of problems setting up the computerized Schengen Information System (SIS), a database of undesirables whose entry to the Schengen area local officials wanted to control. A trial application began in early 1995, but the Agreement was to remain informal until the Treaty of Amsterdam brought it under the umbrella of the Union in 1997.

Once the trial application began, almost all customs and passport controls were eliminated by Schengen signatories, which by then included Austria, Greece, Italy, Portugal, and Spain. Denmark did not join until 1996 because of the potential impact of the agreement on the Nordic passport union of Denmark, Finland, Iceland, Norway, and Sweden. Following negotiations, all five Nordic union members signed on, bringing membership to 15. Britain has not yet joined, citing concerns about security and its special problems and needs as an island state, although it has opted into selected elements, including the SIS and police and legal cooperation on criminal matters. Ireland also has been unable to join because of its customs arrangements with Britain.

The agreement has not extended to the A-10; travel requires a passport or identity card, and internal border controls will only be removed once all parties are sure that the free movement of undesirables has been brought under control. The EU-15 have been allowed to keep their restrictions on the free movement of workers from eastern Europe for at least two years after accession, and potentially for as long as seven years. The result has been the creation of a four-tier Europe: the Schengen signatories, non-signatories, the A-10, and states outside the EU. Another complication has been added by the disruption of historical ties, travel, and the movement of goods between the A-10 and non-EU eastern European countries, creating

Box 7.1 Illegal immigration and terrorism

Just as the United States has long been a magnet for illegal immigrants from Mexico and Latin America, so the EU has the same kind of attraction for workers from eastern Europe, the Balkans, Turkey, North Africa, and the Middle East. The smuggling of people into the EU has become a major industry in recent years, with an estimated value of several billion euros annually. Run mainly by organized crime, the smuggling has grown as a result of a combination of the opening up of eastern Europe and the removal of internal borders among Schengen signatories. There are estimates that as many as half a million people are arriving in the EU each year, entering from North Africa, the Balkans, eastern Europe, and Russia via Spain, Italy, Austria, Germany, and Finland. Most of the illegal immigrants are Afghans, Albanians, Bangladeshis, Iranians, Iraqis, or Kurds. Once inside the EU, many claim to be refugees and apply for asylum (*The Economist*, 20 February 1999).

For its part, terrorism was a problem for Europeans long before Americans were made aware of its harsh brutality in September 2001. Multiple groups were at work in Europe as early as the 1960s and 1970s, ranging from Irish, Basque, and Corsican separatists to the Red Brigades in Italy, and the Red Army Faction and the Baader–Meinhof group in Germany. The cross-border control of terrorists had been discussed since 1975 by senior officials from justice and home affairs ministries, meeting biannually as the Trevi Group to exchange information. They gradually expanded their interests to take in other security threats, such as those posed by organized crime and football hooligans. A particular concern was the relative ease with which terrorists could enter the Community from third countries through those member states with the weakest border controls, such as Greece or Portugal. The threat of terrorism has obviously achieved a new prominence and notoriety since the terrorist attacks on the United States, although the EU has been less of a target than has the United States and US interests overseas.

In order to help deal with concerns arising from the removal of internal border checks, the member states have agreed common measures on visas, immigration, extradition, and political asylum, and have improved cooperation among national police forces, to which end the European Police Office (Europol) was created in 1995 (although it only formally began operations in 1998). Based in The Hague, Europol was initially defined as an intelligence service, responsible for gathering and analysing information about drug-trafficking in support of the work of national police forces. Its interests have since expanded to include terrorism, illicit trafficking in radioactive and nuclear materials and in people, illegal immigration, money laundering, and organized crime, not only from internal sources, but from Turkey, Poland, Russia, and Colombia. Modelled in part on Interpol, the worldwide police organization, Europol cannot carry out investigations or bring prosecutions. It is building a computer base of information that can be accessed by its liaison offices in the member states, and by national police forces in the interests of building cooperation across borders.

– in the words of Polish foreign minister Wlodzimierz Cimoscewicz – a 'glass curtain' between EU and non-EU states in the east (Buonanno and Deakin, 2004).

Fiscal barriers

Control over direct taxation – such as personal income tax and corporation tax – remains firmly in the hands of the government of the member states. For some, notably Britain, suggestions that responsibility for tax policy be shifted to the EU are rejected out of hand; in its approach to the discussions over the draft constitution, for example, the Blair administration described taxation as a 'red line' issue, signalling clearly that it was not open to negotiation. This has left the EU active only on issues relating to indirect taxation, such as excise duties and value-added tax (VAT), a form of sales tax. As regards the single market, the major fiscal barrier to its completion was different levels of indirect taxation, which caused distortion of competition and artificial price differences, thereby posing a handicap to trade. Thanks in part to the influence of the EEC, all member states introduced VAT in the 1970s, but rates in the 1980s varied from as low as 12 per cent in Luxembourg to as high as 22 per cent in Denmark. This was one reason why border controls on the movement of goods persisted: because VAT was paid at the point of purchase, refunds could be claimed for exported goods, and imports possibly subjected to additional charges.

There were also variations in the levels of excise duties among the member states, reflecting different levels of national concern about human health. In the 1980s, for example, smokers in France paid nearly twice as much on cigarettes as those in Spain, smokers in Ireland four times as much, and smokers in Denmark six times as much. The differences were a boon to tourism, because travellers from one country to another could often buy cheaper alcohol, tobacco products, and other consumer items to take home with them. However, the duties were another barrier to the single market.

In 1991 agreement was reached on a minimum rate of 15 per cent VAT, with lower rates on basic necessities such as food, and in 1992 various minimum rates were also agreed on excise duties. In July 1993 an agreement came into force whereby VAT was collected at the local rate in the country to which the goods and services were going. Agreement was subsequently reached on an EU-wide VAT system in which tax is collected only in the country of origin, the ultimate goal being a single rate of VAT, or at least variations within a very narrow band. Rates in 2004 ranged from a low of 16 per cent in Germany and Spain to a high of 25 per cent in Denmark, Hungary, and Sweden.

The idea of minimum rates of VAT has been relatively easy for political and public opinion to accept; much more difficult has been the suggestion that the EU work towards harmonizing tax rates in other areas, notably corporation tax or the setting of minimum withholding tax on savings. Such a suggestion was made by the finance ministers of Germany and France in late 1998, and was immediately opposed by their counterpart in Britain, Gordon Brown. Talk of tax harmonization, no matter how limited the scope, is seen by many as the first step towards the development of EU authority over the setting of income tax, a notion that is deeply troubling to many Euro-doubters.

Technical barriers

Among the most persistent barriers to the single market was the existence of different technical regulations and standards among the member states. Most were based on different safety, health, environmental, and consumer protection standards, and many seemed petty and inconsequential: different definitions of chocolate that prevented British chocolate being sold in many other member states, for example, or the insistence by Germans that no beer could be sold in Germany that did not meet domestic 'purity laws'. Many of these regulations were in the interests of consumer safety, and were thus welcome, but others were criticized for amounting to another form of economic protectionism. The Community tried to remove technical barriers by developing EC standards and encouraging member states to conform, but this was a time-consuming and tedious task, and did little to discourage the common image of interfering Eurocrats. Three breakthroughs helped clear many bureaucratic and political hurdles:

- A 1979 decision by the Court of Justice established the principle of mutual recognition, meaning that if a product met local standards in one country, it could not be blocked from another. West Germany had refused to import a French blackcurrant liqueur, Cassis de Dijon, on the grounds that its wine-spirit content was below the minimum set by the West German government for fruit liqueurs. The importer charged that this was a restriction on imports of a kind prohibited under the Treaty of Rome. The Court of Justice agreed, helping clear the way for free movement in goods and services, and greatly easing the workload for the Commission.
- The 1983 mutual information directive required member states to tell the Commission and the other member states if they planned to develop any new domestic technical regulations, and to allow the others three months to respond if they felt these would create new barriers to trade.

- The Cockfield report included a 'new approach' to technical regulation: instead of the Commission working out agreements on every rule and regulation, the Council of Ministers would agree laws with general objectives, and detailed specifications could then be drawn up by existing private standards institutes, such as the European Standardization Committee (CEN) and ETSI, the European Confederation of Posts and Telecommunications Administrations.

Progress has since been made on removing technical barriers to the single market in a wide variety of areas, from safety and operating standards for road vehicles to the content of processed food. Much work remains to be done in other areas, however, notably the kinds of technical differences that cannot be resolved by the marketplace. One of those involves the standardization of electrical goods and services. An international organization – now called the European Committee for Electrotechnical Standardization, or CENELEC – has been at work on this since just after the Second World War, and has been particularly busy since the signature of the SEA. Based in Brussels, CENELEC has been active in developing Europe-wide standards for performance and safety, and all 25 EU member states – along with Iceland, Norway, and Switzerland – are members. Although there are now more than 5,000 active CENELEC standards, it has been unable to address some of the broader problems that face European consumers moving across borders, such as different voltages (most of Europe uses 220 volts, but some localities use 110 volts), and electrical plugs and sockets whose design differs from one member state to another, obliging travellers to take an adapter with them wherever they go. There have been plans afoot since 1992 to develop a common plug, but the cost of rewiring homes and businesses throughout the EU will almost certainly be prohibitive.

An issue of recent interest has been the internet and electronic commerce. An e-commerce directive adopted by the EU in 2001 applied single market principles of free movement of services to e-commerce, allowing operators to provide services throughout the EU. Many of the issues in the directive were technical, including protection of personal data and rules on unsolicited email advertising and the use of online contracts. The EU has also been keen to see reductions in the costs of using the internet, the integration and liberalization of telecommunications markets, and internet access for all schools in the EU. In an effort to improve trans-European links and to pave the way for increased traffic, basic telephone services have been liberalized in most member states, work is under way on an Integrated Service Digital Network which would allow the transmission of voice, data, and images through telephone lines, and member states are being encouraged to remove the need for different sets of licences and regulatory approval, and to end monopolies on mobile phone services.

Effects of the single market

The Single European Act was, in its time, the most radical of all the steps taken in the process of European integration since the signing of the treaties of Paris and Rome. It not only accelerated the process of economic integration, but it also changed the lives of every European, making economic integration more real to millions of people.

Rights of residence

As noted in Chapter 6, the Treaty of Rome allowed Europeans only limited rights to move for any length of time from one member state to another. Migration was seen mainly in economic terms; it was tied to occupation, and anyone who wanted to move to another member state was assessed on the basis of the skills they brought. Since the completion of the single market, the situation has been very different: almost any legal resident of an EU member state can now live and work in any other EU member state, open a bank account, take out a mortgage, transfer unlimited amounts of capital, and even vote (in some countries) in local and European elections. A few restrictions remain on EU-15 residents, but they are relatively minor. For example, students are given annual residence permits, must be enrolled in a course of study, and must be able to support themselves. Retirees and people of independent means are given five-year renewable residence permits, and pensions are not yet entirely mobile, although work has been under way to make it possible for workers to move their pensions with them. As noted earlier, there are greater restrictions on A-10 residents, because of concerns about migration, but these will ease with time.

Joint ventures and corporate mergers

One of the most notable effects of the single market has been to encourage European corporations to launch joint ventures or to merge with businesses in other EU states in order to build a European base. Companies typically merge for one of four reasons: they want to take over smaller rivals in order to grow bigger, they are looking for larger partners with capital for investment, they want to cut costs by cutting payroll and services, or they are on the defensive because competitors have merged. The single market has removed many of the protections once offered by national governments, with the result that European corporations have been encouraged to become more competitive at the global level, regaining some of the ground that they lost to American and Japanese competition during the 1960s and 1970s.

Transnational corporate mergers have long been a feature of the European business landscape – creating such giants as Unilever and Royal

Dutch/Shell (both Anglo-Dutch), or Asea Brown Boveri (Swedish–Swiss) – but the process has accelerated in the last few years. By 2002, about one-third of the companies listed in the *Fortune* magazine list of the world's 100 biggest were European (including Allianz, Volkswagen, and Siemens from Germany, Total Fina Elf and Carrefour from France, and the Dutch company ING). Where the five biggest of those companies (by revenues) in the late 1990s were American, by mid-2002, two had been displaced by European corporations: BP of Britain (ranked second in mid-2004), and Royal Dutch/Shell (ranked fourth in mid-2004).

The single market programme helped push competitiveness to the top of the European agenda, and the Commission in the late 1980s had become actively involved in trying to overcome market fragmentation and the emphasis placed by national governments on promoting the interests of often state-owned 'national champions'. The Community also launched new programmes aimed at encouraging research in information technology, advanced communications, industrial technologies, and weapons manufacture (Tsoukalis, 1997, pp. 49–51). The single market has helped take down many of the barriers that national corporations once faced, and increased the number of consumers they can reach. The euro has also made it easier for companies in search of acquisitions to borrow money and buy other companies, which has combined with privatization programmes in many countries and the general trend towards globalization to greatly increase the number of acquisition opportunities, joint ventures, and corporate mergers, both within the EU and between European and non-European corporations.

Notable joint ventures have included those between Thompson of France and Philips of the Netherlands on high-definition television, Pirelli of Italy and Dunlop of Britain on tyres, BMW and Rolls-Royce on aeroengines, and among the members of the European Space Agency (ESA). Set up in 1973 in an attempt to promote European cooperation in space research, the ESA now has 15 members: Switzerland, Norway, and all the EU-15 members except Greece and Luxembourg. Europe has also offered competition to the Americans in the field of satellite launching; 12 European countries have worked together in the development of Arianespace, a space-launch consortium owned by governments and state-owned companies (France has a stake of just over 50 per cent). Since the launch of the first in its series of Ariane rockets in 1979 from Kourou in French Guiana, Arianespace has taken over more than half the global market for commercial satellite launches, eating into a business long dominated by the United States. Current prospects are uncertain, however, following the mixed track record of the Ariane 5 launcher, and growing competition from China and India.

Box 7.2 Europe and the aerospace industry

Few areas of multinational business have seen quite such dramatic change in recent years as the aerospace industry, where rationalization, competition, and other economic pressures have cut the number of large civilian aircraft producers in the world from dozens to just two. Famous names of western European aviation – from Vickers to Hawker Siddeley, Messerschmitt and Dassault – have all gone. In Britain, alone, the 19 aircraft producers of the 1940s had been whittled down by 1986 to just one, British Aerospace (Owen and Dynes, 1992, pp. 162–3). The same kind of pressures have led to similar changes in the United States, where Lockheed now focuses on military aircraft and McDonnell-Douglas was taken over in 1997 by Boeing, now the only remaining American manufacturer of large civilian aircraft.

Much of the responsibility for the changes on both sides of the Atlantic lies with the success of Airbus, a European consortium founded in 1970, and whose share of the new civil aircraft market has grown since 1975 from 10 per cent to more than 50 per cent. The Airbus consortium is 80 per cent owned by the European Aeronautic Defence and Space company (EADS), created in 2000 by a merger between Aérospatiale Matra of France, DaimlerChrysler Aerospace of Germany, and Construcciones Aeronauticas (CASA) of Spain; the remaining 20 per cent is owned by BAE Systems of Britain. Airbus produces a line of 12 different airliners, the newest being the controversial 555–seat double-decker A380, the world's largest passenger aircraft, which is currently under construction.

The creation of both Airbus and EADS was prompted by the argument that economies of scale were giving American manufacturers an advantage over their European competitors, whose national markets were too small to sustain them. Similar arguments have encouraged transnational cooperation in western Europe on military aircraft and missiles. Individual member states still make competitive products, such as France's Mirage jet fighters, and Britain's Harrier jump jets, but are finding that it makes better commercial sense to pool resources. Successful collaborations include production of the Tornado fighter-bomber and the Eurofighter, both made by a consortium of EADS and Italy's Alenia (which together have 63 per cent interest), and BAE Systems (37 per cent). In April 2001, BAE, EADS, and Finmeccanica of Italy joined forces to create MBDA, the world's second largest producer of missiles after Raytheon of the United States.

The growth of new pan-European businesses seeking to profit from the opportunities offered by the single market, and looking to create 'world-size' companies to compete more effectively with the United States and Japan, has led to a surge in merger and acquisition activities, notably in the chemicals, pharmaceuticals, and telecommunications industries. In 1989–90 the number of intra-EC mergers overtook the number of national mergers for the first time (Owen and Dynes, 1992, p. 222), since when the European mergers and acquisitions market has grown to be bigger than that in the United States. Notable recent examples are:

- The mergers among a number of British, Canadian and American pharmaceuticals companies to create GlaxoSmithKline.
- A string of takeovers by the French insurance company AXA, now ranked among the three dozen biggest corporations in the world.
- A series of takeovers by the Royal Bank of Scotland – including those of Britain's National Westminster bank, Irish mortgage company First Active, and Charter One bank of the United States – that have made RBS the world's fifth largest bank.
- The mergers and acquisitions which in the space of two years transformed Britain's Vodaphone into one of the world's biggest mobile phone businesses. In 1999 it merged with the US company AirTouch, then with Bell Atlantic in the US to create America's biggest wireless service. In 2000 it took over the much larger German company Mannesmann, which had earlier taken over Orange, Britain's third biggest mobile phone company.
- The mergers in 2003 between Air France and the Dutch airline KLM, and between Britain's P&O Princess and Carnival of the United States to create the world's largest cruise vacation group.
- The 2004 merger between Securicor of Britain and Group 4 Falck of Denmark to create the world's second-largest security company.

The new opportunities offered at home have been accompanied by remarkable growth in the flows of foreign direct investment both into the EU, and from the EU into other countries. In the period 1994–2003, there was more than $3 trillion invested in the EU-15, or more than twice the amount that was invested over the same period in the United States. Belgium/Luxembourg, Britain and France were the main targets, drawing in more than half the EU total among them. In terms of outflows, the EU in that period invested nearly $3.9 trillion, or nearly three times the amount invested by the United States, and nearly 15 times the amount invested by Japan. The biggest spenders were Britain ($879 billion), France ($653 billion) and Germany ($452 billion) (OECD figures, 2004). Among the more notable examples of European companies reaching outside the EU to create large new corporations are:

- The 1998 takeover by British Petroleum of Amoco in the United States, and the subsequent merger between BP Amoco and Atlantic Richfield.
- The 1999 takeover by Germany's Daimler of the US automobile manufacturer Chrysler.

- The 2000 takeover by Germany's Deutsche Telekom of Voicestream in the United States.

Of course, bigger is not necessarily better, because takeovers can reduce competition and consumer choice, and run the danger of creating industries that dominate or monopolize a particular sector of the economy. There are also many examples of international mergers failing, sometimes because they have added little value to the participating companies, and sometimes because of language and cultural problems. Out of a concern to make sure that bigger corporations do not become too dominant, the EU has developed a controversial competition policy to avoid abuses such as price-fixing, and to watch out for 'abuses of a dominant position' by bigger companies (Cini and McGowan, 1998). The 1989 merger regulation allows the European Commission to scrutinize all large mergers (even those involving companies based outside the EU that might have an effect on EU business), and the Commission also keeps an eye on the effect of state subsidies on competition in trade (Allen, 1996), and watches for domestic laws that interfere with competition; for example, in 2003–04 it ordered Germany to cancel a law adopted in the 1960s that prevented the vehicle manufacturer Volkswagen from being taken over by another company.

Reflecting the new economic influence of the EU at the global level, recent targets of Commission investigations have even included American corporations. World headlines were made in March 2004 when the Commission imposed a record fine of €479 million ($622 million) on the software-maker Microsoft, whose Windows operating system can be found in 90 per cent of the world's personal computers. The Commission accused Microsoft of abusing its dominant market position by bundling in its media player with its Windows operating system, thereby discouraging consumers from buying media players made by other companies. The Commission ordered Microsoft to begin offering within 90 days a version of Windows without the media player installed, and to reveal its Windows software codes so that rival companies could more easily design compatible products. Not surprisingly, Microsoft appealed the decision.

Even mergers within the United States have been the target of Commission action: a proposed merger in 2000 between telecom companies MCI/WorldCom and Sprint was blocked by the Commission for fear that two American companies would dominate internet operations in the EU (the merger was eventually abandoned), and another in 2001 between General Electric and Honeywell was blocked by the Commission out of concern for its implications for the market in aircraft jet engines. But the Commission approved the 2002 merger between computer makers Hewlett-Packard and Compaq.

A European transport system

An important element in the successful operation of markets is integrated infrastructure, such as transport, energy, and communications networks. Realizing this, the EU has been actively involved in the development of trans-European networks (TENs) aimed at integrating the different transport, energy supply, and telecommunications systems of the member states. Until 1987, harmonization of the transport sector was one of the great failures of the single market: little of substance had been done to deal with problems such as an airline industry split along national lines (see below), time-consuming cross-border checks on trucks, national systems of motorways that did not connect with each other, air traffic control systems using 20 different operating systems and 70 computer programming languages, and telephone lines incapable of carrying advanced electronic communications. Two phenomena have since begun to make a difference.

First, there has been a dramatic increase in tourism. Not only is Europe the biggest tourist destination in the world, capturing nearly 60 per cent of the world tourist trade (World Tourism Organization figures, 2004), but – even in spite of recent concerns about terrorism – Europeans are now travelling in much greater numbers to each other's countries, which has helped break down prejudices, made Europeans more familiar with each other, and encouraged greater cooperation on transportation by increasing the demand for cheap and easy access. Tourism now employs 21.5 million Europeans (about 13 per cent of the workforce in the EU), and generated revenues in 2004 of about $1.42 trillion, or just under 12 per cent of the GDP of the EU (World Travel and Tourism Council figures, 2004). France and Spain are the two biggest tourist destinations in the world, and Italy, Britain, Austria, and Germany are all ranked in the top ten.

Second, rail transport has been revitalized as a cost-efficient and environmentally friendly alternative to road and air transport. The EU has plans to develop a 35,000km high-speed train (HST) network connecting Europe's major cities, the way being led by France with its high-speed TGV, which needs special new track, and Germany with its ICE network, which can use existing track. With trains travelling at 200–300 kph (some of them with coaches finished to luxurious standards), the HST system has cut travel times considerably. Germany even has hopes over the long term of largely replacing domestic air flights with a system of very high-speed trains (VHSTs) based in part on floating mag-lev technology. Meanwhile, investments have been made in building the tunnels and bridges needed to ensure uninterrupted travel: the completion in 1994 of the $15 billion Eurotunnel under the channel between Britain and France and in 1998 of road/rail bridges linking Denmark and Sweden were important pieces in the jigsaw.

The development of TENs is now one of the priorities of the EU, and the European Commission has a programme aimed at improving transport links within the EU; it will cost a projected €400 billion by 2010, and will involve the building of 70,000km of railway track (including 22,000km of new and upgraded track for HSTs), and 15,000km of new roads, mainly on the outer edges of the EU. Among the priority projects identified by the European Council are a €20 billion north–south HST link between Berlin and Verona, a €13 billion HST link between Paris, Brussels, Cologne, Amsterdam, and London, new motorways for Greece, a motorway link between Portugal and Spain, and a 1400km Ireland–UK–Benelux road link.

Open skies over Europe

One of the most notable changes brought about by the single market programme has been the loosening of regulations on air transport (see Armstrong and Bulmer, 1998, Chapter 7). Because most European states are too small to support a significant domestic industry, the majority of air traffic in Europe is international. Until the 1980s, most European countries had state-owned national carriers – such as Air France, Lufthansa, and Alitalia – which played an influential role in making national air transport policy, and had a national monopoly over most of the international routes they flew; the result was that air transport was highly regulated, and very expensive to consumers.

Changes began in the mid-1980s when the Thatcher government launched a liberalization programme in Britain that led to the privatization of British Airways in 1987, and negotiated bilateral agreements with several other EU member states. Meanwhile, the European Civil Aviation Conference recommended liberalization, as did a number of national and European interest groups (notably those representing consumers' unions), and the idea was taken up in turn by the European Commission and incorporated into the Cockfield report. Britain was most actively in favour, while Germany and France provided limited support, and states with smaller or less efficient national carriers – such as Spain, Italy, and Denmark – were opposed. Against this background, three packages of laws and regulations worked their way through the EU institutions in 1987–92, which substantially opened up the market, and led to a restructuring of the air transport market.

Among the notable trends that have emerged in recent years are:

- An increase in the number of international airline alliances. These include Star (whose members include Lufthansa, Polish Airlines, Austrian, SAS of Scandinavia, and United Airlines), and Oneworld (involving British Airways, Ireland's Aer Lingus, Finnair, Spain's Iberia, and American Airlines). Their purpose is to cut costs, combine ticketing, and consolidate routes.

- Increased pressure for airlines to merge. In 2003, for example, after discussions first with British Airways, Swissair, and the Italian airline Alitalia, Dutch KLM merged with Air France to create Europe's biggest airline. There have also been rumours of British Airways merging with Iberia, and of Germany's Lufthansa taking over Swiss (the airline that replaced Swissair, which declared bankruptcy in 2002).
- A growth in the number of cut-price operators such as easyJet and Ryanair.

The results of these changes have included greater choice for consumers, who can now fly more cheaply than before. The more open markets, though, have not immunized European airlines against the economic downturn that has hit airline travel in recent years.

Considerable progress has been made since 1987 in moving towards the completion of the single market, but work still remains to be done. In June 1997, the Commission launched a Single Market Action Plan aimed at generating a political commitment for the decisive completion of the single market by January 1999. This divided remaining actions into three groups: those that could be implemented in the short run because they did not need new EU legislation, those that had already been proposed but still needed approval from Parliament and the Council of Ministers, and those that were more complex, such as a reworking of the VAT system. Much progress has been made on implementation of the nearly 1340 existing single market-related directives, but the implications of the single market are still not fully understood by Europeans or their leaders, and much still relies not so much on deliberate political decisions as on the pressures of the marketplace to reduce or remove remaining barriers.

A new set of challenges was introduced with eastern enlargement in 2004. The ten new members increased the population of the EU by 20 per cent, but its economic wealth by less than 5 per cent. They have brought greater social and economic diversity into the EU, but they have also widened the gap between wealth and poverty (see Chapter 8 for details). Their rural populations are typically bigger than those of the EU-15, unemployment rates are higher, there has been less investment in infrastructure and communications, and their labour force is less educated. In the years leading up to accession, they made so many changes to their trade and investment policies that – it has been argued – they have already felt most of the economic effects of enlargement, they are already competing in the single market, and there is already free movement of money, goods, and services (but not labour) (Grabbe, 2004). However, improvements in competitiveness are still needed, as well as investments in infrastructure and worker education. Eastern Europe provides many market opportunities, but there are also many challenges that lie ahead.

Inside the euro zone

In March 2002, after years of controversy and often difficult economic adjustment, 12 of the 15 EU member states took one of the most far-reaching steps so far in the history of integration: they abolished their separate national currencies and replaced them with the new European currency, the euro. It was a move that was a long time coming, meeting considerable political resistance along the way and causing economic problems for several member states, and yet it was driven by the understanding that few barriers to the completion of the single market were so fundamental as the existence of 15 different currencies with fluctuating exchange rates. At the same time, the surrender of national currencies posed many troubling questions about sovereignty and independence, because by giving up their national currencies, the governments of the 12 countries in the euro zone were agreeing to give up control over important domestic economic policy choices, such as the ability to be able to adjust interest rates. Critics also saw the adoption of the euro as another step towards the creation of a unified system of government.

It was understood as early as the 1950s that stable exchange rates would be an important part of the functioning of a single market. Fortunately, that stability was provided by the postwar system of fixed exchange rates. It was only when this system began to crumble in the late 1960s, and finally collapsed with the US decision in 1971 to end the link between gold and the US dollar, that monetary union – the agreement of fixed exchange rates and a single currency – began to move up the agenda of European integration. A committee headed by Luxembourg prime minister Pierre Werner met in 1969–70 to discuss the issue, and concluded that the Community should work towards adopting a single currency in stages by 1980. Community heads of government agreed, and attempts were made using a mechanism called the 'snake in the tunnel' to keep exchange rates steady against each other, and jointly against the US dollar. But international currency turbulence in the wake of the energy crises of the 1970s undermined their efforts, and by 1977 only five of the 12 Community member states were still in the scheme.

A renewed attempt to achieve exchange rate stability and keep inflation under control was made in March 1979 with the launch of the European Monetary System (EMS). An artificial currency called the European

Box 7.3 The European Central Bank

Although it has – until recently – been one of the least known of the EU institutions, the ECB is now playing an important role in the lives of Europeans with the euro having replaced most national currencies. As it has become increasingly involved in the direction of European monetary policy, however, worrying questions have been raised about its powers, and about the lack of effective checks on those powers.

First proposed in 1988, the framework of the Bank was described in the Maastricht treaty. It was founded in 1994 as the European Monetary Institute (EMI), and it was finally established in June 1998 as the European Central Bank. Based in Frankfurt, its main job is to ensure monetary stability by setting interest rates in the euro zone. It has a governing body consisting of the central bank governors from each participating state, and a six-member full-time executive board. Directors serve non-renewable terms of eight years and can only be removed by their peers or by an order from the European Court of Justice. The Bank also has links to non-participating countries through a general council composed of the central bank governors of all EU member states. A new exchange rate mechanism (ERM II) links the euro with the national currencies of non-participating countries, and the ECB is allowed to take action to support non-participating countries so long as this does not conflict with its primary task of maintaining monetary stability among participating countries.

Concerned about the need to convince the sceptical German public that the new European currency would be as strong as the Deutschmark (Daltrop, 1987, pp. 175–6), Helmut Kohl insisted that the ECB should be an almost direct copy of the famously independent German Bundesbank. In fact, it makes the Bundesbank seem quite restricted by comparison, and was by 1998 already being described as 'the most powerful single monetary authority in the world' (*European Voice*, April 1998). Neither national nor EU leaders are allowed to try to influence the Bank, its board, or its constituent national central banks, and the only body that can play any kind of watchdog role over the Bank is the monetary subcommittee of the European Parliament, but it so far lacks the resources to be able to hold the Bank or its president – Jean-Claude Trichet of France – particularly accountable. This makes it very different from the United States Federal Reserve, whose chairman is regularly brought to account for its policies before the banking committee of the US Senate.

Currency Unit (ecu) was created, whose value was based on a basket of European currencies, each weighted roughly according to the size of the economies of the different member states (the Deutschmark made up about 30 per cent of the ecu, the British pound about 11–15 per cent, the Italian lira about 9 per cent, and so on). Exchange rates between member states were set in ecus, and countries in the EMS undertook to make sure that those rates fluctuated by no more than 2.25 per cent either way, using a regulatory scheme know as the Exchange Rate Mechanism (ERM). Although several member states again found it difficult to keep their currencies stable relative to the ecu, the EMS contributed to exchange rate stability in the 1980s, and to the longest period of sustained economic expansion since the war. The ecu also helped accustom Europeans to the idea of a single currency.

In 1989 a plan developed under the leadership of Commission president Jacques Delors proposed another staged move towards a single currency: all member states would join the ERM, the band of exchange rate fluctuations would be narrowed and then fixed irrevocably, and the ecu would become the new single currency. Despite the near-collapse of the ERM in 1992–93 – when Britain and Italy pulled out, several other countries had to devalue their currencies, and the bands of exchange rate fluctuation had to be widened to 15 per cent – the Maastricht treaty affirmed the basic principles behind the Delors plan. EU member states wanting to adopt the single currency had to meet several 'convergence criteria' that were considered essential prerequisites:

- A national budget deficit of less than 3 per cent of GDP.
- A public debt of less than 60 per cent of GDP.
- A consumer inflation rate within 1.5 per cent of the average in the three countries with the lowest rates.
- A long-term interest rate within 2 per cent of the average in the three countries with the lowest rates.
- A record of keeping their exchange rates within approved ERM fluctuation margins for two years.

Meeting at the Madrid European Council in December 1995, EU leaders decided to call the new currency the euro, and agreed to introduce it in three stages. The first stage came in May 1998 when it was determined which countries were ready: all member states had met the budget deficit goal, but only seven member states had met the debt target, Germany and Ireland had not met the inflation reduction target, and Greece had not been able to reduce its interest rates sufficiently. Maastricht, however, included a clause that allowed countries to qualify if their debt-to-GDP ratio was 'sufficiently diminishing and approaching the reference value at a satisfactory pace'.

In the event, despite the fact that the national debt in Belgium and Italy was nearly twice the target, all but Britain, Denmark (both of which had met all the criteria), Greece and Sweden announced their intention to adopt the euro. Questions were raised in the minds of Eurosceptics about the seriousness with which member states were approaching the convergence criteria, the wisdom of which had already been questioned by many economists. There were also concerns about the extent to which efforts by governments to meet the criteria had contributed to economic problems in several EU states (notably Germany), and therefore about the strength of the foundations upon which the euro was built.

The second stage came in 1 January 1999 when the euro was officially launched, participating countries fixed their exchange rates, and the new European Central Bank began overseeing the single monetary policy. All its dealings with commercial banks and all its foreign exchange activities were subsequently transacted in euros, and the euro was quoted against the yen and the US dollar. Pause for thought was provided in September 2000 when, in a national referendum, Danes voted against their country adopting the euro. Polls also showed that a majority of Swedes were against adoption, and in Britain found opposition running at three to one. Concerns also arose when the value of the euro against other currencies fell steadily: its value against the US dollar fell from $1.17 to as low as 85 cents. Nonetheless, plans for the transition proceeded, with the printing of 14.5 billion euro banknotes and the minting of 56 billion coins. In January 2001 Greece became the twelfth member state to join the euro zone, having met the targets for reduced inflation and budget deficits.

The final stage began on 1 January 2002, when euro coins and notes became available. The original plan had been for the euro and national currencies to be in concurrent circulation for six months, but it was subsequently decided that Europeans were to be given just two months to make the final transition from national currencies to the euro, and national currencies ceased to be legal tender in the euro zone on 1 March 2002. After centuries of fiscal independence, the 12 members of the euro zone made the final irrevocable step to abolish their national currencies, and Deutschmarks, drachmas, escudos, francs, guilders, liras, marks, pesetas, punts, and schillings faded into history.

In September 2003, a national referendum in Sweden went against that country adopting the euro (by a vote of 56 per cent to 42 per cent). Meanwhile, the Blair administration in Britain has declared itself in favour of joining the euro, and has promised a referendum on British membership, but the date is uncertain, public opinion in Britain is running firmly against the euro, and Britain's finance minister Gordon Brown has set five 'economic tests' for British membership. These include certainty about the compatibility of business cycles and economic structures, and being assured that joining would create better conditions for businesses making long-term decisions to invest in Britain, help the competitive position of the British financial services industry, and promote higher growth, stability, and a lasting increase in jobs. As for the A-10, all are committed to adopting the euro, but they must first show that they can participate fully in the single market, show progress towards achieving the conditions needed for adoption, and meet the convergence criteria. This is likely to take several years.

Opinions have been mixed on the benefits and costs of the euro, and it is probably safe to say that no one chapter in the history of European integration was approached with so many doubts remaining. Its introduction raised questions about the long-term economic effects for Europe, few of which are fully understood, even by economists. Among the benefits:

1. Instead of having to change currencies when they travel from one country to another, and paying for goods and services with unfamiliar banknotes and coins, travellers now use the same currency wherever they go in the euro zone, making them more aware of being part of the common enterprise of integration.
2. There is greater price transparency, because instead of costs being expressed in different currencies from one country to another, they are all expressed in euros, and consumers can make easy comparisons. This promotes competition as businesses try to make their goods and services available at similar prices throughout the euro zone.
3. There are fewer bureaucratic barriers to the transfer of large sums of money across borders, and businesses no longer have to spend time and money changing currency. This saves everyone transaction costs.
4. The stock and bond markets in the euro zone will likely continue their tendency to unify, and investors, instead of focusing on their home markets alone, will become used to the idea of a European stock market.
5. The euro is now a world class currency in the same league as the US dollar and the Japanese yen, providing the euro zone with a tool that allows it to have greater influence over global economic policy, rather than having to react to developments in the United States and Japan.

At the same time, the adoption of the euro has been a gamble. Never before has a group of sovereign states with a long history of independence tried combining their currencies into one on a similar scale, and the risks have been significantly greater than those involved in completing the single market. Furthermore, all the key preparatory decisions about the euro were taken by European national leaders with little or no regard to public opinion, which was often hostile to the idea, and uncertain about the implications. The potential costs of the euro include the following:

1. Different countries have different economic cycles, and separate currencies allow them to devalue, borrow, adjust interest rates, and take other measures in response to changed economic circumstances. Such flexibility is no longer available in the euro zone, because the

European Central Bank cannot follow different fiscal policies for different parts of the EU. The members of the euro zone must sink or swim together.

2. Some economists were concerned about the underlying weaknesses in EU economies in 1997–98, and raised questions about the extent to which figures relating to the convergence criteria were being fudged to allow countries that had not met those criteria to take part. Some feared that these weaknesses could result in a high-credibility Deutschmark being replaced with a low-credibility euro, undermining economic health throughout the EU. The most sceptical even doubted that all the euro-zone countries would be able to keep within the ERM.

3. Unless Europeans learn each other's languages and are able to move freely in search of jobs, the euro could perpetuate the pockets of poverty and wealth that already exist across the EU, thereby interfering with the development of the single market. Having a common currency in a country as big as the United States works mainly because people can move freely; this is not true of the EU, where there are still physical, fiscal, technical and social barriers to movement.

Some of the problems inherent in the euro became clear even before it was finally adopted, with the signature in 1997 – at the insistence of Germany – of the 'stability and growth pact'. Generated by concerns that governments in the euro zone might try to get around ECB monetary policies by increasing spending and running large budget deficits, the pact – which was signed by all 15 EU member states – required that they keep their budget deficits to less than 3 per cent of their gross domestic product, and placed a 60 per cent limit on government borrowing. Any country that was in breach of the pact could be fined by the European Commission. Unfortunately, recession came to most industrialized countries in 2002–03, and France, Germany, Italy and Portugal quickly found themselves either in breach of the deficit limit or running the danger of crossing the 3 per cent barrier; they were later joined by Greece and the Netherlands. While there was general agreement on the principle of the pact, there was criticism that it was too inflexible (in that it made no distinctions among countries with different economic bases) and that its focus on curbing inflation left it poorly equipped to deal with slow economic growth. Commission president Romano Prodi even went so far in October 2002 as to describe attempts to enforce the pact without taking heed of changing circumstances as 'stupid'.

By the second half of 2003 the European Central Bank was warning that most euro-zone countries were in danger of failing to meet the target on budget deficits, thereby damaging the prospects for economic growth. In November 2003, the two biggest euro-zone economies – France and

Germany – both broke the limits and prevented other EU finance ministers from imposing large fines on the two countries (a decision that was annulled by the European Court of Justice in July 2004). Its ministers, along with their British counterpart, argued that the rules of the pact were too rigid and needed to be applied more flexibly if they were to work. By December the pact had all but collapsed and new rules were being explored in 2004 to promote fiscal stability in the euro zone, including the granting of permission to selected countries in difficulties to temporarily carry larger deficits.

Conclusions

Although the work of the European Union has been driven most obviously by economic factors – and particularly by the goal of free trade in a single market – European leaders have found, through neofunctionalist logic, that economic integration has had a spillover effect on many other policy areas. Most notably, they have found that completion of the single market was a more complex notion than originally expected. The primary objective of the single market was the removal of tariffs and non-tariff barriers to trade, but behind that seemingly harmless term – non-tariff barriers – lay a multitude of problems, handicaps, and obstacles.

Among other things, economic integration has meant removing cross-border checks on people and goods, controlling the movement of drugs and terrorists, agreeing standard levels of indirect taxation, harmonizing technical standards on thousands of goods and services, agreeing regulations in the interests of consumer safety, reaching agreement on professional qualifications, allowing Europeans to take capital and pensions with them when they move to another country, opening up the European market for joint ventures and corporate mergers, developing trans-European transport and energy supply networks, providing the means by which Europeans can communicate with each other electronically, developing common approaches to working conditions, establishing common European environmental standards, promoting the development of poorer rural and urban areas in order to avoid trade distortions, and creating an equitable and efficient agricultural sector.

In a sense, however, everything that was agreed during the 1960s, the 1970s, and the 1980s – the thousands of decisions taken by prime ministers, chancellors, presidents, ministers, and European bureaucrats, and the thousands of directives, regulations, and decisions developed and agreed by the different EU institutions – was simply a prelude to the biggest project of all, the conversion to a single currency. In March 2002, 12 of the 15 member states abolished their national currencies and adopted the euro, while three – Britain, Denmark, and Sweden – opted to remain out, at least temporarily. Many questions remained about the wisdom of the positions taken both by the champions and the opponents. Have the former been too hasty in their decision to press on, regardless of their domestic economic problems? Are Britain and Denmark being wisely cautious or typically Eurosceptic in their decisions to wait and see? Will the adoption of the euro prove to be a disruptive step too far, or one of the most far-sighted and creative decisions ever taken by Europe's leaders? What impact will it have, directly or indirectly, on economic development in eastern Europe?

Whatever happens over the next few years, the single market has had widespread and irreversible implications for everyone living in the European Union, and for all the EU's trading partners. It has helped create new wealth and opportunity, has brought down many of the economic barriers that have for decades divided Europeans, and has paved the way for the creation of trans-European economic ties that have reduced national differences and promoted the idea of Europe as a powerful new actor on the world stage.

Chapter 8

Improving the Quality of Life

Building an even playing field
Agricultural policy
Regional policy
Social policy
Environmental policy
Conclusions

> *The European Dream, with its emphasis on inclusivity, diversity, quality of life, sustainability, deep play, universal human rights and the rights of nature, and peace is increasingly attractive to a generation anxious to be globally connected and at the same time locally embedded.*
>
> Jeremy Rifkin, *The European Dream* (2004)

For most of its early life, the work of the European Economic Community as its title implied – was focused on quantitative issues: rebuilding the economies of western Europe, agreeing a customs union and building a single market in order to promote economic development, and seeking ways to make the European marketplace more open, more efficient, more competitive, and more profitable. True, one of the core motivations was to improve the quality of life of the people of Europe, but this would be an effect rather than a primary motive.

It quickly became clear that wealth and efficiency would not be evenly distributed in the Community as long as there were differences in opportunity, economic and social standards, personal income, education, and the overall quality of life both within and among member states. There would be no level playing field on which Europeans could compete, some would be handicapped by local problems while others had easier access to jobs and wealth, and differences in regulatory standards, access to natural resources, access to funds for investment, and environmental quality would all stand as barriers to the completion or at least the effective operation of the single market.

For these reasons, the Community began to focus increasingly on qualitative issues, and on setting up the mechanisms needed to transfer resources to those parts of the Community suffering the most difficulties and the greatest handicaps. The result was the development of common policies in four major areas:

- *Agricultural policy*, which was factored in to the Treaty of Rome, was designed to ensure that Community farmers had a market for their produce. The Common Agricultural Policy eventually became the most expensive and the most controversial of all the activities undertaken jointly by the member states.
- *Regional policy*, which aims to even out the economic differences within and among the member states by regenerating old industrial areas, investing in rural development, and connecting producers and markets, was also an early goal of the Community. It was only in the 1970s, though, that it became a priority.
- *Social policy*, which focuses on issues relating to employment (encouraging job creation, the free movement of labour, improved living and working conditions, and the rights and benefits of workers) was all but ignored until the 1970s, when immigration and growing economic disparities made it more urgent.
- *Environmental policy*, concerns for which were all but unknown in the 1950s, but which grew in the 1960s as the air and water pollution created by economic growth promoted a reaction from increasingly affluent Europeans. Differences in environmental quality also posed a barrier to the single market, so that by the 1980s there was new support for addressing the problem.

This chapter, in contrast to the primarily economic issues covered in the pervious chapter, looks at the impact of European integration on the quality of life in Europe, and at the character of joint responses to shared or common problems.

Building an even playing field

As with all societies, the European Union contains many economic and social divisions. It is home to some of the wealthiest communities in the world, particularly in its major cities, but the rich do not have to look far to find decaying industrial areas, underdeveloped rural areas, pockets of poverty and high unemployment, and regions heavily dependent on low-profit agriculture or fisheries. This has been especially true since the 2004 enlargement, when 15 countries with a combined gross domestic product (GDP) of more than $8.5 trillion were joined by ten countries with a combined GDP of just over $400 billion.

The statistics clearly show the economic and social disparities with which the EU is struggling:

- Expressing the average per capita GDP for the EU as 100, levels varied in 2004 from a high in Luxembourg of 208 to lows in Estonia, Latvia,

Lithuania, Poland and Slovakia of about half the EU average (see Figure 8.1).

- Unemployment rates in mid-2003 ranged from a low of 4–5 per cent in Austria, Ireland, Luxembourg, and Britain to 9–10 per cent in Finland, France, and Germany, and to a high of 17–19 per cent in Poland and Slovakia (about twice the EU average) (see Figure 8.2).

Figure 8.1 *Per capita GDP in the European Union*

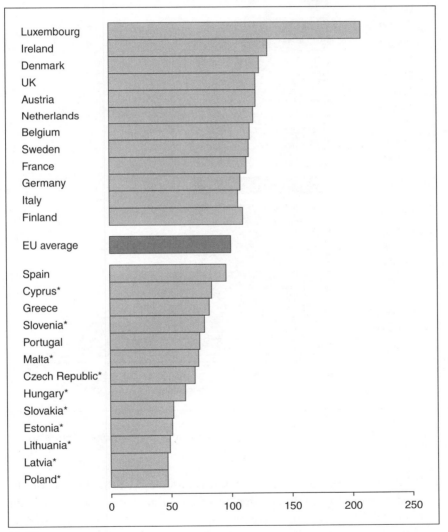

*A-10 states.
Source: Eurostat web page, http://europa.eu.int/comm/eurostat, 2004. Figures are for 2004, and are expressed in relation to the EU average of 100.

Figure 8.2   *Unemployment in the European Union*

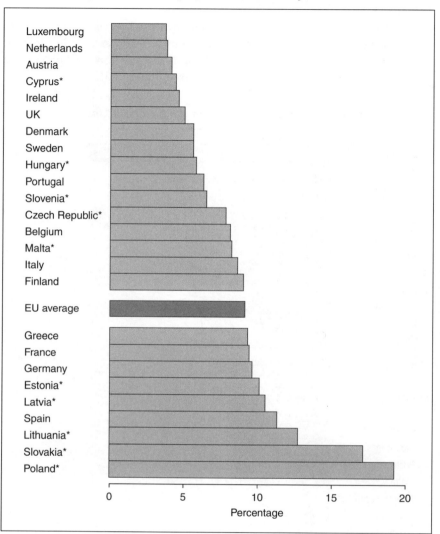

*A-10 states.
Source: Eurostat web page, http://europa.eu.int/comm/eurostat, 2004. Figures are for 2003.

- While about 70–72 per cent of the economic wealth of most of the wealthier EU-15 countries is generated by services and just 1–3 per cent by agriculture, services account for just 61–62 per cent of GDP in Slovenia and Lithuania, 57 per cent in the Czech Republic, and 54 per cent in Ireland (see Figure 8.3). In both Greece and Lithuania, farming accounts for about 7 per cent of GDP.

Figure 8.3 *Economic structure of EU member states*

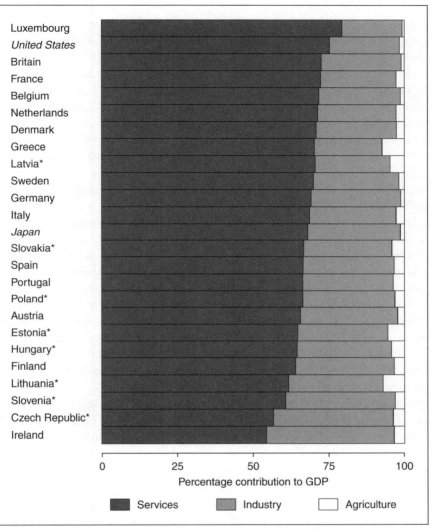

Percentage contribution to GDP

■ Services   ▨ Industry   □ Agriculture

*A-10 states. Figures for the United States and Japan are included for comparison. *Source:* World Bank website, http://www.worldbank.org/data, 2004. Figures are for 2002, except 2001 for Ireland, Japan and the United States. No figures available for Cyprus or Malta.

The wealthiest parts of the EU are in the north–central area, particularly in and around the 'golden triangle' between London, Dortmund, Paris and Milan. The poorest parts are on the eastern, southern, and western margins: the A-10, eastern Germany, Greece, southern Italy, Spain, Portugal, Ireland, Northern Ireland, and western Scotland. The relative poverty of these regions has several different sources: some are depressed agricultural areas with little industry and high unemployment, some are declining industrial areas with outdated plants, some (notably islands) are geographically isolated from the prosperity and opportunity offered by bigger markets, and most suffer relatively low levels of education and health care and have underdeveloped infrastructure, especially roads and utilities.

The preamble to the Treaty of Rome included the sentiment that economic unity and 'harmonious' development required that the member states work to reduce 'the differences existing between the various regions and the backwardness of the less favoured regions'. As well as the obvious moral need to address poverty and economic handicaps wherever they existed, there was a clear strategic need as well: variations in the economic wealth of the member states would interfere with the smooth functioning of the single market. As a result, jobs would move to the poorer parts where cheaper labour was available, inequality would interfere with the development of a skilled labour force, Europe would lack the well-educated and affluent consumers needed for a successful marketplace, and poorer regions would not attract the kind of investment and infrastructure needed to help Europe compete at the global level.

Recognizing these problems, the EU has given priority to achieving 'cohesion', or a reduction in economic disparities in the interests of promoting 'economic and social progress'. In order to do this, the EU has increased efforts to help bring the poorer member states closer to the level of their wealthier partners. While free marketeers have always hoped that the single market would have a 'trickle-down' effect by directing more investment towards the poorer parts of Europe, the EU has taken a more proactive approach by setting up several structural funds, aimed at spending in the interests of cohesion. They include the following:

- The European Regional Development Fund (ERDF), which is spent mainly on underdeveloped areas (particularly those affected by the decline of traditional industries such as coal, steel, and textiles) and inner cities. It is the biggest of the structural funds, and spending has grown rapidly – up from $11 billion in 1994 to $20 billion in 2002.
- The European Social Fund (ESF), which is designed to promote employment and worker mobility, combat long-term unemployment and help workers adapt to technological change; particular attention is paid to the needs of migrant workers, women, and the disabled. Sixty billion euros are budgeted to be spent under the fund in 2000–06. Major recipients to date have been eastern Germany, Greece, Ireland, southern Italy, Portugal, and Spain.
- The Cohesion Fund, which targets member states with a per capita GDP of less than 90 per cent of the EU average (that is, Greece, Ireland,

Portugal, and Spain). It compensates these states for the additional costs incurred by the tightening of environmental regulations, and provides financial assistance for transport projects.

- The Guidance Section of the European Agricultural Guidance and Guarantee Fund (EAGGF), which is part of the Common Agricultural Policy (see below) and is aimed at the reform of farm structures and rural areas.

Among them, the structural funds account for just under one-third of EU spending, and they have played a major role in spreading wealth and opportunity to poorer parts of the EU, and helping level the playing field of the single market. The challenge of repeating this record in the A-10 is of a greater order, but the principle will still apply. The free market is likely to play a much greater role, with investment flows from the west exploiting new opportunities, consumers, and pools of labour in the east.

Agricultural policy

Agriculture is not a headline issue in most industrialized countries, because it accounts for only a small fraction of economic activity. But in the EU it has long been a contentious issue: it employs barely 7 per cent of European workers, and accounts for just 3 per cent of the combined GDP of the EU, but it is the most expensive, the most complex, and sometimes the most politically charged of the policy areas in which the EU has become involved. The EU has more powers over agriculture, has passed more legislation on agriculture, spends almost as much of its budget on agriculture as on all other policy areas combined, and has seen more political activity on agriculture than on probably any other policy area. Only the foreign ministers meet more often than the agriculture ministers, and the Agriculture DG is the second biggest of all the Commission's directorates-general.

Agricultural policy is also structurally different from other EU policy areas in two important respects. First, while barriers have been removed and markets opened up in almost every area of EU economic activity, agriculture remains heavily interventionist. The EU has taken a hands-on approach to keeping agricultural prices high, drawing criticism not only from within the EU but from the EU's major trading partners. Second, unlike most other EU policy areas, agricultural policy was built into the Treaty of Rome, where the commitment to a common agricultural policy was spelt out more clearly than was the case for any other policy area, although the details were only agreed in the 1960s. Why has agriculture been so prominent?

First, at the time the Treaties of Rome were being negotiated, farming was important to European economies, societies, and cultures. It accounted for about 12 per cent of the GNP of the Six, and for about 20 per cent of the workforce. The Second World War had also made Europeans aware of how much they depended on imported food, and of just how prone those imports were to disruption. Many farms in the Six were small and vulnerable, and several national governments operated agricultural support and protection programmes that, for political reasons, could not be ended. At the same time, separate national systems might have interfered with the common market, so the suggestion was made for a Community support system.

Second, it was a key element in the trade-off between France and Germany when the terms of the EEC were under negotiation (Grant, 1997, pp. 63–8). France was concerned that the common market would benefit German industry while providing the French economy with relatively few benefits. In the mid-1950s France had a large and efficient agricultural sector, which contributed significantly to employment and economic activity. Concerns that the common market would hurt its farmers encouraged the French government to insist on a protectionist system. Even though this was to prove expensive, threats to change the system even now bring protesting French farmers out in their thousands.

Third, agricultural prices are more subject to fluctuation than prices on most other goods, and since Europeans spend about a quarter of their incomes on food, those fluctuations can have knock-on effects throughout the economy. Price increases can contribute to inflation, while price decreases can force farmers to go deeper into debt, perhaps leading to bankruptcies and unemployment. The problem of maintaining minimum incomes has been exacerbated by mechanization, which has led to fewer people working in farming in Europe. European governments felt that subsidies could help prevent or offset some of these problems, encouraging people to stay in the rural areas and discouraging them from moving to towns and cities and perhaps adding to unemployment problems.

Finally, farmers in the richer EU states have traditionally had strong unions working for them. As well as national unions, more than 150 EU-wide agricultural organizations have been formed, many of which directly lobby the EU. Among these is the Committee of Professional Agricultural Organizations (COPA), which represents farmers generally on a wide range of issues. Not only are farmers an influential lobby in the EU, but there are many other people who live in rural areas, and many rurally based services. The residents of small towns and villages add up to a sizeable proportion of the population, and of the vote. No political party can afford to ignore that vote, especially as there is little organized resistance to the agricultural or rural lobbies, either at the national or at the EU level.

At the core of agricultural issues in the EU is the Common Agricultural Policy (CAP), which has three underlying principles: the promotion of a single market in agricultural produce, a system of protectionism aimed at giving advantages to EU produce over imported produce, and joint financing (that is, the costs of CAP must be shared equitably across all the member states). What this has meant in practical policy terms is that EU farmers have been guaranteed the same minimum price for their produce, irrespective of how much they produce, of world prices, or of prevailing levels of supply and demand. Meanwhile, the EU's internal market is protected from imports by tariffs, and the member states share the financial burden for making this possible.

CAP is not so much a common agricultural policy as a common system of agricultural subsidies. Annual prices for all farm produce are fixed by the agriculture ministers meeting in the spring (usually April or May). On the basis of discussions and negotiations that usually have been going on since the previous September and have pulled in the Commission, the Agriculture Council, interest groups, and national governments, the ministers set several kinds of prices:

- *target prices*, or the prices they hope farmers will receive on the open market in order to receive a fair return on their investments. These are usually set high above world prices in order to ensure a minimum standard of living for farmers, and they are supported by levies on imports and subsidies to promote exports.
- *intervention prices*, or the prices the EU will pay as a last resort to take produce off the market if it is not meeting the target price.
- *threshold prices*, or the prices for imports from outside the EU at which levies will be charged in order to make them less competitive.
- *entry prices*, or the minimum price at which a commodity can be imported into the EU.

This price-setting arrangement has become more expensive and more complex as EU farmers have produced more than consumers need. The EU has had to buy up the surplus of commodities such as butter, cereals, beef, and sugar, some of which is stored while the rest is sold outside the EU (much to the irritation of other farming countries, such as the United States), given as food aid to poorer countries, destroyed, or converted into another product. For example, excess wine might be turned into spirits, which take up less space, or even into heating fuel. The EU has also tried to discourage production by paying farmers not to produce food.

The costs of CAP come out of the European Agricultural Guidance and Guarantee Fund (EAGGF), which has been the single biggest item on the EU budget since it was launched in 1962 (although agricultural spending has fallen from about 85 per cent of the budget in 1970 to about 46 per cent in 2004). The bulk of funds are spent in the Guarantee Section, which is used to buy and store surplus produce, and to encourage agricultural exports. Most of that money goes to the producers of dairy products, cereals, oils and fats, beef, veal, and sugar. Meanwhile, the Guidance Section is one of the elements that makes up the EU's structural funds (see later in this chapter), and is used to improve agriculture by investing in new equipment and technology, and helping those working in agriculture with pensions, illness benefits, and other supports.

In terms of its original goals – increasing productivity, ensuring a fair standard of living for farming communities, stabilizing markets, securing supplies, and protecting European farmers from the fluctuations in world prices – CAP has been an outstanding success. European farmers are wealthier then before, and their livelihoods have become more predictable and stable. The EU is the world's largest exporter of sugar, eggs, poultry, and dairy products, and accounts for nearly 20 per cent of world food exports. Encouraged by guaranteed prices, European farmers have squeezed more and more from their land, so that production has gone up in virtually every area, and the EU is now self-sufficient in almost every product it can grow or produce in its climate (including wheat, barley, wine, meat, vegetables, and dairy products), and produces far more butter, cereals, beef and sugar than it needs. The successes cannot all be ascribed to CAP, however, because farmers have also been helped by intensification, mechanization, and the increased use of agrochemicals.

Unfortunately, CAP has also created many problems:

- EU-15 farmers produce much more than the market can bear, creating stockpiles of surplus production: literally, there have been warehouses full of surplus cereal, powdered milk, beef, olive oil, raisins, figs, and even manure. By the late 1990s, the stockpiles had largely disappeared, but there were warnings that rising world prices could lead to a reappearance of these stockpiles.
- CAP funds have been used fraudulently. Differences between EU prices and world prices have meant high refunds that provide an irresistible temptation for less honest farmers and – in Italy – organized crime (Grant, 1997, pp. 99–101).
- CAP has created economic dependency (sustaining farmers who would have gone out of business), has pushed up the price of agricultural land, and has failed to close the income gap between rich and poor farmers. While mechanization and intensification have brought new profits to farmers in states with efficient agricultural sectors, such as Denmark, France, and the Netherlands, those in less efficient states, such as Greece, Italy, and Portugal, remain relatively poor. The gap has grown with the enlargement of the EU to eastern Europe.

- CAP has encouraged the increased use of chemical fertilizers and herbicides, and encouraged farmers to cut down hedges and trees and to 'reclaim' wetlands in the interests of making their farms bigger and more efficient.
- CAP has made food more expensive for consumers, despite the surpluses. The contradictions between high prices and warehouses full of stored food has been a major source of public scepticism about the wisdom of European integration.
- Because nearly 46 per cent of EU revenues (nearly €46 billion in 2004) are swallowed up by agriculture, and because there is a cap on the size of the EU budget, there is less available for spending in other areas.
- CAP has distorted world agricultural prices, soured EU relations with its major trading partners, and perpetuated the idea of a protectionist European Union.

With growing political and public pressure for change, numerous attempts have been made over the years to reform EU agricultural policy. The first came at the end of the 1960s when rising concerns about the cost of price supports prompted the suggestion by the Commission that small farmers be encouraged to leave the land, and that farms be amalgamated into bigger and more efficient units. This was vehemently opposed by small farmers in France and Germany. Following several other failed attempts to reform the system, Agriculture Commissioner Ray MacSharry addressed the issue in 1991, warning of the rising volume of stored agricultural produce. He proposed moving away from guaranteed prices, reducing subsidies on grain, beef, and butter, and encouraging farmers to take land out of production (Lewis, 1993, p. 337). Despite the opposition of many farmers and their unions, and despite warnings from the Court of Auditors that they increased the opportunities for fraudulent claims, the Agriculture Council finally approved the proposals in May 1992 after 18 months of talks. Food surpluses have since fallen, farm incomes have risen, and the rise in world cereal prices has helped negate the effects for farmers of CAP price cuts. The pressure for change has continued unabated, however, with proposals in 1998 by MacSharry's successor – Franz Fischler – for a shift away from compensating farmers when prices fell below a certain level and towards subsidizing them for certain kinds of production.

Further reforms were agreed in 2003. From 2005, the link between subsidies to farmers and the amount they produce will be broken, and farmers will instead receive a single payment (although individual member states will be allowed a limited reversion to the old system if there is a danger of significant job losses). Intervention prices on milk powder, butter, and other products will be reduced and direct payments for bigger farms will be cut. At the same time, member states such as Britain that

Box 8.1 The Common Fisheries Policy

The fishing industry in the EU employs just 0.2 per cent of the workforce, but the state of the industry has implications for coastal communities all around the EU. Disputes over fishing grounds in European waters have also led to sometimes bitter confrontation between EU partners and their neighbours. There were, for example, the infamous cod wars of the 1960s between Britain and Iceland over access to fisheries in the north Atlantic. Similarly, in 1984 French patrol boats fired on Spanish trawlers operating inside the Community's 320-km limit, and more than two dozen Spanish trawlers were intercepted off the coast of Ireland. Spain's fishing fleet was bigger than the entire EC fleet at the time, and fishing rights were a major issue in Spain's negotiations to join the EC. More recently, Spanish fishing boats became an issue in domestic British politics when Eurosceptics in the Major government quoted their presence in traditional British waters as one of their many complaints about the effects of British membership of the EU.

For all these reasons, fishing has been an unusually prominent issue in policy developments in the EU, which since 1983 has pursued a Common Fisheries Policy (CFP). The main goal of this is to resolve conflicts over territorial fishing rights and to prevent overfishing by setting catch quotas. The goals of the policy are pursued in four main ways. First, all the waters within the EU's 320-km limit have been opened up to all EU fishing boats, although member states have the right to restrict access to fishing grounds within 19 km of their shores. Second, the CFP prevents overfishing by imposing national quotas (or Total Allowable Catches) on the take of Atlantic and North Sea fish, and by regulating fishing areas and equipment, for example by setting standards on the mesh size of fishing nets. Third, it set up a market organization to oversee prices, quality, marketing, and external trade. Finally, it guides negotiations with other countries on access to waters and the conservation of fisheries.

want to move ahead with more radical reforms will be allowed to do so. Fischler argued that the reforms would make CAP less trade-distorting and more market-oriented, that they would offer more opportunities for farmers to diversify, and that they would give the EU a stronger hand in negotiations within the World Trade Organization. Opponents demurred, arguing that it would be several years before the long-term effects became clear.

Eastward enlargement has added a new dimension to the issue, because of the small size of most eastern European farms and the low productivity of its farmers. Investment in agriculture also has greater political, economic and social significance, given the relatively large farming populations in the east (see Figure 8.4). Opening CAP immediately to the new member

Figure 8.4   *Population engaged in agriculture*

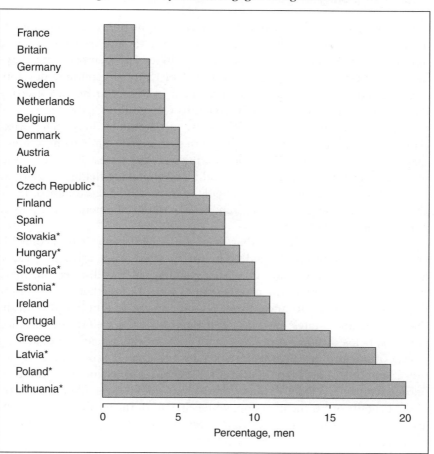

*A-10 states.
Source: World Bank Web site, http://www.worldbank.org/data, 2004. Figures are for 2002, except 2001 for Ireland. No figures available for Cyprus, Luxembourg or Malta.

states would likely have bankrupted the EU, but special efforts also needed to be made to make sure that A-10 farmers did not feel like second-class citizens. The compromise agreed was to allow them a small but growing proportion of agricultural payments. At the same time, €22 billion ($26 billion) was budgeted to be spent in the period 2000–6 under a programme called SAPARD (designed to help applicant countries prepare for CAP), a rural development package worth €5.1 billion ($6.1 billion) was made available for 2004–6, and it was agreed that direct aids would be phased in over ten years, starting at 25 per cent in 2004 and moving up in annual increments of 5 per cent.

Regional policy

The EU's regional policy is aimed at investing in the poorer parts of the EU in such a way as to reduce disparities of wealth and to provide more opportunity for their inhabitants. The wealthier EU member states have long had their own domestic programmes of regional economic development, aimed at encouraging new investment in poorer areas, at offsetting the effects of rural decline, and at trying to revive old industrial areas and the centres of large cities. While these programmes may help offset economic disparities *within* member states, there is a limit to how much they can deal with such disparities *among* member states. And as long as those differences exist, attempts to build a level playing field for economic activity throughout the European single market will be undermined. Little surprise, then, that the EU has given priority to development in the poorer parts of the member states.

Armstrong (1993) suggests that there are several benefits to a joint EU approach: it ensures that spending is concentrated in the areas of greatest need, it ensures coordination of the spending of the different member states, and it encourages the member states to work together on one of the most critical barriers to integration. A common regional policy also means that the member states have a vested interest in the welfare of their EU partners, helps member states deal with some of the potentially damaging effects of integration (such as loss of jobs and greater economic competition), and introduces an important psychological element: citizens of poorer regions receiving EU development spending are made more aware of the benefits of EU membership, while citizens of the wealthier states that are net contributors have a vested interest in ensuring that such spending is effective.

European regional policy dates back to the 1950s when provision was made by the European Coal and Steel Community for grants to depressed areas for industrial conversion and retraining. Funds were later provided under the Common Agricultural Policy for the upgrading of farms and farming equipment, the improvements of farming methods, and the provision of benefits to farmers. In 1969, the Commission proposed a common regional policy, including the creation of a regional development fund, but found little support among the governments of the member states.

The climate changed after the first round of enlargement in the early 1970s, when a complex pattern of political and economic interests came together to make the idea of a regional policy more palatable. Most importantly, the 'rich man's club' of the 1950s (Italy excepted) had been joined by Britain and Ireland, two countries with regional problems. Their accession not only widened the economic disparities within the EEC, but also strengthened Italy's demands for a regional policy. The Commission-sponsored Thomson Report argued in 1973 that regional imbalances were acting as a barrier to one of the goals of the Treaty of Rome ('a continuous and balanced expansion' in economic activity), threatened to undermine plans for economic and monetary union, and could even pose a threat to the common market (Commission of the European Communities, 1973). Agreement was reached to create a European Regional Development Fund in 1975.

The distribution of funds was originally based on a quota system, under which Britain, Italy, and Ireland were net beneficiaries of spending under the ERDF, and the other six Community members were net contributors. Reforms in the late 1970s led to the introduction of a small 'non-quota' element (5 per cent of the total could be determined by the Commission on the basis of need) and suggestions that the wealthier countries should give up their quotas altogether since they could afford their own internal development costs. More reforms in 1984 led to a tighter definition of the parts of the Community most in need of help, pushed up the non-quota segment to 20 per cent, and replaced the fixed quotas with minimum and maximum limits. Hence Germany had a limit of 3 per cent, France 10 per cent, Britain 19 per cent, Spain 24 per cent, and Italy 29 per cent.

The Single European Act brought new attention to regional policy, introducing a new Title V on Economic and Social Cohesion, and arguing the need to 'clarify and rationalize' the use of the structural funds. Further reforms, agreed in 1988, were based on Britain's insistence on reduced CAP spending and increased spending under the structural funds to 25 per cent of the EC budget by 1993 (in the event they reached nearly 32 per cent of spending). The 1988 reforms were also aimed at improving the efficiency of regional policy by setting up Community Support Frameworks under which the Commission, the member states and the regions would work more closely together on agreeing the means to achieve regional development planning goals.

More changes to regional policy came with Maastricht, under which a Committee of the Regions (COR) was created to give regional authorities a greater say in European policy, and the Cohesion Fund was created. The latter grew out of concern that economic and monetary union might worsen regional disparities, particularly given that poorer countries were going to be handicapped by the requirement (as a prelude to the single currency) for member states to limit their budget deficits to 3 per cent of GDP.

Regional policy is now one of the most important policy concerns of the European Union. In 1975 structural fund spending accounted for less than 5 per cent of the EEC budget, but now it amounts to nearly one-third of all EU spending (nearly €31 billion in 2004) and more than half of all EU citizens now benefit from projects paid for by the structural funds. A total of €213 billion was budgeted to be spent in the period 2000–6. The EU's regional policy has the following goals:

- Help for Objective 1 regions, defined as regions 'where development is lagging', and where per capita GDP is less than 75 per cent of the EU average. These regions include areas with low population density (such as northern Finland and Sweden) and remote areas, such as French overseas departments. Eligible regions contain just over 22 per cent of the EU-15 population, and received just under €20 billion in 2004, or 65 per cent of all spending under the structural funds. The biggest recipients are Spain, Portugal, Greece, Italy, and Germany (for investment in the former East Germany), while Denmark and the Benelux countries receive no funding. Objective 1 projects are funded mainly out of the ERDF and the Cohesion Fund.
- Help for Objective 2 areas, defined as those suffering 'structural difficulties' (including high unemployment and job losses, industrial decline, poverty, or crime), or areas heavily dependent on fishing or agriculture. They include the older industrial regions of Britain, France, Germany, and Spain, containing 18 per cent of the population of the EU-15, and received just over €3 billion in 2004, mainly out of the ERDF.
- The promotion of Objective 3 programmes aimed at developing human resources. The whole of the EU is eligible, and these programmes are aimed at reducing unemployment, improving access to the labour market, and promoting equal opportunities for men and women. They are funded mainly out of the European Social Fund, and Germany, Britain, France, Italy, and Spain (in that order) are the biggest recipients. About €3.1 billion was spent in this area in 2004.
- There are also a host of specialized 'Community Initiatives' with specific objectives, some of which overlap with social policy. These include Interreg III, which promotes cross-border, transnational and interregional cooperation with a view to helping the balanced development of multiregional areas, Urban II, which focuses on regenerating cities and declining urban areas, Leader+, which promotes sustainable rural development, and Equal, which addresses inequalities and discrimination in the labour market. Together they take up about 5 per cent of the structural funds budget.
- Finally, the EU set up programmes that gave pre-accession aid to ten eastern European countries (the eight that joined in 2004, together with Bulgaria and Romania). The oldest of these is PHARE, set up in 1989 to help these countries build the institutions and systems needed to ensure the correct application of EU law, and to invest in infrastructure and

new businesses. The Instrument for Structural Policies for pre-Accession (ISPA) did for the applicant countries what the Cohesion Fund did for existing member states, and the Special Accession Programme for Agriculture and Rural Development (SAPARD) (mentioned earlier) helped them prepare to participate in CAP.

There is little doubt that regional policy is helping to close the gap between richer and poorer member states, and that the balance of economic power among them is changing. There is still a substantial gap in per capita GDP between the richest (Luxembourg) and the poorest (Poland and the Baltic states), but most EU-15 member states have seen their per capita GDP grow, and the A-10 are likely to follow. One of the biggest success stories has been Ireland, whose per capita GDP grew from 61 per cent of the EU average in 1986 to 105 per cent in 1999 and 131 per cent in 2004 (Eurostat figures). Changes of this kind have created new opportunities in the poorer parts of the EU that discourage the outflow of labour, generate new sources of wealth and develop new markets for the rest of Europe.

Social policy

Effective economic integration demands a reduction in the social differences among Europeans. Without equal pay, equal working conditions, comparable standards on workers' rights and women's rights, and an expansion of the skilled workforce, the foundations of a workable single market will be undermined. Poorer European states will suffer the effects of competition from their wealthier partners in the EU, while those with less progressive employment laws will lose jobs to those that offer better working conditions. These concerns combined with the long history of welfare promotion in individual western European states have helped make social policy an important part of the EU agenda.

Social policy deals mainly with questions related to employment, or the rights, opportunities, and benefits provided to potential, actual, or former workers. One EU scholar argues that the EU has engaged not so much in 'social policy' as in 'social regulation', because it has focused on activities that balance quality-of-life issues with economic efficiency, and has not tried to replace the welfare programmes of the member states (Majone, 1993, p. 168). These activities have proved controversial, because social policy treads on sensitive ideological and cultural toes. Conservatives and liberals will never agree on the best way of building a level social playing field, and programmes that may be seen as progressive by one member state may be seen as a threat to economic progress or even cultural identity by another. Generally speaking, national labour unions have been in favour of EU social policy, as have the Commission and Parliament (dominated as it was until the 1999 elections by social democratic parties), while business interests and conservative political parties have been opposed, arguing that social policy could make European companies less competitive in the global market (Geyer and Springer, 1998, p. 208).

Relatively little attention was paid to social issues in the early days of the EEC: concern about the competitive implications of different levels of social security payments and labour costs encouraged the EEC Six to avoid addressing social questions head-on during the negotiations leading up to the Treaty of Rome. The treaty ended up being based on the naive assumption that the benefits of the single market would improve life for all European workers. This proved true to the extent that it helped increase wages, but market forces failed to deal with gender and age discrimination, wage disparities, different levels of unemployment, and safety and health needs in the workplace.

The Treaty of Rome made it the Community's business to deal with such matters as the free movement of workers, equal pay for equal work, working conditions, and social security for migrant workers. However, social issues were pushed down the EEC agenda while governments concentrated on completing the single market and resolving battles over agricultural policy, and the movement of workers was heavily restricted. Restrictions began to be eased so that labour shortages in the larger northern economies could be overcome. This led to an influx of immigrants from southern Europe, mostly from non-EC states such as Greece, Portugal, Spain, and Turkey, and what was then Yugoslavia. Enlargement in 1973 brought an increase in the disparities in levels of economic wealth within the Community, so social policy was pushed up the political agenda. The European Social Fund was set up in 1974, and the first in a series of four-year Social Action Programmes (SAPs) was launched, aimed at developing a plan of action to achieve full employment, improved living and working conditions, and gender equality. However, a combination of recession and ideological resistance from several European leaders ensured that many of the words failed to be translated into practical change on the ground.

Because a core goal of the Single European Act was the freedom of Europeans to live and work wherever they liked in the EC, social policy came to the fore again as questions were raised about the mobility of workers and about 'social dumping': money, services, and businesses moving to those parts of the Community with the lowest wages and social security costs. The Commission tried to focus the attention of national governments on the 'social dimension' of the single market, but economic recession made sure that the SEA initially lacked such a dimension. This encouraged Commission president Jacques Delors – a moderate socialist – to launch an attempt in 1988 to draw more attention to the social consequences of the single market.

The Belgian government had raised the idea of a charter of basic social rights during its presidency of the Council of Ministers in 1987, modelled on its own new national charter. The idea was taken up by Delors, and was given a helping hand by the determination of the socialist government of François Mitterrand to promote social policy during the French presidency of the EC. Other countries with socialist governments – such as Spain and Greece – were in favour, as was the moderately conservative government of Helmut Kohl in Germany. The only opposition came from the conservative government in Britain. Margaret Thatcher considered it 'quite inappropriate' for laws on working regulations and welfare benefits to be set at the Community level, and dismissed the Social Charter as 'a socialist charter – devised by socialists in the Commission and favoured predominantly by socialist member states' (Thatcher, 1993, p. 750).

When the Charter of Fundamental Social Rights of Workers (or the Social Charter) was adopted at the 1989 Strasbourg summit, Britain refused to go along. Plans to incorporate the Social Charter into Maastricht were undermined by the refusal of Thatcher's successor John Major to agree to its content, and it was only when Britain changed its position following the 1997 election of Tony Blair that the charter was incorporated by the Treaty of Amsterdam. Among other things, it notes the right to freedom of movement, to fair remuneration for employment, to social protection (including a minimum income for those unable to find employment), to freedom of association and collective bargaining, to equal treatment, to health, safety, and protection in the workplace, and to a retirement income that allows a reasonable standard of living.

Despite all the rhetoric about social issues, most attention since the 1990s has focused on just one problem: the failure of the EU to ease unemployment, the persistence of which was once described as equivalent to the persistence of poverty in the United States (Dahrendorf, 1988, p. 149). The single market has not been able to generate enough jobs for Europeans, and although unemployment rates in the EU-15 fell during the 1990s, they still do not compare well with the United States and Japan (9.1 per cent for the EU in 2004, compared to 6 per cent for the United States and 5.3 per cent for Japan). The causes are unclear, but at least part of the problem has been the relative weakness of trade unions and the relative ease with which workers can be laid off. Another factor is the size of the informal labour market in Europe, which accounts for as much as one-fifth of GDP in some states and is all but institutionalized in southern Italy, where it overlaps with organized crime. The EU has launched a host of retraining programmes, and is shifting resources to the poorer parts of the EU through various regional and social programmes, but with mixed results. Geyer and Springer (1998, p. 210) argue that EU employment policy has had 'high visibility but little focus', and that the search for solutions is hampered by a lack of support in the member states, which have been responsible for employment policy. They also note that the EU has the problem of trying to create jobs through increased competitiveness while preserving the traditional rights of employees.

One of the changes that came with the Amsterdam treaty was the introduction of an employment chapter that called on member states to 'work towards developing a coordinated strategy for employment'. However, it only requires the Commission and the member states to report to each other, and most of the responsibility for employment policy still remains with the member states. Unemployment has been high on the agendas of several recent European Council summits, which have agreed common guidelines on employment policy, including a fresh start for the young and the long-term unemployed, and simplified rules for small and medium-sized enterprises. Although millions of new jobs have been created in the EU since the 1990s, nearly half are temporary or part-time jobs, many of them are in the service sector, and because most are being filled by men and women new to the job market, they have done little to help ease long-term unemployment.

Another issue on the social agenda has been an improvement in the status of women. The position of women in politics and the workforce in the EU is not that different from their relative position in other liberal democracies, but the situation varies significantly from one member state to another, giving added importance to EU social policy and the goal of building economic and social cohesion. In general, women are in a better position in progressive northern European states such as Denmark, Finland, and Sweden, and relatively worse off in poorer states such as Portugal, Spain, Greece, and the A-10.

About one in three European workers are women, but career options are still limited, proportionately more women than men are employed in part-time jobs, and women are more likely to work in traditionally feminized jobs – such as nursing and teaching – than in management, and in the less well-paid and more labour-intensive sectors of industry (Springer, 1992, p. 66). Unemployment figures are higher for women than for men in most EU states, and women are also paid less than men for comparable work – about 80 per cent of the wages earned by a man. On the other hand, about 75 per cent of working women are employed in the expanding service sector, all EU member states are legally obliged to provide maternity leave, several member states offer parental leave, and the public provision of childcare is improving.

Although the rights of working women were mentioned in the Treaty of Rome (which, for example, establishes the principle of equal pay for men and women), it was not until the EEC began to look more actively at social policy in the 1970s that women's issues began to be addressed. The 1974 SAP included the goal of achieving gender equality in access to employment and vocational training, and equal rights at work were promoted by new laws such as the 1975 equal pay directive and the 1976 equal treatment directive. Even though direct and indirect gender discrimination is illegal under EU law, however, women still face invisible barriers and glass ceilings.

Elitism and gender bias in the EU are exemplified by imbalances in the staffing of the major EU institutions, although things are improving. The first woman ever appointed to the College of Commissioners was Vasso Papandreou of Greece in 1991. There were five women in the 1999–2004 College, and thanks to a specific request to governments from president José Manuel Durão Barroso to nominate more women, seven of the 25 new commissioners appointed in 2004 were women. Female membership of the European Parliament has also improved, with about 190 women MEPs (or 30 per cent of the total) in the 1999–2004 Parliament. Meanwhile, however, there are many more men than women in the more senior bureaucratic positions in the Commission and Council of Ministers, and many more women than men in secretarial and clerical positions, only three of the 25 judges on the Court of Justice in 2004 were women, and only two women – Margaret Thatcher and former French prime minister Edith Cresson – have ever taken part in meetings of the European Council.

Environmental policy

As noted earlier, while the Treaty of Rome mentioned the need for improvements in the standard of living for Europeans, little attention was paid to the quality of economic development in the early years of the Community. Certainly the environment was not an issue on the minds of most governments and policy makers, in large part because the environmental implications of economic development were neither appreciated nor understood. The few pieces of 'environmental' law that were agreed in the 1960s were prompted less by concern about environmental quality than by worries over the extent to which different national environmental standards were distorting competition and complicating progress on the common market.

By the early 1970s thinking had begun to change. There was a public reaction against what was seen as uncaring affluence, generated by a combination of improved scientific understanding, worsening air and water quality, several headline-making environmental disasters, and new affluence among the western middle classes (see McCormick, 1995, Chapter 3, for more details). Just as the governments of the member states could not avoid being caught up in the growing demand for a response, so the improvement of environmental quality had to be pushed up the agenda of European integration. The first step was taken with the publication in 1973 of the first Environmental Action Programme. More programmes followed, emphasizing the importance of environmental protection as an essential part of 'harmonious and balanced' economic growth. In 1986 the Single European Act gave the environment legal status as a Community policy concern, while later institutional changes gave the European Parliament a greater role in environmental policy making, and introduced qualified majority voting on most issues related to environmental law and policy.

A multinational response to environmental problems makes sense at several levels:

- Many problems – such as air and water pollution – are not limited by national frontiers, and are best addressed by several governments working together.
- Individual countries working alone may not want to take action for fear of saddling themselves with costs that would undermine their economic competitiveness; they have fewer such fears when several countries are working towards the same goals at the same time. As states become more dependent on trade and foreign investment, and the barriers to trade come down, so parochial worries about loss of comparative economic advantage become less important.
- The economic benefits of removing barriers to free trade (including different environmental standards) help offset some of the costs of taking action.
- Rich countries can help poor countries address environmental problems through funding assistance and a sharing of technical knowledge, and over the long term will see fewer factories closing and being moved to countries with lower environmental standards.

Community policy was initially based on taking preventive action and working to make sure that divergent national policies did not act as barriers to free trade, a problem noted by the Court of Justice in 1980 when it argued that competition could be 'appreciably distorted' in the absence of common environmental regulations. States with weak pollution laws, for example, had less of a financial or regulatory burden than those with stricter ones, and might attract corporations that wanted to build new factories with a minimum of built-in environmental safeguards.

By the early 1980s the Community had switched to a focus on environmental management as the basis of economic and social development. Environmental factors were consciously considered in other policy areas, notably agriculture, industry, energy and transport, and were no longer taking second place to the goal of building a single market. The logic of this idea was taken a step further in the 1990s when the EU adopted the

---

Box 8.2 Principles of European environmental policy

The goals of EU environmental policy are outlined in the treaties and the six Environmental Action Programmes, but they are broad and generalized. They include the improvement of the quality of the environment, the protection of human health, the prudent use of natural resources, increased environmental efficiency (meaning improvements in the efficiency with which resources are used so that consumption is reduced), and the promotion of measures at the international level to deal with regional or global environmental problems.

Whatever the goals say, EU policy has so far focused on problems that are better dealt with jointly than nationally, such as the control of chemicals in the environment, the reduction of air and water pollution, the management of waste, fisheries conservation, and the control of pesticides. The EU has also been active in areas not normally defined as 'environmental' at the national level, including noise pollution and the control of genetically modified organisms. It has been less involved in the protection of ecosystems, natural habitats, and wildlife, the management of natural resources such as forests and soil, and the promotion of energy conservation and alternative sources of energy. Among the underlying principles of EU policy are the following:

- *Sustainable development*: renewable natural resources such as air, water, and forests should be used in such a way as to ensure their continued availability for future generations.
- *Integration*: environmental protection must be a component of all EU policies that might have an environmental impact. This principle applies in only three other EU policy areas: consumer protection, culture, and human health.
- *Prevention*: the EU emphasizes action to prevent the emergence of environmental problems, rather than just responding to problems as they arise.
- *Subsidiarity*: the EU restricts itself to issues that are best dealt with jointly, leaving the rest to be addressed by the member states.
- *Derogation*: member states unable to bear the economic burden of environmental protection are given longer deadlines, lower targets, or financial assistance.

principle of sustainable development, agreeing that no economic development should take place without careful consideration of its potential impact on the environment.

There has been strong public support for EU activities on the environment. Eurobarometer polls have found that most Europeans rank environmental protection above finance, defence, or employment as an issue of EU concern, that most feel pollution is an 'urgent and immediate problem', and that most agree that environmental protection is a policy area better addressed jointly by EU states than by member states alone. Underpinning these opinions has been the growth in support for green political parties. In the 1989 EP elections, 30 green members were returned from seven member states; in 2004 there were members from about a dozen (mainly western) member states. By the late 1990s greens were also sitting in the national legislatures of most EU-15 member states, and were members of coalition governments in Belgium, Finland, Germany, and Italy.

A substantial body of environmental law has been agreed by the EU, covering everything from environmental impact assessment to controls on lead in fuel, sulphur dioxide and suspended particulates, lead in air, pollutants from industrial plants and large combustion plants, nitrogen dioxide, and vehicle exhaust emissions. Six action programmes have been published (the sixth covers the period 2000–10), a plethora of green and white papers has generated discussion on a wide range of issues, and the goals of EU policy have been given new definition since 1995 by the work of the European Environment Agency (EEA), a data-gathering agency that provides information to the other EU institutions. The EEA has been involved in the publication since 1995 of a series of triennial regional assessments of the state of the European environment.

Environmental management is now one of the most important areas of policy activity for the EU, ranking only behind foreign policy cooperation, economic issues and agriculture in terms of the level of political activity involved. Environmental policy in western Europe is now made more at the EU level than at the level of the member states. In the cases of countries such as Portugal and Spain, which had done very little on the environment before joining the Community, their national laws are now almost entirely driven by the requirements of EU law.

Although there has been progress on environmental policy making, the record on implementation is not so good, and experience in this field says something more broadly about the difficulties that policy making faces at the level of the EU. The record on the environment is explained by several factors:

- A lack of financial and technical resources.
- Organizational problems within EU institutions.

- The fact that most EU law has focused on developing policies rather than the means of implementing and enforcing them.
- The failure of all the parties involved in making policy to recognize the difficulty of meeting the goals they have set.
- The limited ability of the Commission to ensure that member states implement EU law.
- The long-term lack of a legal basis to EU environmental policy.

It is also explained by differences between the regulatory programmes and systems of the member states. Where Greece and Spain have had a poor record on implementation because their local government is relatively poorly organized and under-equipped, Germany and the Netherlands have a bad record because they have sophisticated systems of domestic environmental law, and lack the motivation to fully adapt their own measures to EU requirements. Meanwhile Denmark has a good record on implementation, helped by a high degree of public and official environmental awareness, effective monitoring systems, and the involvement of the Danish parliament in negotiating new environmental law (Collins and Earnshaw, 1993).

It has been argued that the Commission – through the European Environment Agency – should be given the power to carry out inspections and ensure compliance by member states, but this would raise worries about loss of sovereignty and the 'interference' of the Commission in the domestic affairs of member states. Besides, effective inspections would need huge resources: even the United States Environmental Protection Agency – with a staff of 18,000 and a multibillion dollar budget – is hard-pressed to keep up with everything it is expected to do. For the foreseeable future the Commission will have to continue to rely – as it has done for many years – on whistle-blowing by environmental interest groups, and on cases being brought before national courts and the European Court of Justice.

Regional cooperation among countries promises a quicker and more effective resolution of transnational environmental problems than any other approach, at least among countries with similar political systems and similar levels of economic development. The 2004 enlargement muddied the waters considerably because of the significantly different environmental standards inherited by eastern Europe from the Soviet era. But free-market forces of the kind brought by the European Union are likely to have a more efficient and effective result than the imposition of regulations that give developing industries little incentive to think about environmental planning. Given the extent to which the causes and effects of environmental problems do not respect national frontiers, and the extent to which shared responses are more effective than unilateral responses, the EU model may provide the only adequate response to such problems, mainly because it encourages different states to cooperate rather than to adopt potentially conflicting objectives.

Conclusions

The EU approaches to agricultural, social, regional, and environmental policy provide illustrations of the kinds of forces that are at work in the process of European integration, aimed at levelling the playing field and at both creating new opportunities and removing barriers to free trade.

The case of agricultural policy has been something of an aberration, the result of a political pact between two of the founding member states. In practice it is interventionist, but in principle it began as an attempt to offer equal opportunities to farmers across the EU, and to invest in rural economies that might otherwise have been left behind. It has been almost too successful, offering a blank cheque that has invited European farmers to produce as much as the land would sustain, rather than being driven by what the market would bear. But this is now changing.

Regional development has meant an attempt to help the poorer regions catch up with their richer neighbours, with the utopian goal of encouraging an equitable distribution of the benefits of integration. The EU has tended to equate development with growth, but whether quantity and quality go hand in hand has long been debatable. It is also debatable whether the free market can ever entirely eliminate inequalities of opportunity, which is why regional policy has been based on a kind of grand welfare system that sees the redistribution of wealth as a means of encouraging equal opportunity. It remains to be seen how long it will take to bring the different parts of the EU to the same economic level, assuming this is even possible.

Social policy has been aimed at reducing differences in income, working conditions, and worker skills with a view to creating an even playing field in the labour market. The attempt to build a common approach has stepped on ideological toes, but has ultimately brought all the member states around to a standard set of objectives. The biggest failure has been the inability to reduce unemployment across the EU, a problem which promises to compromise some of the achievements of the single market unless it can be relatively quickly turned around.

In the case of the environment, there is little question that international cooperation is desirable and even inevitable. Problems such as air and water pollution ignore national boundaries, and there are repeated examples from around the world of one state being a producer and downwind or downstream states being recipients. As the global economy expands, the barriers posed to trade by different environmental standards add a new dimension. There will always be strong ideological disagreement about the extent to which the state should manage natural resources and regulate industry, but there is a strong internal logic to international cooperation on environmental management. There is an emerging consensus that the EU has been a positive force in environmental protection, and that European environmental problems are better dealt with at the EU level than at the national or local level.

Chapter 9

The EU and the World

Building a European foreign policy
Towards a European defence policy
Europe as an economic power
Relations with the United States
Relations with eastern Europe
Development cooperation
Conclusions

Europe's citizens need Europe to be strong and united. They need it to be a power in the world ... Europe today is no longer just about peace, it is about projecting collective power.

Tony Blair, British prime minister, 2000

The EU presents a confusing image to the outside world. It is more than an international organization but less than a state, which leaves outside actors wondering whether they should still think of the 25 member states separately, or should instead think of the European Union as a single large bloc. The states still go their own way in many areas, such as defence and security issues, but when trade negotiations are on the agenda, third parties must deal with the EU as a whole, because the member states usually allow the Commission to represent their collective interests.

The lack of focus, the long-time absence of policy leadership, and the frustration felt by other countries was neatly summed up in a (sadly, apocryphal) question credited to former US Secretary of State Henry Kissinger: 'When I want to speak to Europe, whom do I call?' The problem was resolved to some extent in 1999, when a single external relations portfolio was created in the Commission, and a High Representative was appointed who would be the first point of contact on issues of European foreign and security policy. Another step is proposed under the draft constitution, by which a minister of foreign affairs will be responsible for 'conducting' the EU's foreign and security policy. That policy has been given more definition in recent years as the leaders of the EU member states have reached agreement on a broader set of issues, allowing them to take common positions in their dealings with third parties.

But the deliberations and the decisions of those leaders may ultimately prove to have been just a prelude to the new global role thrust on the EU by a series of unconnected developments: the 2001 terrorist attacks on the

United States, the 2002 launch of the euro, the 2003 US-led invasion of Iraq, and the 2004 enlargement of the EU into eastern Europe. The United States – or at least the Bush administration – has been widely criticized for its failure to provide leadership in the global war on terrorism, and for launching a war in Iraq that was without strategic merit. With its credibility harmed, and many outside the United States looking for alternative analyses of global problems, and a different set of solutions, an opportunity has arisen for the EU to both crystallize its own objectives and to provide a new source of leadership.

While the steps taken by the EU to build a common foreign and security policy have been halting, there are no longer any doubts about its status as an economic superpower. It is the world's biggest and richest marketplace, with more than 454 million consumers, more than 28 per cent of global GDP, 35 per cent of imports, and 34 per cent of exports. It is the dominating actor in global trade negotiations, the biggest market in the world for mergers and acquisitions, and the biggest source of foreign direct investment. Its influence over the global economy continues to grow as the euro takes root, posing formidable competition to the US dollar and the Japanese yen. Much more is now expected of the EU as a global actor, both by its own members and by other countries. The result has been new momentum on the development of common foreign and security policies, and a new assertion of European influence in the world. This chapter argues that European integration has clearly moved beyond internal economic issues, and thanks to a combination of the changing nature of power, the changing opinions of Europeans, and the declining credibility of US foreign policy, Europe – once a bystander in the cold war – is now a potent actor in world affairs.

Building a European foreign policy

In their attempts to build a common European foreign policy, EU leaders have found themselves being pulled in two directions. On the one hand it is clear that the EU will have more power and influence in the world if its member states act as a group rather than independently. On the other hand there is the fear that coordination will interfere with the freedom of member states to address matters of national rather than of European interest, and will lead inexorably to the surrender of national sovereignty and the creation of a European federation. The tension between these two views has undermined attempts to build common policy positions, let alone a common foreign policy.

The Treaties of Rome make no mention of foreign policy, and the EEC long focused on domestic economic policy, although the logic of spillover implied that the development of the single market would make it difficult to avoid the agreement of common external policies. There were several abortive moves in that direction in the early years of integration, including the European Defence Community (EDC) and the European Political Community, and Charles de Gaulle's plans for regular meetings among the leaders of the Six to coordinate foreign policy. The EDC was proposed in 1950, was pursued most actively by the French, and was to have been built on the foundations of a common European army and a European minister of defence. However, Britain was opposed to the idea, preferring to pursue the goals of the Treaty of Brussels (see below) and to bring Italy and West Germany into the fold. All prospects of an EDC finally died in 1954 when the French National Assembly turned it down (Urwin, 1995, pp. 60–8).

Community leaders subsequently focused on building the single market, and it was only at their summit in The Hague in 1969 that they decided to look again at foreign policy. The following year they agreed to promote European Political Cooperation (EPC), a process by which the six foreign ministers would meet to discuss and coordinate foreign policy positions. EPC was not incorporated into the founding treaties, it remained a loose and voluntary arrangement outside the Community, no laws were adopted on foreign policy, each of the member states could still act independently, and most of the key decisions on foreign policy had to be unanimous. Nonetheless, consultation became habit-forming, and the European Council was launched in 1974 in part to bring leaders of the member states together to coordinate policies.

The EPC process was strictly intergovernmental, and was overseen by the foreign ministers meeting as the Council of Ministers, with overall leadership coming from the European Council. Regular meetings of senior officials from all the foreign ministries provided continuity, and a small secretariat was set up in Brussels to help the country holding the presidency of the Council of Ministers, which provided most of the momentum. Larger or more active states such as Britain and France had few problems providing leadership, but policy coordination put a strain on smaller and/or neutral countries such as Ireland and Luxembourg. The shifting of responsibilities every six months gave each member state its turn at the helm, but complicated life for non-Community states, which had to switch their attention from one member state to another, and to establish contacts with ministers and bureaucrats in six, then nine, then 12 capital cities.

EPC was given formal recognition with the Single European Act, which confirmed that the member states would 'endeavour jointly to formulate and implement a European foreign policy'. But then came the Gulf War of 1990–91, which found the Community both divided and unprepared.

Box 9.1 The EU on the world stage

How does the EU fit into the global system? It can adopt laws that are binding on its member states, but can it also negotiate with third parties on behalf of the member states, and enter into binding agreements with those parties? The answer depends on where one looks.

The Treaty of Rome included a Common Commercial Policy, which gave the Commission authority to negotiate with third parties, and to make recommendations to the Council of Ministers on agreements with third parties. It also allowed the Council to authorize the Commission to open and conduct the necessary negotiations. But there were questions about the policy areas to which this applied, and it took a 1971 case before the Court of Justice (*Commission* v. *Council (AETR)*) to clarify matters. The immediate issue was a dispute between the Commission and the Council over an international agreement on road transport. The Commission claimed that it had competence, because the power to develop a common transport policy included the right to reach agreements with third parties. The Council disagreed, arguing that the Treaty of Rome only allowed the Commission to reach such agreements in areas specifically listed in the treaty.

The Court sided with the Commission, arguing that there were implied powers for the Commission to conclude treaties with third parties in areas which flowed from 'other provisions of the Treaty and from measures adopted ... by the Community institutions'. In other words, the Court concluded that whenever the Community adopted common rules in a particular area, the member states no longer had the right – individually or collectively – to enter into agreements with third parties that affected those rules: 'as and when those rules come into being, the Community alone is in a position to assume and carry out contractual obligations with third countries affecting the whole sphere of application of the Community legal system'.

The result was that in policy areas within which the EU has sole authority (that is, competence), or a large measure of authority, the Commission can sign an international agreement without the member states also signing. These areas include the Common Agricultural Policy, the Common Commercial Policy, competition, and common policies on fisheries and air transport. In such cases, the EU has only one vote. Conversely, in policy areas where the EU has little or no competence – including criminal justice, education, and taxation – the member states alone have the power to sign, in which case they have 25 independent votes. However, because there are political and practical difficulties in defining the boundaries between domestic and external policy, and between economic and non-economic policy, authority is sometimes shared, and the result is what are called 'mixed agreements': they are signed both by the EU and the member states (Smith, 1997).

When Iraq invaded Kuwait in August 1990, the United States orchestrated a multinational campaign involving 13 countries in defence of Saudi Arabia, followed by a six-week air war against Iraq and a four-day ground war in February 1991. The Community was united in quickly banning Iraqi oil imports, suspending trade agreements, freezing Iraqi assets in the EC, and giving emergency aid to frontline states (Ginsberg, 2001, p. 193), but in terms of hard military action, Community member states took quite different positions (van Eekelen, 1990; Anderson, 1992):

- Britain committed 35,000 troops, 60 warplanes and 15 naval vessels to the war effort, placing them under US operational command.
- France committed 12,500 troops, 40 warplanes, and 14 naval vessels, but placed more emphasis on diplomatic resolution in order to maintain good relations with Arab oil producers and protect its weapons markets.
- Germany's options were limited by a strong postwar tradition of pacifism and constitutional limits on the deployment of the German troops; it sent minesweepers and provided the United States and Britain with financial support.
- Belgium refused to sell artillery shells to Britain and, along with Portugal and Spain, refused to allow its naval vessels to be involved in anything other than minesweeping or enforcing the blockade of Iraq.
- Ireland stayed neutral.

The Community response, charged Luxembourg foreign minister Jacques Poos, underlined 'the political insignificance of Europe'. For Belgian foreign minister Mark Eyskens, it showed that the EC was 'an economic giant, a political dwarf, and a military worm' (*New York Times,* 25 January 1991). Commission President Jacques Delors noted that while the member states had taken a firm line against Iraq on sanctions, once it became obvious that the situation would have to be resolved by force, the Community realized that it had neither the institutional machinery nor the military force to allow it to act as one (Delors, 1991).

The divisions over the war – coupled with the dramatic changes then taking place in eastern European and the former USSR – emphasized the need for Europe to address its foreign policy more forcefully, and political pressure grew for a review of EPC. The result was its replacement under Maastricht by the Common Foreign and Security Policy (CFSP). Despite the new label, however, the goals of the CFSP were only loosely defined, with vague talk about the need to safeguard 'common values' and 'fundamental interests', 'to preserve peace and strengthen international security', and to 'promote international cooperation'.

How has the CFSP fared? On the one hand there has been a steady convergence of positions among the member states on key international issues. Their ambassadors to the United Nations meet frequently to coordinate policy, and the EU states mainly vote together on resolutions in the Security Council, where the EU – through Britain and France – holds two of the five permanent seats. The EU has agreed several 'common strategies', such as those on Russia and the Ukraine, 'joint actions', such as transporting humanitarian aid to Bosnia and sending observers to elections in Russia and South Africa, and 'common positions' on EU relations with other countries, including the Balkans, the Middle East, Myanmar, and Zimbabwe. The EU has also flexed its economic muscle to political ends, for example becoming embroiled in several trade disputes with the United States (see later in this chapter).

The EU also coordinated western aid to eastern Europe, Russia and the former Soviet republics during the 1990s, and has become the major supplier of aid to developing countries (see later in this chapter). The president of the European Commission attends meetings of the G8 along- side the leaders of Russia and the seven most industrialized countries (four of which are EU member states), as well as meeting annually with the president of the United States. The significance of the EU as an actor on the global stage is also reflected in the fact that almost every country in the world now has diplomatic representation in Brussels (both for Belgium and for the EU), and that the Commission has opened more than 130 overseas delegations. In his study of the EU's international political influence, Ginsberg (2001) concludes that it has had more impact, and on a wider range of issues, than is generally recognized.

On the other hand there have been many examples of weakness and division, most notably over the Balkans (see Peterson, 2003). The EU failed to broker peace in Bosnia (a job subsequently completed under US leadership), and failed to act on a 1996 dispute between Greece and Turkey over an uninhabited Aegean island. The latter prompted Richard Holbrooke, the US assistant secretary of state for European affairs, to accuse the EU of 'literally sleeping through the night'. Then there was the EU's feeble response to the 1998 crisis in the Yugoslav province of Kosovo. When ethnic Albanians in Kosovo began agitating for independence from Serb-dominated Yugoslavia, the government of Slobodan Milosevic re- sponded with force, leading to a massive refugee problem and reports of massacres of both Kosovars and Muslims. The West's initial position on the conflict seemed to be aimed at discouraging separatism rather than stopping the violence, and the Milosevic government took this as a signal to continue its offensive. When the military response eventually came, in March 1999, it was led not by the EU but by the United States under the auspices of NATO.

The problems with the CFSP have in part been a consequence of weaknesses in the policy-making machinery of the EU. The core difficulty is that while the Commission carries out trade negotiations on behalf of the EU, discussions on the CFSP have rested more firmly with the Council of Ministers, and so have been more driven by national interests, and more prone to intergovernmental disputes. Changes made to the CFSP by the Treaty of Amsterdam were designed to respond to such problems. As well as opening up the possibility of limited majority voting on foreign policy issues, the rotation of countries holding the presidency of the EU was changed so that large member states alternated with small ones, more effectively balancing leadership. Amsterdam also led to the creation of a Policy Planning and Early Warning Unit in Brussels to help the EU anticipate foreign crises, and the old habit of having four different regional external affairs portfolios in the European Commission ended with the creation of a single foreign policy post and the appointment of a High Representative on foreign policy; the first office-holder was Javier Solana, former secretary-general of NATO. Under the new constitution, the tasks of the European commissioner and the High Representative will be combined into a single EU foreign minister, who will be able to speak for the EU as a whole in areas where there is a common position. The minister will be supported by an expanded EU diplomatic service.

Ironically, while the leaders of the member states have sometimes equivocated, and are divided on the idea of relinquishing more powers over foreign policy to the EU institutions, there is widespread public support for the idea of a common European foreign and security policy. Eurobarometer polls in recent years have consistently found more than two-thirds of Europeans in favour, support being highest in Italy, Luxembourg, Greece and Germany (80–83 per cent in favour) and lowest in Finland, Austria, Sweden and Britain (52–57 per cent) (Eurobarometer 61, Spring 2004).

Towards a European defence policy

Dealing with the 'foreign' element of the CFSP – while not easy – has been less politically troubling than dealing with the 'security' element. Together the EU member states constitute a formidable military power, and the EU could theoretically be a military superpower. But European governments have independent opinions and priorities when it comes to committing their forces, there is still only limited coordination on policy, and progress on setting up a European defence force has been slow. There has also been an ongoing division of opinion within the EU about how to relate to NATO and the United States (see Box 9.2).

Box 9.2 A European or an Atlantic defence?

One of the core issues in the debate about European foreign policy is the question of how the EU should relate to the United States. Among governments, there are two main schools of thought:

- Atlanticists such as Britain, the Netherlands, Portugal, and many of the A-10 emphasize the importance of the security relationship with the United States, and are loath to do anything that could be interpreted as undermining or replacing the transatlantic security relationship.
- Europeanists such as France, Italy, Spain, and sometimes Germany look more towards European independence, and believe that the EU should reduce its reliance on the American defensive shield.

During the cold war (1945–91), Atlanticists had the upper hand because the main defence issue was security against a Soviet attack, something that fell squarely under the remit of the US-dominated North Atlantic Treaty Organization (NATO). Furthermore, member states had different policy positions and different defence capacities: the British and the French had special interests in their colonies and former colonies, the Germans and the Dutch saw their armed forces as part of the broader NATO system, and several countries – notably Ireland – were neutral. Europeans became used to coordinating their defence policies within the NATO framework, guided by US leadership.

With the end of the cold war, Europeanists appeared to gain ground, in part thanks to changes in US policy. President Kennedy had spoken during his inauguration in 1960 of the willingness of the United States to 'bear any burden' and 'meet any hardship ... to assure the survival and success of liberty'. By the mid-1990s, though, American public opinion had turned against such an idea, and the term 'burden sharing' became more common in transatlantic discussions, with demands for the EU to take on greater responsibility for addressing its own security threats. Meanwhile, the ability of the EU to respond to security threats was clearly inadequate, a problem that became more critical during the 1990s as US defence spending fell (Barber, 1998). Then came the divisions over how to conduct the war on terrorism, and the transatlantic fallout over the 2003 US-led attack on Iraq, the latter in particular showing that European public opinion was taking an increasingly independent view. According to the Eurobarometer poll taken in 2003 (in the EU-15 only), 75–77 per cent of Europeans favoured foreign policy independence from the United States, building on the steady 63–67 per cent support since 1994 for a common foreign and security policy. Where 46 per cent of Europeans felt that decisions on European defence policy were better taken by the EU, just 14 per cent said they were better taken by NATO.

Maastricht stated that one of the goals of the EU should be 'to assert its identity on the international scene, in particular through the implementation of a common foreign and security policy including the eventual framing of a common defence policy'. But while the CFSP moved defence more squarely onto the EU agenda, Maastricht provided a loophole by committing member states to a common policy that would 'include all questions related to the security of the Union, including the *eventual* framing of a common defence policy, *which might in time* lead to a common defence' (emphasis added).

Nothing so clearly illustrates the problem of developing a common security policy as the independent stance taken by France over the years. After withdrawing its forces from the integrated NATO military command in 1966, France more often preferred to go its own way than to cooperate with either NATO or its European partners. Driven by a combination of its concern about US influence in Europe through NATO, and its own political marginalization, it has adopted policy positions that have often run counter to those of its neighbours, and of the EU as a whole. For example, it tried to prevent the creation of a new consultative council bringing together NATO countries and former Warsaw Pact members, it refused to place its warships under NATO command during the UN blockade of Serbia and Montenegro in 1993–6, it has pursued its own independent interests in its former African colonies, and it unilaterally resumed nuclear testing in the Pacific in 1995.

As if the lack of policy agreement is not enough, Europe also lacks the necessary institutional machinery for a common defence policy. One option lay in the revival during the 1980s and 1990s of the Western European Union (WEU), which traced its roots back to the Brussels treaty for collective self-defence, signed in 1948 by Britain, France, and the Benelux countries. The WEU was long overshadowed by NATO, but was reactivated in 1984 following the failure of a plan to give EPC a security dimension (van Eekelen, 1990). The WEU passed its first modest test in 1987–90 when it coordinated minesweeping by its members in the Persian Gulf during the Iran–Iraq war, but the 1990–1 Gulf War stretched it far beyond its limits.

A significant attempt to build a common European military came in May 1992 with the founding of Eurocorps, set up by France and Germany to replace an experimental Franco-German brigade set up in 1990. Headquartered in Strasbourg, the 60,000–member Eurocorps became operational in November 1995 and was joined by contingents from Belgium, Luxembourg, and Spain. It was conceived as a step towards the development of a European army that would give substance to the Common Foreign and Security Policy, give the EU an independent defence capability, and provide insurance should the United States decide to withdraw its forces from Europe. Germany insisted that Eurocorps would complement NATO and that it would be placed under NATO 'operational command' in the event of a threat to western European security, but Britain, the Netherlands, and the United States suspected that France's objective – as it has been since the time of de Gaulle – was to displace the US dominance of NATO. Britain preferred that Eurocorps operate under the auspices of the WEU, while France preferred to see the WEU and Eurocorps as the basis of an EU defence wing.

In June 1992, the WEU foreign and defence ministers – meeting at Petersberg, near Bonn – issued a declaration in which they agreed that military units from member states, acting under the authority of the WEU, could be used to promote the 'Petersberg tasks': humanitarian, rescue, peacekeeping, and other crisis management jobs (including peacemaking). The WEU went on to work with NATO in monitoring the UN embargo on Serbia and Montenegro, helped set up a unified Croat–Muslim police force to support the administration of the city of Mostar in Bosnia in 1994–6, and helped restructure and train the Albanian police force in 1997.

With its membership expanding and the acknowledgement under the terms of Maastricht that it should be 'developed as the defence component of the EC, and as a means to strengthen the European pillar of the Atlantic Alliance', the WEU underwent an overhaul. Its secretariat was moved from London to Brussels in January 1993, and the 1997 Treaty of Amsterdam resulted in closer association between the WEU and the EU, and the incorporation of the Petersberg tasks into the EU treaties. That same year, Tony Blair became prime minister of Britain and signalled his willingness to see Britain play a more central role in EU defence matters. He and French president Jacques Chirac explored the potential of the Anglo-French axis in European security matters, and – after a December 1998 meeting in St. Malo, France – the two leaders declared that the EU should be in a position to play a full role in international affairs, 'must have the capacity for autonomous action, backed up by credible military forces, the means to decide to use them, and the readiness to do so', and suggested the creation of a European rapid reaction force. This was later endorsed by German chancellor Gerhard Schröder (for more details, see Collester, 2000).

Another chapter was added to the story with the launch in 1999 of the European Security and Defence Policy (ESDP) (see Howarth, 2003). An integral part of the CFSP, this was to consist of two key components: the Petersberg tasks, and a 60,000–member Rapid Reaction Force that could be deployed at 60 days' notice and sustained for at least one year, and could carry out these tasks. The Force – championed mainly by Britain and France – was not intended to be a standing army, was designed to complement rather than compete with NATO, and could only act when

NATO had decided not to be involved in a crisis. Meanwhile, WEU resources were steadily merged into the EU, and political and military committees were established to work on the rapid reaction force. The plan was to have it ready by the end of 2003, but while it was declared partly operational in December 2002 and carried out its first missions in early 2003 – a police mission to Bosnia and a peacekeeping operation in Macedonia – it was not until November 2004 that EU defence ministers finally reached agreement. The force is due to be set up by 2007, with units of 1500 troops each from France, Italy, Britain, and Spain, to be followed by other EU member states.

The terrorist attacks on the World Trade Center in New York and on the Pentagon in Washington DC in September 2001 brought new issues into the equation. The meaning of 'war' and 'defence' had already been changing with the end of the cold war, but the attacks – and the response to the attacks – forced a change in consideration of defence policy on both sides of the Atlantic: terrorism (especially when it involved suicide attacks) could not be met with conventional military responses, it transcended national borders, it was not a problem that could be resolved by interstate conflict, and it showed that the United States still needed the help of the Europeans for intelligence-gathering, diplomatic ventures, and bases from which to launch military responses.

Many European leaders hoped that the tragedy would herald a new era in US foreign policy, with an emphasis on multilateralism and diplomacy. While they – and European public opinion – were initially deeply sympathetic to the United States, and provided both political support and hard military support for the subsequent US-led invasion of Afghanistan, there was a dramatic parting of the ways over the problem with Iraq. The Bush administration charged Iraqi leader Saddam Hussein with possessing weapons of mass destruction (notably chemical and biological agents), aspiring to build nuclear weapons, and being a threat to neighbouring states and to American interests, and tried to win passage of a UN resolution condemning Iraq and authorizing military action. When this failed, the United States and Britain launched an attack on Iraq in March 2003.

The crisis saw European governments split into three camps: supporters of US policy included Britain, Denmark, Italy, the Netherlands, Spain, and many in eastern Europe; opponents included Austria, Belgium, France, Germany, and Greece; those that took no position included Finland, Ireland, Portugal and Sweden. US Defense Secretary Donald Rumsfeld caused much bafflement when, in January 2003, he dismissed France and Germany as 'old Europe' and as 'problems' in the crisis over Iraq, contrasting them with the eastern European governments that supported US policy. A new element was added to the debate when, in April 2003,

Belgium, France, Germany, and Luxembourg announced plans to establish an independent European military headquarters that could plan operations undertaken by EU member states, and to launch a European Security and Defence Union.

Whatever the divisions of opinion among European leaders, far more significant was the remarkable uniformity of public opposition to the war in the EU. Opinion polls found that 70–90 per cent were opposed in Britain, Denmark, France, Germany, and even in several eastern European countries such as the Czech Republic and Hungary. Several pro-war governments – notably those in Britain and Spain – found themselves in trouble with their electorates, and British prime minister Tony Blair saw his approval ratings fall rapidly. Massive public demonstrations were held in most major European capitals, including Berlin, London, and Rome. A June 2003 survey found reduced faith in American global leadership, with less than half of those questioned wanting to see a strong global US presence. In Germany, long a staunch US ally, 81 per cent of respondents felt that the EU was more important than the United States to their vital interests, up from 55 per cent in 2002 (German Marshall Fund survey, September 2003). Most remarkably, another survey found that 53 per cent of Europeans viewed the United States as a threat to world peace on a par with North Korea and Iran (Eurobarometer poll, October 2003).

Against the background of a rapidly changing transatlantic relationship, the draft EU constitution includes the stipulation that the EU should take a more active role in its own defence, talking of the 'progressive framing of a common Union defence policy' leading to a common defence 'when the European Council, acting unanimously, so decides'. Even if they were to be limited to the Petersberg tasks, the question still remained as to how European defence forces should be organized. Europeanists such as France continue to want to develop an independent EU capability. The United States is content to see the Europeans taking responsibility for those tasks from which NATO should best keep its distance, but insists that there should be no overlap or rivalry in the event of the creation of a separate European institution. Meanwhile, Atlanticists such as Britain continue to feel nervous about undermining the US commitment to Europe.

While there is no questioning the American superiority in the field of military power (the United States spends more on defence every year than the next ten countries combined), an issue often overlooked in the debate about the global role of the EU is the question of 'soft power'. Defined by Joseph Nye as 'the ability to get what you want through attraction rather than coercion' (Nye, 2004, p. x), and centred on culture, political ideals, and policies rather than on the threat of violence, the argument can be made that – particularly under the Bush Doctrine – the United States has become associated in the minds of many with hard power rather than soft power, which has been one of the causes of the decline in the credibility of US foreign policy. By contrast, lacking the resources or the joint command structures (or the freedom from US influence in the hallways of NATO) to launch an effective independent military operation of any substance, the EU has become adept at using soft power in its dealings with other countries. In a world in which violence is increasingly rejected as a tool of statecraft (at least among wealthy liberal democracies), the use of diplomacy, political influence, and the pressures of economic competition may be giving the EU a strategic advantage which reduces the need to develop a significant common military capacity.

Europe as an economic power

While the prospects of the EU becoming a major military power are uncertain, there are no doubts at all about its new status as an economic superpower. The common external tariff is in place, the single market is complete, most of the western member states have adopted a single currency, the Commission has powers to represent the governments of all the member states in negotiations on global trade, and it is now well understood by everyone that the EU is the most powerful actor in those negotiations. There has also been rapid economic growth in most parts of the EU over the last twenty years, with even some of the poorer parts catching up as a result of the opportunities opened up by the single market and investments made under the structural funds.

The figures paint an incontestable picture of European economic power:

- With just over 7 per cent of the world's population, the European Union accounts for more than 28 per cent of the world's GDP (more even than the United States). It also accounts for more than one-third of global merchandise trade (nearly three times the share of the United States) (see Figure 9.1).
- With enlargement in 2004, the population of the EU grew from 375 million to 454 million, giving the EU nearly 60 per cent more consumers than the United States. More importantly, the personal wealth of western Europeans – combined with the largely open internal market that now exists in the EU – means that the EU is the largest capitalist market in the world. Just as multinational corporations have found it essential since the Second World War to sell to the US market in order to maximize their profits, so they now seek a foothold in the European market, which is more accessible thanks to the completion of the single market and adoption of the euro.
- Twelve of the 25 member states (which among them account for 74 per cent of the GDP and 67 per cent of the population of the EU) now have

Figure 9.1 *The EU in the global economy*

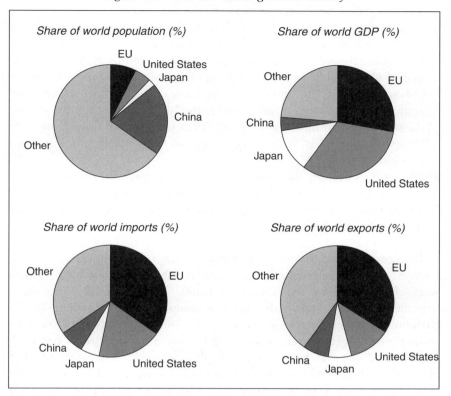

Sources: Population and GDP figures from World Development Indicators Database, World Bank website, 2004, http://www.worldbank.com. Figures are for 2002. Trade figures from World Trade Organization home page, 2004, http://www.wto.org, and are for merchandise trade in 2001.

a common currency that stands alongside the US dollar and the Japanese yen in terms of credibility and influence. It is increasingly usual to hear analysts describing the euro as a challenger to the status of the US dollar in global trade and finance, and arguing that it might eventually replace the dollar as the primary international reserve currency. Governments and corporations are increasingly borrowing in euros, nearly 40 per cent of foreign exchange transactions are now carried out in euros, central banks are holding more of their reserves in euros, and euros are increasingly used by consumers outside the euro zone, notably in eastern Europe.

- One-third of the corporations in the Fortune 100 list of the world's largest industrial corporations are European – mainly German, French, British, Italian and Dutch. They include Royal Dutch/Shell, BP,

DaimlerChrysler, Allianz, Total Fina Elf, Volkswagen, Siemens, AXA, Vivendi Universal, Fiat, and Peugeot.

- As noted in Chapter 7, the EU has become the biggest mergers and acquisitions market in the world, thanks to the unprecedented surge of corporate takeovers and mergers that has occurred in the EU since the mid-1980s, notably in the chemicals, pharmaceuticals, and electronics industries. European multinationals have also become increasingly aggressive in pursuing targets outside the EU, such that the EU is now the source of two-thirds of all foreign direct investment flowing into the United States, with millions of American jobs reliant on European investment.

- The EU has become the engine of economic growth for eastern Europe and the former USSR, which have a combined population of nearly 262 million, enormous productive potential, and a wealth of largely untapped natural resources.

The economic wealth of the EU has been built on the foundations of the removal of trade restrictions and the lowering of customs barriers that were championed by the Treaty of Rome. This outlined a Common Commercial Policy, stating that the Community would contribute 'to the harmonious development of world trade, the progressive abolition of restrictions on international trade, and the lowering of customs barriers'. To this end the EU has built a complex network of multilateral and bilateral trading networks and agreements, some based on proximity (agreements with eastern Europe and Mediterranean states), some on former colonial ties (see the section on development cooperation below) and some on expediency (agreements with the United States and Japan).

The growth of European economic power has also been helped by an institutional structure that – unlike the structure set up for security policy – promotes common positions among the member states. The Council of Ministers is responsible for making the final decisions, but it uses qualified majority voting, and the Commission plays an active role at every level. The latter generates policy initiatives, is responsible for investigating and taking action against unfair trading practices, and makes suggestions to the Council of Ministers when it thinks that agreements need to be negotiated with other countries or international organizations. Most importantly, once the member states have agreed a position among themselves, they leave it up to the Commission to negotiate almost all external trade agreements on behalf of the EU as a whole. So if Henry Kissinger was to ask to whom he should speak in Europe regarding trade matters, the answer would be clear.

The new economic significance of the EU is particularly clear in the role it has played in global trade negotiations. In 1948, the General Agreement on Tariffs and Trade (GATT) was founded to oversee a programme aimed at removing trade restrictions and liberalizing trade; it was replaced in 1995 by the World Trade Organization (WTO). The GATT/WTO negotiations have taken place in successive rounds lasting several years, the lengthiest and most contentious of which was the Uruguay round, launched in 1986 by 105 countries (there were 117 by the time it concluded in December 1993). EU states negotiate not in an individual capacity, but as the EU, and are typically represented by the European commissioner for trade.

During the Uruguay round, a combination of the Community's position on global trade negotiations, its focus on internal economic issues, and its promotion of special arrangements with ACP states (see below) led to talk about 'Fortress Europe', particularly from political and corporate leaders in the United States worried about the implications of the single market and about the EC's unwillingness to cut agricultural subsidies. The Europeans eventually made concessions on production and export subsidies, their experience clearly showing the benefits of policy collaboration and speaking with a single voice (Woolcock and Hodges, 1996).

The most recent round of negotiations – which began in 2001 in Doha, Qatar – was designed to open up world markets for agricultural and manufactured goods. They collapsed in Cancun, Mexico, in September 2003 because rich and poor countries could not agree. The poor countries accused the EU in particular of supporting and protecting its farmers through CAP export subsidies (which has made European farmers more competitive and productive), and of 'dumping' their produce cheaply in poor countries, undermining the efforts of local farmers. (The United States was also criticized for its subsidies, particularly to cotton farmers.) The talks were finally concluded in Geneva in August 2004 after the EU and the United States agreed to reduce the subsidies, in return for which they would be given better access to markets in poorer countries, a position the EU had been promoting. EU and US trade negotiators had met the month before to discuss their negotiating positions, as had the foreign ministers of the EU states.

Relations with the United States

The transatlantic relationship has blown hot and cold, which is only to be expected given that the EU and the United States are both major allies and major competitors (see Lundestad, 2003). Relations were strong after the Second World War, the United States having played a critical role in ridding Europe of Nazism, then contributing centrally to European reconstruction and integration with the investments it made under the

Marshall Plan and the security umbrella it provided for western Europe during the cold war. US administrations saw integration as a way of helping the region recover from the ravages of war and of improving European (and American) security in the face of the Soviet threat. Relations cooled in the early 1960s with Charles de Gaulle's concerns about American influence in Europe, and continued to cool as the Europeans fell out with the United States over Vietnam, and over German diplomatic overtures to eastern Europe.

The 1971 collapse of the Bretton Woods system – precipitated by the decision of the Nixon administration to abandon the gold standard – not only marked the beginning of a steady withdrawal of the US responsibility for global leadership, but also emphasized to many Europeans the unwillingness of the United States always to take heed of European opinion on critical issues. The Community was by then rapidly catching up with the United States in economic wealth, it traded less with the United States and more with eastern Europe, and the revival of the western European antinuclear movement in the early 1980s placed a further strain on transatlantic relations.

Trade was the focus of early EC–US relations, the United States preferring to deal with security matters either through NATO or bilaterally with allies such as Britain and West Germany. The end of the Soviet hegemony in eastern Europe in the late 1980s led to a new volatility in Europe that encouraged the first Bush administration to call for stronger transatlantic ties on political matters. The result was the signature in November 1990 of a Transatlantic Declaration committing the United States and the Community to regular high-level meetings. Contacts were taken a step further in 1995 with the adoption of a New Transatlantic Agenda and a Joint EU–US Action Plan under which both sides agreed to move from consultation to joint action aimed at promoting peace and democracy around the world, expanding world trade, and improving transatlantic ties. Biannual meetings have since taken place between the presidents of the United States, the Commission and the European Council, between the US secretary of state and EU foreign ministers, and between the Commission and members of the US cabinet.

The EU and the United States are each other's major trade partners, and the largest sources and destinations of foreign direct investment. They continue to hold many common views on foreign policy and on the promotion of democracy and capitalism around the world, but divisions of opinion have become more common and more substantial with time. This is hardly surprising, because there has been a reassertion of European economic power since the end of the cold war, a relative decline of US influence, a revision of US economic and security priorities, and a recalculation of international relations in the vacuum left by the collapse of the USSR. An early example of a disagreement was the slowness of the Community to criticize the 1979 Soviet invasion of Afghanistan, and the unwillingness of any EC member state except West Germany to support the resulting US-led boycott of the 1980 Moscow Olympics. Since then (see Box 9.3), the two sides have disagreed over a wide variety of political, economic, and security issues. The new economic power of the EU has been exemplified by a series of transatlantic trade disputes over issues such as agricultural exports, steel tariffs, tax breaks for exports, and dealings with Cuba.

As noted earlier, though, the most serious breakdown in transatlantic relations came as a result of the US-led invasion of Iraq in 2003. It is still too early to fully appreciate its impact on transatlantic relations, but there is no question that they have changed. At one level, the dispute could be dismissed as just another of the many that have coloured US–European relations since 1945, and perhaps as more reflective of the short-term goals and values of the Bush administration than of long-term US policy on Europe. But the depth of public opposition to US policy was remarkable, as was the division among the leaders of the EU's four major powers: Germany, Britain, France, and Italy. For some, the dispute has shown that the worldviews of the United States and the European Union are now so different, and the opportunity so clear for an influential actor to emerge that can offer alternative analyses and prescriptions for global problems, that the war on terrorism may ultimately be seen as the beginning of a fundamental change not just in the nature of the transatlantic relationship, but in the balance of influence in the post-cold war world. It is certainly difficult to imagine the effects being quickly forgotten.

Relations with eastern Europe

The dominant presence of the United States in the external relations of the EU has been supplanted to some extent in recent years by the growing importance of central and eastern Europe. Not only is the EU the major source of foreign aid for the eastern bloc, but the EU has now enlarged into eastern Europe, with important political and economic implications for the whole region.

A common EU response to changes in eastern Europe was agreed at the December 1988 Rhodes European Council. With the encouragement of the United States, the EU took responsibility for coordinating western economic aid to the east, a role that was formalized at the July 1989 meeting of the Group of Seven industrialized countries (G7), and strengthened in December 1989 with the launch of a programme to help with economic restructuring in Poland and Hungary. Known as PHARE, the programme

Box 9.3 The European superpower

Since the end of the cold war and the collapse of the Soviet Union, it has become increasingly common to hear the United States described as the world's last remaining superpower. 'We live in a one-superpower world,' argues American political scientist John Ikenberry, 'and there is no serious competitor in sight' (Ikenberry, 2002, p.1). For former US national security adviser Zbigniew Brzezinski, the United States is the first, last and only global superpower (quoted by Huntington, 1999). But this idea of a single dominating power – the unipolar analysis – shows signs of tiring, and there are many who now argue that American power is in decline. Analysts quote historical precedent, noting that the dominance of a single power – a hegemon – has often encouraged the rise of other powers to balance against it (see, for example, Waltz, 1991; Layne, 1993; Huntington, 1999). Charles Kupchan (1998), while noting that the peace and prosperity of the late 1990s rested on American power, has argued that America's will to underwrite the international order would not last indefinitely, and that its global influence would decline as other large countries become less enamoured of following the US lead.

Increasingly, the EU is seen as the major challenger to US hegemony. Not only is it now quite clearly an economic superpower, but it no longer needs the security umbrella provided by the United States during the cold war, and so has been more inclined to assert its policy differences with the United States. The two actors may be agreed in general on the promotion of capitalism and democracy, and they may be deeply intertwined with each other through trade and investment, but they increasingly see the world from different perspectives (see Kagan, 2003, for a controversial assessment of transatlantic differences). Iraq was a notable case in point, but Americans and Europeans have also been out of step on issues as varied as the Arab–Israeli conflict, climate change, capital punishment, support for the United Nations, how to deal with Iran and North Korea, and participation in the International Criminal Court.

The United States is not just at odds with the EU, but with much of the rest of the world. Its policy choices – particularly under the Bush administration – are driven increasingly by unilateralism, by the use of force to achieve its objectives, and by a domestic electorate that is becoming more socially conservative in its views. Furthermore, the credibility of its claims to be the champion of democracy are undermined by significant flaws in the practice of American democracy, in particular the many questions recently raised about the American electoral process.

For these reasons – historical precedent, economic growth, and the declining credibility of the US role in the world – the European Union has the opportunity to exert itself as a superpower. Building on the foundation of a different set of values, it can offer a different set of analyses of international problems, a different set of solutions, and an approach to international relations based more on diplomacy and multilateralism.

was later extended to other eastern European states and the Baltic states. The EU's influence was also boosted by the creation in 1990 of the European Bank for Reconstruction and Development (EBRD), which subsequently channelled public money from the EU, the United States, and Japan into development of the private sector in the east. Based in London, the EBRD is not actually part of the EU, but its foundation was an EU initiative, it derives 51 per cent of its capital from the EU, deals in euros, and has had a growing influence on EU decisions. Much like the International Bank for Reconstruction and Development (the World Bank), the EBRD was founded to provide loans, encourage capital investment, and promote trade, but its specific focus has been on helping east European countries make the transition to free-market economics.

Meanwhile, trade and cooperation agreements were signed by the EU with almost all eastern European states during the 1990s, several billion dollars in loans were made available by the European Investment Bank, the EU sent food aid to the east, and several programmes were launched to help east European social reform, including help to upgrade university departments in the east under the Tempus programme. The Commission coordinated the aid efforts of the G24 countries: the EU, what remained of EFTA, and the United States, Canada, Japan, Australia, New Zealand, and Turkey. The EU's leading role in this programme not only helped define EU foreign policy, but also made the EU a major independent actor in the economic and political future of eastern Europe.

More significantly, the end of the cold war produced a growing number of eastern European requests for associate or full membership of the EU. Europe Agreements came into force in 1994 with Hungary and Poland, in 1995 with Bulgaria, the Czech Republic, Romania, and Slovakia, and in 1998 with the three Baltic states. These Agreements were seen as a step beyond associate membership, and were designed to integrate eastern European economies with those of the EU as quickly as possible through the staged removal of barriers to trade in industrial and agricultural goods, and of barriers to the movement of workers. The Treaty of Amsterdam paved the way for eastward expansion, which was confirmed in 1998 when membership negotiations began with the Czech Republic, Estonia, Hungary, Poland, and Slovenia.

In order to help these countries make the transition and prepare them for EU membership, the EU launched the Agenda 2000 programme in 1997. Essentially a working programme for the EU until 2006, it included a list of all the measures that the Commission believed were needed to bring the eastern European states into the EU without risking institutional paralysis and substantially increased costs for the existing members. The measures included reform of the structural funds to ensure that they were spent in the regions of greatest need, the reduction of subsidies under CAP, and a new focus under PHARE on training local specialists in fields such as law and administration. The EU also agreed 'pre-accession strategies' with all applicant countries, and began publishing reports every year on the progress each country was making towards aligning their national laws and standards with those of the EU.

The enlargement of May 2004 brought eight eastern European states into the EU, including three former republics of the Soviet Union: Estonia, Latvia, and Lithuania. Earlier rounds of enlargement to poorer states such as Greece, Portugal, and Spain had created problems enough in the 1980s (which were partly overcome by huge EU investments in infrastructure in the three countries) but the challenge of integrating eastern European members is of a different order. Their governments and citizens are still struggling with the task of transforming their economies from central planning to the free market, and their political systems from one-party authoritarianism to multiparty democracy. Eastern Europe is also relatively poor. While per capita GNP is in the $15–30,000 range in most EU-15 states, it is in the $1,000–5,000 range for most eastern European states. The ten countries that joined in 2004 increased the population of the EU by 20 per cent, but its wealth by less than 5 per cent.

As for the future, any European country that meets the 'Copenhagen conditions' outlined in Chapter 3 (democracy, a free market, and the ability to adopt all existing EU laws) can be considered for membership. Bulgaria and Romania have already been shortlisted as the next two countries to join the EU, some time after 2007, after which the possibilities become less clear. Much depends on how the first few years of eastern European membership of the EU evolve. Optimists hope that it will open up new investment opportunities, and will pull eastern Europe into a strategic relationship with the west that could be useful if relations with Russia deteriorate. The expansion of membership has also changed the relationship among the existing EU member states, most notably reducing the influence of France and Germany, a development that has been welcomed by a number of smaller member states, but that could have troublesome implications for decision making. Finally, it has forced a much-needed reappraisal of the EU decision-making process, although critics argue that the changes agreed under Nice, Amsterdam, and the draft constitution are too little and too late.

Development cooperation

The long history of European colonialism has left the European Union with a heritage of close economic and political ties to the South: Latin America, south Asia, and Africa. Several of the founding members of the

Community – notably France and Belgium – still had large colonies when the Treaty of Rome was signed, and from the time of the first unsuccessful French attempts to have its overseas territories accorded associate status of the EC, the South has been a significant factor in the external relations of the EU. At the heart of that relationship has been a programme of aid and trade promotion involving several dozen former European colonies in sub-Saharan Africa, the Caribbean and the Pacific – the so-called ACP states (Table 9.1).

EU development aid policies have been based partly on remedying quality of life issues such as poverty and hunger, but there are also less altruistic motives: the South accounts for a significant share of EU exports, and the EU continues to rely on the South as a source of oil and of key raw materials such as rubber, copper, and uranium. The EU aid programme

Table 9.1   *The ACP states*

Africa (48)	Mali	Dominica
Angola	Mauritania	Dominican Republic
Benin	Mauritius	Grenada
Botswana	Namibia	Guyana
Burkina Faso	Niger	Haiti
Burundi	Nigeria	Jamaica
Cameroon	Rwanda	St Kitts and Nevis
Cape Verde	Sao Tome and	St Lucia
Central African	Principe	St Vincent and
Republic	Senegal	Grenadines
Chad	Seychelles	Suriname
Comoros	Sierra Leone	Trinidad and Tobago
Congo (Brazzaville)	Somalia	
Congo (Kinshasa)	South Africa	
Djibouti	Sudan	*Pacific (14)*
Equatorial Guinea	Swaziland	Cook Islands
Eritrea	Tanzania	Fiji
Ethiopia	Togo	Kiribati
Gabon	Uganda	Marshall Islands
Gambia	Zambia	Micronesia
Ghana	Zimbabwe	Nauru
Guinea		Niue
Guinea Bissau		Palau
Ivory Coast	*Caribbean (16)*	Papua New Guinea
Kenya	Antigua and Barbuda	Samoa
Lesotho	Bahamas	Solomon Islands
Liberia	Barbados	Tonga
Madagascar	Belize	Tuvalu
Malawi	Cuba	Vanuatu

has several different aspects. As well as allowing all Southern states· to export industrial products to the EU tariff- and duty-free (subject to some limitations on volume), the EU provides food and emergency aid, and sponsors development projects undertaken by non-governmental organizations. The EU has also negotiated a series of cooperative agreements with the ACP countries, mainly non-Asian former colonies of Britain and France. These began with the 1963 and 1969 Yaoundé Conventions (named after the capital of Cameroon, where they were signed), which gave 18 former colonies preferential access to Community markets. The 18 in turn allowed limited duty-free or quota-free access by the EC to their markets. The provision of trade concessions was expanded by the four Lomé Conventions (named after the capital of Togo), which were signed in 1975, 1979, 1984, and 1989.

Lomé IV, which covered the period 1990–2000 and was revised in 1995, had three main elements. First, it provided financial aid to 71 ACP states under the European Development Fund, in the form mainly of grants for development projects and low-interest loans. Second, it provided free access to the EU for products originating in ACP countries, with the exception of agricultural products covered by CAP. About 95 per cent of ACP exports entered the EU duty-free, compared to just 10 per cent of agricultural goods from other countries, and other goods were subject to tariffs in the range of 17–23 per cent. Finally, it offered an insurance fund for ACP exports called Stabex, designed to offset falls in the value of 50 specified ACP agricultural exports. If prices fell below a certain level, Stabex made up the deficit. If they went above that level, ACP countries invested the profits in the fund for future use.

Opinions were mixed about the effects of the Yaoundé and Lomé conventions. On the one hand, they helped build closer commercial ties between the EU and the ACP states, and there was an overall increase in the volume of ACP exports to Europe from the 1960s to the 1990s. On the other hand, the conventions were widely criticized for promoting economic dependence, and for perpetuating the flow of low-profit raw materials from the ACP to the EU, and the flow of high-profit manufactured goods from the EU to the ACP. Questions were also raised about the extent to which they helped the ACP states invest in their human capital, and helped them develop greater economic independence.

Other problems were structural. Stabex did not help countries that did not produce the specified commodities, payments from the European Development Fund were small by the time the fund had been divided among 71 countries, the ACP programme excluded the larger Southern states that had negotiated separate agreements with the EU (for example, India and China), too little attention was paid to the environmental implications of the focus on cash crops for export, and the programme neither helped deal with the ACP debt crisis nor really changed the relationship between the EU and the ACP states.

The biggest problem was internal to the ACP countries themselves. They mostly failed to diversify their exports, to invest in infrastructure, to build up a more skilled labour force, and to become more competitive in the world market. The EU provided them with a generous set of trade preferences, and yet imports from the ACP as a share of the EU total fell from 6.7 per cent in 1976 to just 3 per cent in 1998. Oil, diamonds, gold, and other industrially related products accounted for about two-thirds of ACP exports to the EU, the balance being made up by agricultural products (30 per cent) and fish (5 per cent). Four countries – Nigeria, Ivory Coast, Cameroon, and Mauritius – between them accounted for more than 40 per cent of EU imports from the ACP countries. At the same time, economic growth in many sub-Saharan African states was sluggish, and there was very little trade taking place among African ACP states.

Negotiations began in 1998 on a new EU-ACP agreement, which was signed in Cotonou, Benin, in 2000. Designed to run for 20 years, with revisions every five years, the Cotonou agreement added seven more countries to the ACP group, including Cuba. It places a stronger requirement on ACP states to improve domestic political, economic, and social conditions, and it emphasizes the importance of human rights and democracy, its objectives including the promotion of the interests of the private sector, gender equality, sustainable environmental management, and the replacement of trade preferences with a progressive and reciprocal removal of trade barriers. Whether this will be enough to address the structural problems of ACP programme remains to be seen.

Meanwhile, the EU has become the single biggest source of official development assistance in the world, collectively accounting for just over half the total of $52 billion given in 2001 (compared to 22 per cent from the United States and 19 per cent from Japan) (World Bank figures). Most EU aid (15 per cent of which is channelled through the EU) goes to sub-Saharan Africa, but an increasing proportion is going to Latin America. The EU also provides emergency humanitarian aid (nearly €500 million in 2001), much of which has gone in recent years to the victims of conflicts in Afghanistan, Armenia, Azerbaijan and Tajikistan. It has also become the second largest provider of food aid in the world after the United States, supplying food worth about €500 million per year.

Conclusions

The process of European integration was born as a way to help western Europe rebuild after the Second World War, and to remove the historical causes of conflict in the region. Over time the EC/EU has become increasingly extroverted, and integration now has implications not just for internal European relations, but for Europe's relations with the rest of the world. While the EEC initially focused on bringing down the barriers to internal trade, it very quickly became involved in external trade matters, and the EU has turned increased attention to common foreign and security policies. The process has steadily acquired consistency and regularity, and the development of common foreign and security policies has become one of the core endeavours of European integration.

With the end of the cold war, the clear security threat posed by the Soviet Union was replaced by economic concerns, by regional security problems such as those in the Balkans and the Middle East, and by less easily defined threats such as nationalist pressures in Russia, the movement of political refugees, the spread of nuclear weapons, the implications of new technology, and environmental problems. Meanwhile globalization proceeded under the auspices of the World Trade Organization, and the wealth and competitiveness of China, India and other newly industrializing countries continued to grow, altering the balance of global economic power. Thanks to all these changes, it seemed that the European Union would have difficulty defining its global role.

Then came the September 2001 terrorist attacks in the United States, followed by the US-led invasion of Iraq in March 2003. Coincidentally, the EU was launching its new single currency, expanding its membership deep into eastern Europe, and upgrading the CFSP to the ESDP. Its role in the world was now dramatically redefined. The new economic power of the EU combined with growing alarm at US foreign policy and a growing rejection of US global leadership to suggest that a new role was about to be forced on the Europeans. They were clearly out of step with the United States not just on the immediate problem of international terrorism and the most effective response, but on a wide variety of longer-term issues relating to trade, security, the environment, and more.

The changes of the last few years have made it clear that the EU must work to give its identity clearer definition, to assert itself on the global stage, and to build the kind of political influence that it needs as a new superpower. The world may never wake up to the sight of multilingual soldiers, sailors, and pilots going into combat under the colours of the European flag, following an agreement reached by Europe's political leaders. It may be that Europe becomes more adept at using soft power, and at building on its political, economic, and diplomatic advantages as an alternative to the increasingly discredited policies of the United States. Even though the EU may still present a rather confused and confusing image to the outside world, the outline of that image is slowly becoming sharper.

Conclusions

The rise of the European Union has been one of the most important developments in global politics and economics since 1945. It has also been one of the least understood. For many years, regional integration was little more than a gleam in the eye of a few pan-Europeanists and a huddle of technocrats in Brussels, and it presented a rather dull and uninspiring face to the world. But it has come into its own since the end of the cold war, and now demands both deeper and wider understanding, because it has changed the face not just of politics and economics in Europe, but of the international system. As argued in the Introduction, the change has been the result of two main sets of developments: the deepening and widening of European integration, which has transformed the EU into one of the two biggest economies in the world, and policy differences with the United States, which – particularly in the last few years – have encouraged Europeans and their leaders to think more creatively about a newly independent role for Europe in the world.

Consider, first, the impact of the single market programme. The most obvious effect of bringing down borders has been to create the biggest capitalist marketplace in the world, with more than 450 million consumers. It is still a work in progress, to be sure, but it has come a long way since the days when 'Europe' was mainly about squabbles over farm subsidies. The barriers to the free movement of people, money, goods, and services are now almost gone, giving European corporations a much bigger market in which to sell their goods and services, giving consumers access to a wider array of products, and allowing Europeans increased freedom to move around their region, and no longer just for economic need – as was once the case – but out of personal choice. The freedoms of the new Europe have been underpinned – at least in 12 of the member states – by the adoption of the euro, which has not only made it easier for goods and services to cross national boundaries, but has given the EU a world-class currency that stands alongside the US dollar, giving the EU a new level of influence over international economic and monetary policies.

Consider, second, the importance of the eastward expansion of the EU. Until just the last few years, the EU was an exercise in cooperation among the capitalist economies of western Europe. Eastern Europe still suffered the effects of nearly fifty years of Soviet domination, with a tradition of single-party politics and central planning. It worked hard to rid itself of those influences following the end of the cold war, but there was no escaping the idea that Europe was still divided. This all changed when

233

countries like Poland, Hungary, the Czech Republic, and, most notably, three former Soviet republics (Estonia, Latvia, and Lithuania) joined the EU in 2004. This brought an emphatic end to the cold war, and for the first time in several generations we can now think and talk about 'Europe' as a whole, rather than always qualifying the label with 'western' and 'eastern'. Enlargement has increased the size of the European marketplace and opened eastern Europe to investment from the west, which will help free eastern economies and underpin the process of democratization. Critics have argued that enlargement came too soon and may overextend the EU, even perhaps undermining its new global economic role. But this is a pessimistic view, not borne out by the experience of Greece, Portugal, and Spain, all of which have seen their capitalist and democratic credentials strengthened by membership of the EU.

Consider, finally, the impact of common policies on the member states of the European Union. The development of common European laws has not always been met with enthusiasm by Europeans, but it has been much easier for sceptics to point at the costs of the trivial – common sets of weights and measures, uniform shapes and sizes for fruits and vegetables, and so on – than to consider the longer-term benefits of removing technical barriers to the single market, and of allowing states with progressive laws (for example, on environmental protection) to change procedures in states that have lagged behind. Common agricultural, social, and regional policies have helped European farmers become more productive, and have helped the EU to move new investment to those parts of the continent in greatest need, to invest in transport networks that have underpinned the single market, and to even out the economic playing field. The remarkable changes that have come to Ireland in the last few years, for example, have not all been the result of common EU policies, but the changes might not have happened without those policies.

With all this behind them, the next and most controversial question that Europeans must face relates to political union: will it happen, should it happen, what form will it take, what impact will it have if it succeeds, and what impact will it have if it fails? Concerns about loss of national sovereignty have been part of the debate over Europe almost from the outset, but have deepened in concert with the spread of European integration. 'Federalism' is talked about by some as a goal to which the EU should aspire, and by others as a political lighthouse marking the rocks towards which the European ship of state is headed. Most of those participating in the debate do not really understand federalism, since it has been tried in so few European countries (just Austria, Belgium, Germany, and Switzerland). They rightly argue that national identity and independence in some form must be maintained, but they also exaggerate the abilities of the European institutions to take powers away from the member states. Most notably, they fail to realize that the European Commission (the target of the greatest disdain) has virtually no independent powers, and that most of the key decisions in the EU are still taken by national government leaders meeting as the Council of Ministers or the European Council.

The most immediate challenge faced by the EU is adoption of its new constitution. In principle, the idea of replacing the accumulating and confusing bundle of treaties with a constitution is a good one. It will make the EU easier to understand, it will help the EU adapt to the eastern expansion already achieved and the further expansion on the horizon, and – after several decades of rapid change and growth – it will draw a line in the sand and provide Europeans with an opportunity to take a breath, to think about what they have achieved, and to think about where they want to go next. But its adoption is far from assured – it could be rejected in one or more of the national votes that are scheduled, which would have a more serious impact on European integration than the Danish rejection of Maastricht or the Irish rejection of Nice. But European leaders have proved themselves remarkably capable of reaching compromises and getting past the bumps in the road. A rejection of the constitution is unlikely to be the disaster that so many observers have predicted, but rather would provide another opportunity to fine-tune its content.

So much for the internal changes that have altered the character of the EU. What of the external changes? The most important has been the transformation of the transatlantic relationship. Throughout the cold war western Europe followed the lead of the United States in the struggle against the Soviet Union. Whether inside the hallways of NATO, or during bilateral discussions with the British, the French, or the Germans, it was understood that the United States was the dominating partner in the alliance in both security and economic terms: it had the biggest military, the biggest defence budget by far, the biggest economy and marketplace, and the most successful international corporations. The two sides often disagreed on policy, whether it was over Suez, nuclear weapons, Vietnam, détente, or the Middle East, but the Europeans were rarely in a position to provide much more than symbolic opposition.

The relationship began to change with the end of the cold war, when it became clear that the US protective shield in western Europe was no longer essential. It also became clear that the resurgent European economy was offering real competition to the Americans, as reflected, for example, in the growing number of trade wars between the two sides from the mid-1990s, and in the rise of European corporations such as Airbus. The Europeans proved their military and political weaknesses in their divided responses to the 1991 Gulf War and their failures in the Balkans, but as much as anything these underlined the need for the Europeans to build more effective foreign policies. During the 1990s they flexed their political muscle on a wide variety of international problems, from Iran to Libya, the Kurdish situation, and Cuba, but they always lacked the all-important common foreign and security policy.

The new realities of the transatlantic alliance were brought into the clear light of day by the dispute over the US-led invasion of Iraq in 2003. Most Europeans were already deeply alarmed by the unilateralist postures of George W. Bush, but this was not just about the stance of a single administration: Europeans and Americans had already parted company on a wide variety of fronts, from foreign policy to trade policy and domestic social policy, dating back to the Clinton and Bush Senior administrations and before. What was different in 2003 was that the Europeans finally realized that they had the means to oppose US policy in a meaningful way, and that serious questions could now be posed in public about American motives. They no longer felt obligated to support American policy where the two sides disagreed, and they also saw with new clarity that they needed the security and political assertiveness to back up their uncontested economic position in the world.

Thus, to go back to where this book began, the European Union has finally come into its own. It finally seems to have grown up, and is moving quickly towards the point of fulfilling the promise that its founders and champions have so long predicted. It still has many problems to address, there is still scepticism among many Europeans about its value and impact, it is still widely misunderstood, its decision-making procedures are still often elitist and undemocratic, it still faces the challenge of absorbing the A-10 and dealing with applications from other neighbouring countries (most troublingly, Turkey), and neither Europeans themselves nor the rest of the world have yet become used to the idea of thinking of Europe as a single actor, in addition to – or even instead of – the 25 separate national actors of which it consists. But we have gone far beyond thinking about integration as the tool for keeping peace among Europeans, or as a means of encouraging the French and the Germans to live with each other, or as the channel for opening up Europe's internal borders. All of that has been achieved. Today the most important questions relate to what the new Europe will do with its achievements, and what European integration (dare we even say 'unity'?) means for the rest of the world. These are fascinating times indeed.

Appendix: A Chronology of European Integration, 1944–2004

1944	July	Bretton Woods conference
1945	May	Germany surrenders; European war ends
	June	Creation of United Nations
1947	September	Launch of Marshall Plan
1948	January	Creation of Benelux customs union
	April	Organization for European Economic Cooperation founded
1949	April	North Atlantic Treaty signed
	May	Council of Europe founded
1950	May	Publication of Schuman Declaration
1951	April	Treaty of Paris signed, creating the European Coal and Steel Community
1952	March	Nordic Council founded
	May	Signature of draft treaty creating the European Defence Community (EDC)
	August	ECSC comes into operation
1953	November	Plans announced for European Political Community (EPC)
1954	August	Plans for EDC and EPC collapse
	October	Creation of Western European Union
1956	October	Suez crisis
1957	March	Treaties of Rome signed, creating Euratom and the European Economic Community
1958	January	Euratom and EEC begin to operate
	February	Benelux Economic Union founded
1960	May	Creation of European Free Trade Association
1961	February	First summit of EEC heads of government
	August	Britain, Ireland and Denmark apply for EEC membership
1962	April	Norway applies for EEC membership
1963	January	De Gaulle vetoes British membership of the EEC; France and Germany sign Treaty of Friendship and Cooperation
1965	April	Merger treaty signed

1966	May	Britain, Ireland and Denmark apply for the second time for EEC membership (Norway follows in July)
1967	December	De Gaulle vetoes British membership of the Community
1968	July	Agreement of a common external tariff completes the creation of an EEC customs union; Common Agricultural Policy agreed
1970	June	Membership negotiations open with Britain, Denmark, Ireland and Norway; concluded in January 1972
1971	August	US leaves gold standard; end of the Bretton Woods system of fixed exchange rates
1972	September	Referendum in Norway rejects EEC membership
1973	January	Britain, Denmark and Ireland join the Community, bringing membership to nine
1974	January	Creation of the European Social Fund
1975	January	Creation of the European Regional Development Fund
	March	First meeting of European Council in Dublin
	June	Greece applies for Community membership
1977	March	Portugal applies for Community membership
	July	Spain applies for Community membership
1979	March	European Monetary System comes into operation
	June	First direct elections to the European Parliament
1981	January	Greece joins the Community, bringing membership to ten
1984	January	Free trade area established between EFTA and the EC
1985	June	Schengen Agreement signed by France, Germany and Benelux states
1986	January	Spain and Portugal join the Community, bringing membership to 12
	February	Single European Act signed in Luxembourg
1987	June	Turkey applies for Community membership
	July	Single European Act comes into force
1989	April	Delors report on economic and monetary union
	July	Austria applies for Community membership
	December	Adoption of Social Charter by 11 EC member states; rejection of Turkish membership application
1990	July	Cyprus and Malta apply for Community membership
	October	German reunification brings former East Germany into the Community

1992	February	Treaty on European Union (Maastricht Treaty) signed
	June	Referendum in Denmark rejects terms of Maastricht
1993	May	Referendum in Denmark accepts terms of Maastricht
	November	Treaty on European Union comes into force. European Community becomes a pillar of the new European Union
1994	January	Creation of the European Economic Area
	March	Poland and Hungary become associate members of EU
	May	Opening of Channel Tunnel, linking Britain and France
	June–Nov	Referenda in Austria, Finland and Sweden accept EU membership, but Norwegians say no again
1995	January	Austria, Finland and Sweden join the European Union, bringing membership to 15
	March	Schengen Agreement comes into force
	July	Europol Convention signed
1997	October	Treaty of Amsterdam signed
1998	March	EU membership negotiations open with the Cyprus, Czech Republic, Estonia, Hungary, Poland and Slovenia
	June	Establishment of European Central Bank
1999	January	Eleven member states announce they will adopt the euro
	May	Treaty of Amsterdam comes into force
2000	December	Treaty of Nice signed
2001	March	Switzerland votes against EU membership
	June	Referendum in Ireland rejects terms of Nice
2002	March	Twelve EU member states adopt the euro
2003	March	US-led invasion of Iraq sparks the most serious fallout in postwar transatlantic relations
2004	May	Cyprus, Czech Republic, Estonia, Hungary, Latvia, Lithuania, Malta, Poland, Slovenia, Slovakia join the EU, bringing membership to 25
	June	European Council accepts terms of draft European constitution
	October	European leaders sign the treaty on the European constitution
	November	Lithuania becomes the first EU member to ratify the constitution

Sources of Further Information

The literature on the European Union has grown exponentially in the last few years, with the number of new books, journal articles and websites increasing to match the pace of change in the EU itself, and expanding interest in EU affairs. The following list of sources is not intended to be comprehensive, but to give a taste of what was available as this book went to press. To keep up with developments, you might want to monitor new acquisitions at your nearest library, keep an eye out for new books from the publishers with the best lists on the European Union (including Lynne Rienner, Oxford University Press, Palgrave Macmillan, and Rowman & Littlefield), and search online book dealers such as Amazon.com

Books

Among the growing number of general introductions to the European Union are Dinan (1999, new edition forthcoming 2005), Archer (2000), Van Oudenaren (2000), George and Bache (2001), Nugent (2002), Wood and Yesilada (2002), and Bomberg and Stubb (2003). Edited collections on recent developments in the EU include Laurent and Maresceau (1998), Cram *et al.* (1999), Cowles and Smith (2001), and Cowles and Dinan (2004). For general surveys of the history of the EU, see Black *et al.* (1992), Pinder (1995), Urwin (1995), and Dinan (2004). The best summary of integration theory is Rosamond (2000).

After a long dry spell, the number of books on EU institutions has grown rapidly in the last few years. For surveys of EU institutions and decision making, see Peterson and Bomberg (1999), Hix (2005), Warleigh (2001), and Peterson and Shackleton (2002). The Commission is covered by Cini (1996), Edwards and Spence (1997), Nugent (2000, 2001), and Smith (2004), surveys of Parliament are offered by Corbett (1998), Lodge (2001), and Judge and Earnshaw (2003), and political parties are the focus of a book by Hix and Lord (1997). Most studies of the Court of Justice are written in legal jargon, and there are few general introductions beyond Lasok (1998), Dehousse (1998), and Brown and Kennedy (2000). For an explanation of the EU legal system, see Shaw (2000). Despite its critical role in the EU, the Council of Ministers has been the subject of surprisingly little scholarly literature so far, the only recent full-length studies being Hayes-Renshaw and Wallace (1997, new edition forthcoming 2005), and Sherrington (2000). For an assessment of the role of the presidency of the Council of Ministers, see Kirchner (1992) and Elgström (2003), and for the European Council, see Johnston (1994).

For edited collections dealing with a variety of EU policy areas, see Wallace and Wallace (2000), and Richardson (2001). Tsoukalis (1997) has a general survey of economic policy, while there are now an increasing number of studies of EU activities in many specific policy areas, including agriculture (Grant, 1997), competition (Cini and McGowan, 1998), energy (Matláry, 1997), enlargement (Nugent, 2004), the environment (McCormick, 2001), foreign policy (Rhodes, 1998; Whitman, 1998; White, 2000; Ginsberg, 2001), social policy (Hantrais, 2000; Roberts and Springer, 2001), and technology (Peterson and Sharp, 1998). An area of particular growth since 2002 has been in assessments of the transatlantic relationship and the fallout over the 2003 Iraqi invasion: for example, see Peterson and Pollack (2003), Kagan (2003), Gordon and Shapiro (2004), and Shawcross (2004).

Periodicals and EU publications

The Economist. A weekly news magazine that has stories and statistics on world politics, including a section on Europe (and occasional special supplements on the EU). Selected headline stories can be found on *The Economist* website:

http://www.economist.com

The Economist also publishes two series of quarterly reports that are treasure-houses of information, but they are expensive, and not every library carries them: *Economist Intelligence Unit Country Reports* (these cover almost every country in the world, and include a series on the European Union), and *European Policy Analyst*. Both provide detailed political and economic news and information.

The Economist also publishes *European Voice*, a weekly newspaper published in Brussels that is packed with all the latest news and information on the EU. Selected headline stories can be found on its website:

http://www.european-voice.com

Journal of Common Market Studies. This quarterly academic journal is devoted to the EU and contains scholarly articles and book reviews. Many other academic journals include articles on the EU, of which the most consistently useful are *West European Politics*, *International Organization*, *Parliamentary Affairs*, the *Journal of European Public Policy*, and *Comparative European Politics*.

There are several official sources of EU information, all of which are available on the Web through the Europa website:

http://europa.eu.int

Official Journal of the European Communities. Published daily, this is the authoritative source on all EU legislation, proposals by the Commission for new legislation, decisions and resolutions by the Council of Ministers, debates in the European Parliament, new actions brought before the Court of Justice, opinions of the Economic and Social Committee, the annual report of the Court of Auditors, and the EU budget.

General Report on the Activities of the European Union. This is the major annual report of the EU, with a record of developments in all EU policy areas, and key statistical information.

Bulletin of the European Union. Published ten times per year, this is the official record of events in (and policies of) all the EU institutions. It contains reports on the activities of the Commission and other EU institutions, along with special feature articles. Supplements contain copies of key Commission documents, including proposed legislation.

Directorate-General Documentation. Every DG in the Commission publishes its own periodicals, reports and surveys dealing with its specific areas of interest. One of the most useful of the regular publications is the series of biannual Eurobarometer opinion polls. These have been carried out in the EU since 1973, mainly to provide EU institutions and the media with statistics on public attitudes towards European integration.

Eurostat. An acronym for the Statistical Office of the European Communities, Eurostat collects and collates statistical information of many different kinds from the EU member states. Much of this is available on the Web; all of it is published in the form of yearbooks, surveys, studies, and reports.

EUR-Lex. This is the definitive source on EU legislation, containing all the directives, regulations, and other legal instruments adopted by the EU, as well as internal and external agreements.

Websites

The variety of useful websites changes often, as do their URLs, so instead of listing useful sites here, I have set up a short series of links on my home page. The URL is:

http://mypage.iu.edu/~jmccormi

Palgrave also has a Web page for books in the European Union series which provides information on key developments and links to other internet sources. The URL is:.

http://www.palgrave.com/politics/eu/euontheweb.htm

Bibliography

Allen, David (1996) 'Competition Policy: Policing the Single Market', in Helen Wallace and William Wallace (eds), *Policy-Making in the European Union*, 3rd edn (Oxford: Oxford University Press).

Anderson, Scott (1992) 'Western Europe and the Gulf War', in Reinhardt Rummel (ed.), *Toward Political Union: Planning a Common Foreign and Security Policy in the European Community* (Boulder, CO: Westview).

Archer, Clive (2000) *The European Union: Structure and Process*, 3rd edn (New York: Continuum).

Armstrong, Harvey (1993) 'Community Regional Policy, in Juliet Lodge (ed.), *The European Community and the Challenge of the Future* (London: Continuum and New York: Palgrave Macmillan).

Armstrong, Kenneth and Simon Bulmer (1998) *The Governance of the Single European Market* (Manchester: Manchester University Press).

ASEAN home page (2004) World Wide Web http://www.asean.or.id.

Aspinwall, Mark and Justin Greenwood (1998) 'Conceptualising Collective Action in the European Union: An Introduction', in Mark Aspinwall and Justin Greenwood (eds), *Collective Action in the European Union: Interests and the New Politics of Associability* (London: Routledge).

Bainbridge, Timothy and Anthony Teasdale (1995) *The Penguin Companion to European Union* (London: Penguin).

Barber, Lionel (1998) 'Sharing Common Risks: The EU View', *Europe*, no. 374, pp. 8–9.

Barnes, Ian and Pamela M. Barnes (1995) *The Enlarged European Union* (London: Longman).

Black, Cyril E. *et al.* (1992) *Rebirth: A History of Europe Since World War II* (Boulder, CO: Westview).

Bomberg, Elizabeth and Alexander Stubb (2003) *The European Union: How Does it Work?* (Oxford: Oxford University Press).

Bradford, Michael (1998) 'Education and Welfare', in Tim Unwin (ed.), *A European Geography* (Harlow, Essex: Longman).

Brewin, Christopher and Richard McAllister (1991) 'Annual Review of the Activities of the European Community in 1990', *Journal of Common Market Studies*, vol. 29, no. 4 (June), pp. 385–430.

Brown, L. Neville and Tom Kennedy (2000) *The Court of Justice of the European Communities*, 5th edn (London: Sweet & Maxwell).

Bugge, Peter (1995) 'The Nation Supreme: The Idea of Europe 1914–1945', in Kevin Wilson and Jan van der Dussen (eds), *The History of the Idea of Europe* (London: Routledge).

243

Buonanno, Laurie and Ann Deakin (2004) 'European Identity', in Neill Nugent (ed.), *European Union Enlargement* (Basingstoke and New York: Palgrave Macmillan).

Carr, William (1987) *A History of Germany, 1815–1985*, 3rd edn (London: Edward Arnold).

Cini, Michelle (1996) *The European Commission: Leadership, Organization and Culture in the EU Administration* (Manchester: Manchester University Press).

Cini, Michelle and Lee McGowan (1998) *Competition Policy in the European Union* (Basingstoke and New York: Palgrave Macmillan).

Collester, J. Bryan (2000) 'How Defense "Spilled Over" into the CFSP: Western European Union (WEU) and the European Security and Defense Identity (ESDI)', in Maria Green Cowles and Michael Smith (eds), *The State of the European Union: Risks, Reform, Resistance and Revival* (Oxford: Oxford University Press).

Collins, Ken and David Earnshaw (1993) 'The Implementation and Enforcement of European Community Environment Legislation', in David Judge (ed.), *A Green Dimension for the European Community: Political Issues and Processes* (London: Frank Cass).

Commission of the European Communities (1973) *Report on the Regional Problems of the Enlarged Community* (The Thomson Report), COM(73)550 (Brussels: Commission of the European Communities).

Commission of the European Communities (1985) *Completing the Internal Market* (The Cockfield Report), COM(85)310 (Brussels: Commission of the European Communities).

Commission of the European Communities (2001) *European Governance: A White Paper*, COM(2001)428 (Brussels: Commission of the European Communities).

Corbett, Richard (1998) *The European Parliament's Role in Closer EU Integration* (Basingstoke and New York: Palgrave Macmillan).

Corbett, Richard (2001) 'The European Parliament's Progress, 1994–99', in Juliet Lodge (ed.) *The 1999 Elections to the European Parliament* (Basingstoke and New York: Palgrave Macmillan).

Cowles, Maria Green and Michael Smith (eds) (2001) *The State of the European Union: Risks, Reform, Resistance, and Revival* (Oxford: Oxford University Press).

Cowles, Maria Green and Desmond Dinan (2004) *Developments in the European Union 2* (Basingstoke and New York: Palgrave Macmillan).

Cram, Laura, Desmond Dinan and Neill Nugent (eds) (1999) *Developments in the European Union* (Basingstoke and New York: Palgrave Macmillan).

Dahrendorf, Ralf (1988) *The Modern Social Conflict* (London: Weidenfeld & Nicolson).

Daltrop, Anne (1987) *Politics and the European Community* (London: Longman).

Dehousse, Renaud (1998) *The European Court of Justice* (Basingstoke and New York: Palgrave Macmillan).

Delanty, Gerard (1995) *Inventing Europe: Idea, Identity, Reality* (Basingstoke and New York: Palgrave Macmillan).

Delors, Jacques (1991) 'European Integration and Security', *Survival*, vol. 33, no. 2 (Spring), pp. 99–109.

den Boer, Pim (1995) 'Europe to 1914: The Making of an Idea', in Kevin Wilson and Jan van der Dussen (eds), *The History of the Idea of Europe* (London: Routledge).

de Rougemont, Denis (1966) *The Idea of Europe* (London: Macmillan).

Dinan, Desmond (1999) *Ever Closer Union? An Introduction to European Integration*, 2nd edn (Boulder, CO: Lynne Rienner and Basingstoke: Palgrave Macmillan).

Dinan, Desmond (2004) *Europe Recast: A History of European Union* (Boulder, CO: Lynne Rienner and Basingstoke: Palgrave Macmillan).

Edwards, Geoffrey and David Spence (eds) (1997) *The European Commission*, 2nd edn (London: Cartermill).

Elgström, Ole (ed.) (2003) *European Council Presidencies: A Comparative Perspective* (London: Routledge).

Eurobarometer polls can be found on the Europa Web page at http://europa. eu.int/comm/public_opinion/index_en.htm

Eurostat Web page http://europa.eu.int/comm/eurostat

Featherstone, K. (1994) 'Jean Monnet and the "Democratic deficit" in the EU', *Journal of Common Market Studies*, vol. 32, no. 20, pp. 149–70.

Fernández-Armesto, Felipe (ed.) (1997) *The Times Guide to the Peoples of Europe* (London: Times Books).

Franklin, Mark (1996) 'European Elections and the European Voter', in Jeremy Richardson (ed.), *European Union: Power and Policy-Making* (London: Routledge).

Gallagher, Michael, Michael Laver and Peter Mair (1992) *Representative Government in Modern Europe*, 2nd edn (New York: McGraw-Hill).

George, Stephen (1996) *Politics and Policy in the European Community*, 3rd edn (Oxford: Oxford University Press).

George, Stephen and Ian Bache (2001) *Politics in the European Union* (Oxford: Oxford University Press).

Geyer, Robert and Beverly Springer (1998) 'EU Social Policy After Maastricht: The Works Council Directive and the British Opt-Out', in Pierre-Henri Laurent and Marc Maresceau (eds), *The State of the European Union*, Vol. 4 (Boulder, CO: Lynne Rienner).

Gillingham, John (1991) *Coal, Steel, and the Rebirth of Europe, 1945–1955* (Cambridge: Cambridge University Press).

Ginsberg, Roy H. (2001) *The European Union in International Politics: Baptism by Fire* (Lanham, MD: Rowman & Littlefield).

Gordon, Philip H. and Jeremy Shapiro (2004) *Allies at War: America, Europe, and the Crisis over Iraq* (New York: McGraw-Hill).

Grabbe, Heather (2004) 'What the New Member States Bring into the European Union' in Neill Nugent (ed.), *European Union Enlargement* (Basingstoke and New York: Palgave Macmillan).

Grant, Wyn (1997) *The Common Agricultural Policy* (Basingstoke and New York: Palgrave Macmillan).

Greenwood, Justin (2003) *Interest Representation in the European Union* (Basingstoke and New York: Palgrave Macmillan).

Haas, Ernst B. (1968) *The Uniting of Europe: Political, Social, and Economic Forces, 1950–57* (Stanford, CA: Stanford University Press).

Hantrais, Linda (2000) *Social Policy in the European Union* (Basingstoke and New York: Palgrave Macmillan).

Hardgrave, Robert L. and Stanley A. Kochanek (2000) *India: Government and Politics in a Developing Nation* (Fort Worth, TX: Harcourt College Publishers).

Hay, David (1957) *Europe: The Emergence of an Idea* (Edinburgh: Edinburgh University Press).

Hayes-Renshaw, Fiona and Helen Wallace (1997) *The Council of Ministers* (Basingstoke and New York: Palgrave Macmillan).

Heater, Derek (1992) *The Idea of European Unity* (London: Continuum and New York: Palgrave Macmillan).

Heisler, Martin O., with Robert B. Kvavik (1973) 'Patterns of European Politics: The European Polity Model', in Martin O. Heisler (ed.), *Politics in Europe: Structures and Processes in Some Postindustrial Democracies* (New York: David McKay).

Hix, Simon (2005) *The Political System of the European Union*, 2nd edn (Basingstoke and New York: Palgrave Macmillan).

Hix, Simon and Christopher Lord (1997) *Political Parties in the European Union* (Basingstoke and New York: Palgrave Macmillan).

Hobsbawm, Eric (1991) *The Age of Empire 1848–1875* (London: Cardinal).

Hoffman, Stanley (1964) 'The European Process at Atlantic Crosspurposes', *Journal of Common Market Studies* vol. 3, pp. 85–101.

Hogan, Michael J. (1987) *The Marshall Plan: America, Britain, and the Reconstruction of Western Europe, 1947–52* (New York: Cambridge University Press).

Howarth, Jolyon (2003) 'Foreign and Defence Policy Cooperation' in John Peterson and Mark A. Pollack (eds), *Europe, America, Bush: Transatlantic Relations in the Twenty-First Century* (London: Routledge).

Huntingon, Samuel (1999) 'The Lonely Superpower', *Foreign Affairs*, vol. 78, no. 2.

Ikenberry, G. John (2002) 'Introduction' in G. John Ikenberry (ed.), *America Unrivaled: The Future of the Balance of Power* (Ithaca, NY: Cornell University Press), p. 1.

Ionescu, Ghita (1975) *Centripetal Politics: Government and the New Centres of Power* (London: Hart-Davis McGibbon).

Johnston, Mary Troy (1994) *The European Council: Gatekeeper of the European Community* (Boulder, CO: Westview Press).

Judge, David and David Earnshaw (2003) *The European Parliament* (Basingstoke and New York: Palgrave Macmillan).

Kagan, Robert (2003) *Of Paradise and Power: America and Europe in the New World Order* (New York: Alfred Knopf).

Keating, Michael and Liesbet Hooghe (1996) 'By-passing the Nation State? Regions and the EU Policy Process', in Jeremy Richardson (ed.), *European Union: Power and Policy-Making* (London: Routledge).

Keohane, Robert O. and Stanley Hoffmann (eds) (1991) *The New European Community: Decisionmaking and Institutional Change* (Boulder, CO: Westview Press).

Kirchner, Emil Joseph (1992) *Decision-Making in the European Community: The Council Presidency and European Integration* (Manchester: Manchester University Press).

Kupchan, Charles A. (1998) 'After Pax Americana: Benign Power, Regional Integration, and the Sources of a Stable Multipolarity', in *International Security*, vol. 23, no. 2, pp. 40–79.

Laffen, Brigid (1997) *The Finances of the European Union* (Basingstoke and New York: Palgrave Macmillan).

Lasok, Dominik (1998) *Law and Institutions of the European Communities*, 7th edn (London: Lexis Law Publishing).

Laurent, Pierre-Henri and Marc Maresceau (eds) (1998) *The State of the European Union, Vol. 4: Deepening and Widening* (Boulder, CO: Lynne Rienner).

Layne, Christopher (1993) 'The Unipolar Illusion: Why New Great Powers Will Arise', *International Security*, vol. 17, no. 4, pp. 5–51.

Lewis, David P. (1993) *The Road to Europe: History, Institutions and Prospects of European Integration 1945–1993* (New York: Peter Lang).

Lindberg, Leon N. and Stuart A. Scheingold (1971) *Regional Integration: Theory and Research* (Cambridge, MA: Harvard University Press).

Lodge, Juliet (2001) *The 1999 Elections in the European Parliament* (Basingstoke and New York: Palgrave Macmillan).

Lundestad, Geir (2003) *The United States and Western Europe Since 1945: From 'Empire' by Invitation to Transatlantic Drift* (Oxford: Oxford University Press).

Majone, Giandomenico (1993) 'The European Community Between Social Policy and Social Regulation', *Journal of Common Market Studies*, vol. 3, no. 2, pp. 42–58.

Mancini, G. Federico (1991) 'The Making of a Constitution for Europe', in Robert O. Keohane and Stanley Hoffmann (eds), *The New European Community: Decisionmaking and Institutional Change* (Boulder, CO: Westview Press).

Matláry, Janne Haaland (1997) *Energy Policy in the European Union* (Basingstoke and New York: Palgrave Macmillan).

Mazey, Sonia and Jeremy Richardson (1996) 'The Logic of Organisation: Interest Groups', in Jeremy Richardson (ed.), *European Union: Power and Policy-Making* (London: Routledge).

McCormick, John (1995) *The Global Environmental Movement*, 2nd edn (London: John Wiley).

McCormick, John (2001) *Environmental Policy in the European Union* (Basingstoke and New York: Palgrave Macmillan).

Milward, Alan S. (1984) *The Reconstruction of Western Europe, 1945–51* (Berkeley, CA: University of California Press).

Minshull, G. N. and M. J. Dawson (1996) *The New Europe into the 21st Century*, 5th edn (London: Hodder & Stoughton).

Mitrany, David (1966) *A Working Peace System* (Chicago, IL: Quadrangle).

Monnet, Jean (1978) *Memoirs* (Garden City, NY: Doubleday).

Moravcsik, Andrew (1998) *The Choice for Europe* (Ithaca, NY: Cornell University Press).

Neal, Larry and David Barbezat (1998) *The Economics of the European Union and the Economies of Europe* (New York: Oxford University Press).

Nugent, Neill (ed.) (2000) *At the Heart of the Union: Studies of the European Commission,* 4th edn (Basingstoke and New York: Palgrave Macmillan).

Nugent, Neill (2001) *The European Commission* (Basingstoke and New York: Palgrave Macmillan).

Nugent, Neill (2002) *The Government and Politics of the European Union,* 5th edn (Basingstoke: Palgrave Macmillan and Raleigh, NC: Duke University Press).

Nugent, Neill (ed.) (2004) *European Union Enlargement* (Basingstoke and New York: Palgrave Macmillan).

Nye, Joseph S. (1971) 'Comparing Common Markets: A Revised Neofunctionalist Model', in Leon N. Lindberg and Stuart A. Scheingold (eds), *Regional Integration: Theory and Research* (Cambridge, MA: Harvard University Press).

Nye, Joseph (2004) *Soft Power: The Means to Success in World Politics* (New York: Public Affairs).

OECD home page (2004) http://www.oecd.org

Owen, Richard and Michael Dynes (1992) *The Times Guide to the Single European Market* (London: Times Books).

Palmer, Michael (1968) *European Unity: A Survey of European Organizations* (London: George Allen & Unwin).

Peters, B. Guy (1992) 'Bureaucratic Politics and the Institutions of the European Community,' in Alberta Sbragia (ed.), *Euro-Politics: Institutions and Policy-making in the 'New' European Community* (Washington, DC: Brookings Institution).

Peterson, John (2003) 'The US and Europe in the Balkans', in John Peterson and Mark A. Pollack (eds), *Europe, America, Bush: Transatlantic Relations in the Twenty-First Century* (London: Routledge).

Peterson, John and Elizabeth Bomberg (1999) *Decision-Making in the European Union* (Basingstoke and New York: Palgrave Macmillan).

Peterson, John and Mark A. Pollack (eds) (2003) *Europe, America, Bush: Transatlantic Relations in the Twenty-First Century* (London: Routledge).

Peterson, John and Michael Shackleton (eds) (2002) *The Institutions of the European Union* (Oxford: Oxford University Press).

Peterson, John and Margaret Sharp (1998) *Technology Policy in the European Union* (Basingstoke and New York: Palgrave Macmillan).

Pinder, John (1995) *European Community: The Building of a Union,* 2nd edn (Oxford: Oxford University Press).

Pye, Lucien (1966) *Aspects of Political Development* (Boston, MA: Little, Brown).

Reiff, K. and H. Schmitt (1980) 'Nine Second-Order National Elections: A Conceptual Framework for the Analysis of European Election Results', *European Journal of Political Research*, vol. 8, no. 1, pp. 3–44.

Rhodes, Carolyn (ed.) (1998) *The European Union in the World Community* (Boulder, CO: Lynne Rienner).

Richardson, Jeremy (ed.) (2001) *European Union: Power and Policy-Making,* 2nd edn (London and New York: Routledge).

Rifkin, Jeremy (2004) *The European Dream: How Europe's Vision of the Future is Quietly Eclipsing the American Dream* (New York: Tarcher/Penguin).

Roberts, Ivor and Beverley Springer (2001) *Social Policy in the European Union: Between Harmonization and National Autonomy* (Boulder, CO: Lynne Rienner).

Rosamond, Ben (2000) *Theories of European Integration* (Basingstoke and New York: Palgrave Macmillan).

Salmon, Trevor and Sir William Nicoll (eds) (1997) *Building European Union: A Documentary History and Analysis* (Manchester: Manchester University Press).

Schultz, D. Mark (1992) 'Austria in the International Arena: Neutrality, European Integration and Consociationalism', in Kurt Richard Luther and Wolfgang C. Muller (eds), *Politics in Austria: Still a Case of Consociationalism?* (London: Frank Cass).

Shackleton, Michael (1990) *Financing the European Community* (New York: Council on Foreign Relations Press).

Shaw, Jo (2000) *Law of the European Union*, 3rd edn (Basingstoke and New York: Palgrave Macmillan).

Shawcross, William (2004) *Allies: The US, Britain, Europe, and the War on Iraq* (New York: Public Affairs).

Sherrington, Philippa (2000) *The Council of Ministers: Political Authority in the European Union* (London: Pinter).

Smith, Andy (2004) *Politics and the European Commission* (London: Routledge).

Smith, Michael (1997) 'The Commission and External Relations', in Geoffrey Edwards and David Spence (eds), *The European Commission*, 2nd edn (London: Cartermill).

Springer, Beverly (1992) *The Social Dimension of 1992: Europe Faces a New EC* (Westport, CT: Praeger).

Taylor, Paul and A. J. R. Groom (1975) 'Functionalism and International Relations', in A. J. R. Groom and Paul Taylor (eds), *Functionalism: Theory and Practice in International Relations* (London: University of London Press).

Thatcher, Margaret (1993) *The Downing Street Years* (New York: HarperCollins).

Tsoukalis, Loukas (1997) *The New European Economy Revisited: The Politics and Economics of Integration,* 3rd edn (Oxford: Oxford University Press).

Union of International Associations home page (2004) http://www.uia.org/welcome.htm

Urwin, Derek (1995) *The Community of Europe*, 2nd edn (London: Longman).

van Eekelen, Willem (1990) 'WEU and the Gulf Crisis', *Survival*, vol. 32, no. 6, pp. 519–32.

Van Oudenaren, John (2000) *Uniting Europe: European Integration and the Post-Cold War World* (Lanham, MD: Rowman & Littlefield).

Wallace, Helen (1992) 'What Europe for Which Europeans?', in Gregory F. Treverton (ed.), *The Shape of the New Europe* (New York: Council on Foreign Relations Press).

Wallace, Helen and William Wallace (2000) *Policy-Making in the European Union*, 3rd edn (Oxford: Oxford University Press).

Wallace, William (1990) *The Transformation of Western Europe* (London: Royal Institute of International Affairs).

Wallace, William (1996) 'Government Without Statehood: The Unstable Equilibrium', in Helen Wallace and William Wallace (eds), *Policy-Making in the European Union*, 2nd edn (Oxford: Oxford University Press).

Waltz, Kenneth N. (1991), 'America as a Model for the World? A Foreign Policy Perspective', *PS*, vol. 24, no. 4 (December), p. 669.

Warleigh, Alex (2001) *Understanding European Union Institutions* (London: Routledge).

Weigall, David and Peter Stirk (eds) (1992) *The Origins and Development of the European Community* (London: Pinter).

Westlake, Martin (1994) *A Modern Guide to the European Parliament* (London: Pinter).

Wexler, Immanual (1983) *The Marshall Plan Revisited: The European Recovery Program in Economic Perspective* (Westport, CT: Greenwood).

White, Brian (2000) *Understanding European Foreign Policy* (Basingstoke and New York: Palgrave Macmillan).

Whitman, Richard G. (1998) *From Civilian Power to Superpower? The International Identity of the European Union* (Basingstoke and New York: Palgrave Macmillan).

Williams, Shirley (1991) 'Sovereignty and Accountability in the European Community', in Robert O. Keohane and Stanley Hoffmann (eds), *The New European Community: Decisionmaking and Institutional Change* (Boulder, CO: Westview Press).

Wood, David and Birol Yesilada (2002) *The Emerging European Union*, 2nd edn (London: Longman).

Woolcock, Stephen and Michael Hodges (1996) 'EU Policy in the Uruguay Round', in Helen and William Wallace (eds), *Policy-Making in the European Union* (Oxford: Oxford University Press).

World Bank Web home page (2004) http://www.worldbank.org/data

World Tourism Organization Web home page (2004) http://www.world-tourism.org

World Travel and Tourism Council Web home page (2004) http://www.wttc.org

Zurcher, Arnold J. (1958) *The Struggle to Unite Europe, 1940–58* (New York: New York University Press).

Index

Abbé de Saint-Pierre 32
ACP programme 229–31
ACP states 229
acquis communitaire 73
Adonnino report 139, 140, 148
Adenauer, Konrad 34, 52, 54, 61,
    65
African Union 25
Agenda 2000 124, 227–8
agricultural policy (EU) 64, 112, 182,
    187–93, 206
    see also Common Agricultural
        Policy
Agriculture and Fisheries
    Council 89
air transport in Europe 171–3
Airbus 167
Amsterdam, Treaty of (1997) 71, 74,
    79, 99, 103, 119–20, 127, 139, 153,
    154, 155, 160, 199, 200, 214, 217,
    227
Andean Group 20
Arab Common Market 23
Arab League 23
Arab Monetary Fund 23
Arianespace 166
Asia Pacific Economic Cooperation
    (APEC) 21
assent procedure 99
Association of Southeast Asian Nations
    (ASEAN) 21–2
asylum policy (EU) 70, 73
Atlanticism 215, 219
Attlee, Clement 54–5
Austria 43, 44, 46, 47, 50, 118, 124,
    133, 146, 160, 183, 218
    and ECSC 61
    and EEC 65, 67, 74
    and EFTA 65
    joins EU 74
    postwar situation 54

Balkans 38, 104, 213
Barroso, José Manuel 86, 201
Belarus 37
Belgium 39, 44, 46, 50, 94, 118, 146,
    148, 175, 204, 216, 218
    and 1990–1 Gulf war 212
    postwar situation 55
    regionalism in 115
Benelux customs union 55, 62
Benelux Economic Union 55
Bentham, Jeremy 32
Berlin airlift 56
Berlusconi, Silvio 106
Blair, Tony 117, 199, 217, 219
Bosnia 213, 217, 218
Bosnia and Herzegovina, 8
Brandt, Willy 68
Bretton Woods conference 55–6
Bretton Woods system 68, 78, 224
Briand, Aristide 34
Britain 37, 39, 44, 45, 46, 48, 50, 53,
    56, 58, 59, 60, 62, 70, 94, 118, 133,
    168, 171, 183, 195, 196, 217
    and 1990–1 Gulf war 212
    and 2003 Gulf war 218
    and ECSC 61
    and EEC 64–5, 65–7
    and EEC budget 123, 124
    and EFTA 65
    and the euro 76, 175, 176, 180
    and European security policy 210,
        217
    and Exchange Rate Mechanism 69
    and fisheries 192
    joins EEC 67, 194
    postwar situation 54–5, 57, 78
    regionalism in 115
    and Social Charter 119, 199
Brown, Gordon 163, 176
budget (EU) 11, 88, 121–5, 139,
    189–90

Bush Doctrine   219
Bush, George H.W.   21, 236
Bush, George W.   236
Buttiglione, Rocco   99
Brussels, Treaty of (1948)   210, 216
Bulgaria   196, 227

Caetano, Marcello   67
Canada   18, 19–20, 56, 59
Carl Gustav, King   42
Cassis de Dijon case   163
Channel tunnel   170
Charlemagne   30, 32
Chirac, Jacques   42–3, 117, 217
Christian democracy   44
Churchill, Winston   34, 59
citizenship   *see* European Union,
    'citizenship'
Clinton, Bill   21, 236
Cockfield report (1985)   159, 164, 171
codecision procedure   73, 97–8
cohesion   69, 71, 186, 195
Cohesion Fund   71, 186–7, 195, 196
cold war   34, 38, 51, 59, 215, 226
Committee of Permanent
    Representatives   *see* COREPER
Committee of the American Chamber
    of Commerce   151
Committee of Professional Agricultural
    Organizations (COPA)   188
Committee of the Regions   73, 95,
    150, 153, 154, 195
Common Agricultural Policy   53, 64,
    118, 123, 124, 157, 158, 182,
    189–91, 194, 197, 211, 223, 227
  reform of   124, 191–3
Common Commercial Policy   211,
    222
Common Fisheries Policy   192, 211
Common Foreign and Security
    Policy   73, 212–14, 214, 216
  common positions   213
  common strategies   213
  High Commissioner for   208, 214
  joint actions   213
common external tariff   53, 63, 123,
    157, 158
common market   *see* single market
Common Transport Policy   102

Community method   119
competence (EU)   100
competition policy (EU)   169
confederalism   6–9, 106, 114, 126, 129
constitutions
  European Union   76–7, 80–2, 84,
    92, 127, 208, 219, 235
  United States   81
consultation procedure   97
Convention on the Future of the
    European Union   76, 81
convergence criteria   76, 175–6
cooperation procedure   97
Copenhagen conditions   72–4, 228
Copernicus   31
COREPER   90, 92
corporate mergers   165–9, 222
Cossiga, Francisco   42
Cotonou agreement   231
Coudenhove-Kalergi, Count
    Richard   33–4, 35
Council of Arab Economic Unity   23
Council of Europe   59, 60
Council of European Professional and
    Managerial Staff
    (EUROCADRES)   151
Council of Ministers   5, 6, 8, 69, 73,
    75, 79, 80, 88, 89–94, 97, 102, 103,
    106, 107, 132, 136, 153, 155, 164,
    201
  and interest groups   150, 151
  origins   63
  powers and role   89, 92, 117, 222
  permanent representatives   80, 90,
    92, 137
  presidency   90, 92, 104, 105
  and public accountability   137
  reform of powers   154
  Secretariat-General   92, 105
  voting options   92–3
Council of the European Union   *see*
    Council of Ministers
Court of Auditors   95, 153
Court of First Instance   69, 102, 154
Cresson, Edith   201
culture   110, 115, 142
customs union   63, 68, 157, 158, 159
Cyprus   38, 43, 67, 77
Czech Republic   49, 77, 94, 184, 227

Davignon report (1970)   71–2
Delors, Jacques   69, 73, 84, 159, 199, 212
democratic deficit   132, 135, 137–9
    closing the gap   153–5
Denmark   39, 49, 50, 53, 56, 98, 133, 143, 148, 160, 162, 190, 196, 200, 205, 218
    and ECSC   61
    and EEC   65, 66, 67
    and EFTA   65
    and the euro   76, 175, 176, 180
    joins EEC   67
    and Maastricht   72, 133, 149
    postwar situation   55
derogation   203
development cooperation   228–31
direct actions (EU)   102
directives (EU)   83
    daughter   117
    e-commerce   164
    equal pay   201
    equal treatment   201
    framework   116–7
    mutual information   163
Dubois, Pierre   31
Duc de Sully   32

EADS   167
East African Community   24
eastern Europe
    EU enlargement to   77, 172–3, 192–3, 205, 209, 227, 228, 233–4
    EU relations with   225, 227–8
    postwar situation   55
Ecofin   89
economic and monetary union   68, 69, 112
    see also euro
Economic and Social Committee   95, 150, 154
Economic Community of West African States (ECOWAS)   24–5
Eden, Anthony   58
elections
    in Europe   44–5
    European Parliament   44, 64, 97, 104, 146–8
Elizabeth II, Queen   42

employment policy (EU)   200
enlargement   53, 65–7, 72–4, 77, 124, 133, 172–3
Environmental Action Programmes   202, 203, 204
environmental policy (EU)   151, 182, 201–7
Erasmus programme   143
Erasmus Mindus programme   143
Estonia   37, 43, 77, 182, 227
Equal   196
Eurelectric   152
euro   11, 76, 112, 118, 158, 173–9, 179–80, 209, 220–1
    adoption   175–6
    and eastern Europe   176–7
    pros and cons   177–8
    public opinion on   133
    see also single currency
Eurobarometer   132, 136, 142, 204, 215
Eurocommunism   43
Eurocorps   216–7
Europe
    administrative structures   45–7
    agricultural sector   47
    boundaries   36–9, 74
    culture of   110, 115, 142
    economic structures   47–50
    electoral systems   44–5
    identity of   27–36, 50–1, 109–10
    languages in   36, 102, 114, 141, 143
    political structures   39–45
    postwar conditions   54–5, 56
    regionalism in   114, 115
    standard of living   48
Europe Agreements   227
Europe Day   140
Europe of Democracies and Diversities   98
European Aeronautic Defence and Space company   *see* EADS
European Agency for the Evaluation of Medicinal Products   95
European Agricultural Guidance and Guarantee Fund   187
European Atomic Energy Community (Euratom)   63

European Bank for Reconstruction and
    Development (EBRD)   227
European Capitals of Culture   142
European Central Bank   11, 95, 136,
    154, 174, 176, 178, 189
European Centre for Disease
    Prevention and Control   95
European Chemical Industry
    Council   152
European Civil Aviation
    Conference   171
European Coal and Steel
    Community   16, 52, 13, 194
  creation   61–2
  motives for creation   60–1
European Commission   6, 8, 11, 50,
    63, 75, 82–9, 92, 97, 102, 103, 105,
    106, 107, 131, 132, 136, 145, 155
  origins   63
  College of Commissioners   79,
    83–4, 99, 154, 201
  directorates-general   86, 119, 187
  and interest groups   150, 151, 152
  powers and role   80, 82, 87–9, 117,
    122, 205, 208, 211, 213, 222
  president   84, 86, 137, 154, 213
  and public accountability   135, 137
  and public misconceptions   138
  reform of powers   154
European Committee for
    Electrotechnical Standardization
    (CENELEC)   164
European Confederation of Posts and
    Telecommunications
    Administrations   164
European Constitution, Treaty on   77
European Council   6, 8, 69, 76–7, 77,
    79, 86, 87, 103–6, 132
  and European Political
    Cooperation   210
  and Maastricht   72
  origins   64
  powers and role   80, 104, 106
  summits   104–6; Brussels
    2003   106; Copenhagen
    1993   72; Edinburgh 1992   72;
    Fontainebleu 1984   72, 123,
    139; Gotebörg 2001   105;
    Laeken 2001   76;

  Maastricht 1991   72; Madrid
    1995   175; Rhodes 1988   225;
    Strasbourg 1989   199;
    Stuttgart 1983   70
  see also constitutions, European
    Union
European Court of Justice   6, 8, 11,
    69, 87, 99–103, 107, 131, 136, 145,
    153, 154, 179, 201, 202, 205, 211
  advocates-general   101
  Cassis de Dijon case   163
  chambers   101
  judges   100–101
  origins   63
  powers and role   79, 80, 83, 100,
    117
  and public accountability   137
  president   101
European Crop Protection
    Association   152
European Cultural Month   142
European currency unit (ecu)   68–9,
    173–4, 175
European Defence Community   58,
    62, 210
European Development Fund   230
European Economic Area   74
European Economic Community   16,
    52, 198
  budget   122
  creation   63, 127
European Environment Agency   95,
    204, 205
European Environmental Bureau   152
European Free Alliance   98
European Free Trade Association
    (EFTA)   65, 74
European Investment Bank   63, 95,
    227
European Liberal Democratic and
    Reform Group   98
European Monetary Institute   174
European Monetary System   68, 69,
    103, 173–5
European Parliament   11, 68, 69, 75,
    87, 94–9, 102, 106, 107, 131, 145,
    153, 155
  committees   96–7
  elections   44, 64, 97, 104, 146–8

Members of the European
    Parliament 94, 96, 147, 201
origins 63
powers and role 73, 79, 80, 88, 89,
    92, 94, 97–8, 99, 117, 122, 137,
    202
reform of powers 153–4
site 94, 96
political parties 98, 204
president 96
European People's Party and European
    Democrats, 98
European Police Office *see* Europol
European Political Community 62,
    71, 210
European Political Cooperation 69,
    72, 210
European Regional Development
    Fund 71, 186, 194, 195
European Round Table of
    Industrialists 151
European Security and Defence
    Policy 217
European Security and Defence
    Union 219
European Social Fund 63, 71, 124,
    186, 196, 198
European Space Agency 166
European Standardization
    Committee 164
European Trade Union Confederation
    (ETUC) 151
European Union
  as a global actor 211
  as superpower 209, 220–3, 226
  budget 11, 88, 121–5, 139, 189–90
  character/identity 5–6, 10, 108–9,
    125–9, 208
  'citizenship' 73, 144
  confederal features 8–9, 106, 114,
    127, 129, 145
  constitution *see* constitutions,
    European Union
  economic disparities 182–6
  enlargement 53, 65–7, 72–4, 124,
    133, 172–3
  federal features 10–12, 129
  flag 140
  institutions 119, 128

interest groups in 150–2
law 8, 11, 83, 87–8, 89, 92–3, 100
and member states 108–15, 129–30
membership requirements *see*
    Copenhagen conditions
official languages 143
ombudsman 145
passport 139
policies 115–21, 234;
    agriculture 64, 112, 182,
    187–93, 206 (*see also* Common
    Agricultural Policy);
    asylum 70, 73;
    competition 169;
    development
    cooperation 228–31;
    employment 200;
    environmental 151, 182,
    201–7; Europeanization
    of 150; fisheries 192;
    foreign 72, 88, 112, 209,
    209–14 (*see also* Common
    Foreign and Security Policy);
    immigration 70, 73, 161, 198;
    labour 64, 140–1, 160, 165,
    198; monetary 112;
    regional 71, 114, 182, 194–7,
    206; regionalism in 114, 115;
    security 112, 208, 214–20,
    232; single market 53, 64, 68,
    69–70, 78, 118, 157, 158–64,
    165–73, 198, 233; social 70–1,
    112, 182, 197–201, 206; tax 8,
    162–3; trade 50, 64, 112,
    222–3 (*see also* Common
    Commercial Policy);
    transport 112, 114, 170–1, 211
public opinion in 132–3, 155, 214
    (*see also* Eurobarometer)
relations with United States 223–5,
    232
women, status of 200–1
European Union, Treaty on
    (1992) 46, 68, 72, 117, 118, 127,
    131, 133
  content and effects 73, 88, 103,
    142, 144, 145, 174, 175, 195, 216
European United Left 98
Europeanization 150

Europol   73, 95, 161
executives   39, 42–3
Exchange Rate Mechanism   68, 69,
    174, 175
Eyskens, Mark   212

federalism   9–12, 46–7, 106–7, 118,
    126, 129
Finland   43, 49, 50, 146, 160, 183, 196,
    200, 204
  and ECSC   61
  and EEC   74
  joins EU   74
  neutrality   119
  postwar situation   55
Fischler, Franz   191, 192
fisheries policy (EU)   192
foreign direct investment   168–9
foreign policy (EU)   72, 88, 112, 209,
    209–14
  see also Common Foreign and
      Security Policy
Fouchet plan (1961)   71
France   37, 42, 44, 49, 56, 58, 59, 60,
    94, 98, 135, 146, 148, 160, 162,
    168, 170, 183, 190, 195, 196,
    218
  and 1990–1 Gulf war   212
  and agriculture   118, 188
  and ECSC   61
  and European security   216
  and the euro   178
  and language concerns   143
  postwar situation   54, 78
  regionalism in   115
Franco, Francisco   55, 67
free trade area of the Americas   21
Friends of the Earth   151
functionalism   13–15

Gasperi, Alcide de   54
Gasset, Ortega y   34
Gaulle, Charles de   65–6, 68, 122, 210,
    217, 224
General Agreement on Tariffs and
    Trade (GATT)   64, 222–3
George of Bohemia, King   31
Germany   37, 42, 43, 44, 46, 48, 50,
    58, 59, 60, 61, 62, 94, 98, 143, 146,

    160, 162, 168, 170, 183, 195, 196,
    204, 205, 216, 218
  and 1990–1 Gulf war   212
  beer purity law   163
  and confederalism   7
  and ECSC   61
  and EEC budget   124
  and euro   76
  and federalism   12, 46, 47, 118
  postwar situation   54, 56, 78
Giscard d'Estaing, Valéry   76
Goethe   142
governance   10
Greece   48, 50, 53, 77, 124, 133, 160,
    184, 186, 190, 196, 198, 200, 205,
    213, 218
  and EEC   67
  and euro   76, 175, 176, 178
  joins EEC   67
  postwar situation   55
Greenland   149
Greenpeace   152
Group of Eight (G8)   90, 225
Gulf war
  1990–1   72, 210, 212, 216
  2003–   209, 218–19

Herriot, Edouard   34
high politics   112
Hitler, Adolf   34
Holbrooke, Richard   213
Hugo, Victor   33
Hungary   39, 43, 49, 58, 77, 94, 162,
    225, 227
Hussein, Saddam   218

Iceland   39, 49, 56, 70, 74, 160, 192
  postwar situation   55
immigration policy (EU)   70, 73, 161,
    198
India   22, 47
integrative potential   16–17
interest groups   150–2
intergovernmental conferences
    (IGCs)   127
  Messina   63, 127
  on monetary union   127
  on political union   72, 127
  on single market   127, 159

intergovernmental organizations   4
intergovernmentalism   5, 6, 18, 27,
    126, 128
internal market   *see* single market
international non-governmental
    organizations   4
international organizations   1, 4–5,
    110, 127
Interreg III   196
Investment for Structural Policies for
    pre-Accession (ISPA)   197
Iraq   72, 104, 209, 212
Ireland   48, 50, 53, 70, 117, 118, 133,
    135, 146, 148, 162, 175, 183, 186,
    195
  and ECSC   61
  and EEC   65, 66, 67
  and Exchange Rate Mechanism   69
  and Treaty of Nice   75–6, 133, 149
  joins EEC   67, 194
  neutrality   119, 212, 215
  postwar situation   55
Italy   42, 43, 44, 45, 48, 56, 58, 148,
    160, 175, 178, 190, 195, 196, 204,
    218
  and Exchange Rate Mechanism   69
  postwar situation   54

Japan   48
joint ventures   165–9
Jospin, Lionel   43

Kant, Immanual   32
Kennedy, John F.   215
Keynes, John Maynard   56
Kissinger, Henry   208, 222
knowledge deficit   136
Kohl, Helmut   174, 199
Kosovo   213

'lands between'   37, 51
languages in Europe   36, 102, 114,
    141, 143
  official languages of EU   143
Latin American Free Trade
    Association   20
Latin American Integration
    Association   20
Latvia   37, 77, 182

Leader +   196
League of Nations   34
legislatures (national)   43, 112
Leonardo da Vinci programme   143
Levy, Paul   140
liberal intergovernmentalism   17
Lithuania   37, 77, 183, 184
Lomé Conventions (1975–89)   230
low politics   112, 114
Luxembourg   39, 94, 146, 182, 183,
    197, 216
  postwar situation   55

Maastricht treaty   *see* European
    Union, Treaty on
Macedonia   218
MacSharry, Ray   191
Major, John   199
Malta   43, 65, 67, 77, 94
Marini, Antoine   31
Marshall, George   57
Marshall Plan   56, 57, 224
Martel, Charles   30
Masaryk, Thomas   34
member states and EU   108–15,
    129–30
Mercosur   20–1
Merger Treaty (1965)   63–4
mergers   *see* corporate mergers
Michelangelo   142
Microsoft   169
Milosevic, Slobodan   213
Mitrany, David   14
Mitterrand, François   72, 199
Moldova   37, 42
monarchies in Europe   39
monetary policy (EU)   112
Monnet, Jean   14–15, 16, 52, 60–1, 62,
    65, 127
Moro, Aldo   72
Mozart   142
multi-speed integration   119–20
mutual recognition   163

Nagy, Imre   58
Napoleon   33
Nasser, Gamal Abdel   58
nation   3
nationalism   1, 33, 34, 58–9

neoconservatism   13
neofunctionalism   16–17, 19, 68
Netherlands   39, 43, 48, 49, 50, 55, 98,
    124, 143, 146, 178, 190, 205, 217,
    218
New Transatlantic Agenda   224
Newton, Sir Isaac   31
Nice, Treaty of   74–6, 79, 103, 104,
    117, 120, 127, 133, 153, 154, 155
Nordic Council   55
Nordic Green Left   98
North American Free Trade Agreement
    (NAFTA)   17, 18–20
North Atlantic Treaty   56
North Atlantic Treaty Organization
    (NATO)   4, 38, 56–8, 213, 215,
    216, 217, 218, 220
Norway   39, 43, 56, 70, 160
    and ECSC   61
    and EEC   65, 67, 74
    and EFTA   65
    postwar situation   55

official development assistance   213
ombudsman   *see* European Union,
    ombudsman
Organization for Economic
    Cooperation and Development
    (OECD)   4
Organization for European Economic
    Cooperation (OEEC)   57, 60
own resources   122

Paneuropa   35
Pan-European Union   34
Papandreou, Vasso   201
Paris, Treaty of (1951)   61, 127, 148
parliamentary government   39, 43
Party of European Socialists,   98
Penn, William   32
People's Europe   131–2, 139–45, 155
Petersberg Declaration/tasks   217,
    219
PHARE   196–7, 225, 226
Philip II, King   32
Picasso   142
pillars of the EU   73
Poland   38, 39, 42, 43, 49, 77, 146, 183,
    197, 225, 227

policies (EU)   69, 73, 74, 78, 87–8,
    115–21, 128, 234
    compromise and bargaining   118
    Europeanization of   150
    formal/informal pressures   120
    incrementalism   120–1
    multi-speed integration   119–20
    political games   118–9
    pressures on   116–7
    spillover   16, 111, 113, 117, 121,
        179, 209–10
    *for specific policies see by subject
        area, or see* European Union,
        policies
political parties
    in European Parliament   98, 204
    in Europe   43–4
political union   68, 71, 74
Pompidou, Georges   34, 68
Poos, Jacques   212
population density   49
population growth   49–50
Portugal   37, 42, 43, 48, 53, 56, 94,
    118, 133, 146, 148, 160, 178, 186,
    187, 190, 196, 198, 200, 204, 212
    and ECSC   61
    and EEC   65, 67
    and EFTA   65
    and Exchange Rate Mechanism   69
    joins EEC   67
    postwar situation   55
post-industrialism   47
Prodi, Romano   86, 178
professional qualifications   141
proportional representation   44, 45,
    97, 148

qualified majority voting   93, 202

Rapid Reaction Force   217–18
realist theory   13
referenda   149–50
    Britain, on EEC membership   149
    Britain, on the euro   150, 176
    Denmark, on Maastricht   72, 133,
        149
    Denmark, on the euro   176
    and EEC/EU membership   135, 149
    on EU treaties   149

on the EU constitution 150
and the euro 133, 150
Ireland, on Treaty of Nice 75–6,
    133, 149
and Maastricht 135
Norway, on EC membership 67, 74
Sweden, on the euro 176
Switzerland, on EU membership 74
regional integration 25–6
costs and benefits 15
defined 2
in Africa 24–5
in Asia 21–3
in the Americas 18–21
in the Middle East 23–4
motives behind 12
theories of 13–17
regional policy (EU) 71, 114, 182,
    194–7, 206
regulations (EU) 83
merger regulation 169
Roman Empire 29
Romania 196, 227
Rome, Treaty of (1957) 63, 65, 68, 69,
    70, 100, 102, 127, 133, 148, 157,
    163, 165, 186, 187, 195, 198, 201,
    209, 211, 222, 229
Rousseau, Jean-Jacques 32
Rumsfeld, Donald 218
Russia 37–8, 47, 49

Salazar, Antonio 55
Santer, Jacques 84
SAPARD 193, 197
Schengen Agreement (1985) 70, 119,
    158, 160
Schiller, Friedrich von 31, 140
Schröder, Gerhard 217
Schuman, Robert 14, 16, 52, 60, 61, 65
Schuman Declaration 61
security policy (EU) 112, 208, 214–20,
    232
Serbia and Montenegro 8
Shakespeare, William 142
single currency 68, 73, 74, 76, 78
Single European Act 53, 64, 68, 70,
    87, 107, 127, 140, 158, 159, 195
content and effects 69, 103, 198,
    202, 210

single market 53, 64, 68, 69–70, 78,
    118, 157, 158–64, 198, 233
effects of 165–73
fiscal barriers 162–3
physical barriers 159–62
technical barriers 159, 163–4
Single Market Action Plan 172
Skouris, Vassilios 101
Slavs 38
Slovakia 43, 49, 77, 146, 183, 227
Slovenia 77, 184, 227
snake in the tunnel 173
Social Action Programmes 198, 201
Social Charter 71, 119, 199
social democracy 43–4
social policy (EU) 70–1, 112, 182,
    197–201, 206
Socrates programme 143
soft power 219–20
Solana, Javier 214
South Asian Association for Regional
    Cooperation (SAARC) 22–3
South Asian Preferential Trading
    Agreement (SAPTA) 23
sovereignty 10, 125
Spaak, Paul-Henri 63
Spain 37, 39, 48, 53, 98, 118, 124, 133,
    143, 148, 160, 162, 186, 195, 196,
    198, 200, 204, 205, 212, 216, 218
and ECSC 61
and EEC 65, 67
and Exchange Rate Mechanism 69
and fisheries 192
joins EEC 67
postwar situation 55
regionalism in 115
spillover (EU) 16, 111, 113, 117, 121,
    179, 209–10
Stabex 230
stability and growth pact 178–9
state 1, 2–3, 125
Stockholm Convention (1960) 65
Strauss, Richard 34
structural funds 71, 124, 186–7, 195–6
subsidiarity 111, 129, 203
Suez crisis 54, 58, 64
superpower
    European Union as 209, 220–3, 226
    United States as 56

supranationalism   5–6, 126, 128, 129
sustainable development   203, 204
Sweden   39, 48, 49, 50
    and ECSC   61
    and EEC   65, 74
    and EFTA   65
    and the euro   76, 175, 180
    joins EU   74
    postwar situation   55
Switzerland   7–8, 39, 42, 46, 47, 65, 74

Tatishchev, Vasily   37
tax policy (EU)   8, 162–3
Tempus programme   227
terrorism   161, 170, 218
terrorist attacks, September
    2001   208–9, 218, 232
Thatcher, Margaret   123, 159, 199,
    201
Thomson report (1973)   195
Tito, Josep Broz   38
tourism   141, 170
trade policy (EU)   50, 64, 112, 222–3
    see also Common Commercial
        Policy
Transatlantic Declaration   224
Trans-European Networks   170–1,
    179
transparency   132, 139
transport policy (EU)   112, 114,
    170–1, 211
treaties of the EU   116
    see also Amsterdam, Treaty of;
        European Constitution, Treaty
        on;   European Union, Treaty
        on; Merger Treaty; Nice,
        Treaty of; Paris, Treaty of;
        Rome, Treaty of; Single
        European Act
Trevi Group   161
Trichet, Jean-Claude   174
Truman, Harry S.   57
Turkey   38, 198, 213
    and EEC   67
    and EU membership   77

Ukraine   37, 42
unemployment   71, 183, 199–200
Union for Europe of the Nations   98

Union of Industrial and Employers'
    Confederations of Europe
    (UNICE)   151
Union of Soviet Socialist Republics
    (USSR)   56, 59, 78
unipolarity   226
unitary states   45–6, 118
United Kingdom   see Britain
United Nations   1, 4, 88, 109
United States of America   48, 49
    and 1990–1 Gulf war   212
    and 2003 Gulf War   209, 215,
        218–19
    and cold war   59, 60
    and confederalism   6–7
    and European foreign direct
        investment   168–9, 224
    European opinions about   219
    and European security   56, 215, 217
    and federalism   9, 11–12, 46, 47
    and FTAA/APEC   21
    and Kosovo   213
    and NAFTA   17
    and neoconservatism   13
    relations with EU   223–5, 226, 232,
        235–6
    and Suez crisis   58
    constitution   81
Ural Mountains   37
Urban II   196
urbanization in Europe   49–50

value-added tax   123, 159, 160, 162–3,
    172
Versailles Treaty of (1919) 33, 34
Voltaire   30, 142

Warsaw Pact   58
Werner Committee   173
Western European Union   58, 216, 217
workers, free movement of   64, 140–1,
    160, 165, 198
World Trade Organization (WTO)   4,
    88, 109, 192, 223, 232
World Wide Fund for Nature   152

Yaoundé conventions (1963/69)   64,
    72, 230